N.N.

WILD WALKS

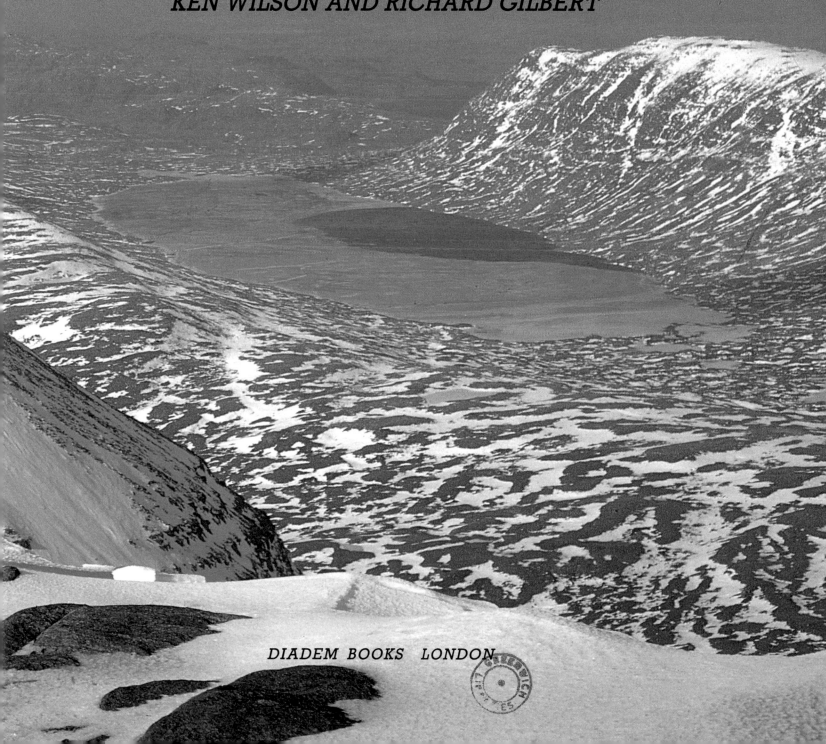

MOUNTAIN, MOORLAND AND COASTAL WALKS IN BRITAIN AND IRELAND

WILD WALKS

COMPILED BY
KEN WILSON AND RICHARD GILBERT

DIADEM BOOKS   LONDON

Other books in this series:

Hard Rock*

Classic Rock*

The Big Walks

Classic Walks

Cold Climbs

Extreme Rock

*Published by Grafton Books

First page (half title): Mountain Ash in Glen Etive.
Photo: John Beatty

Frontispiece: A Flowerdale Forest panorama – the view
to Baosbheinn, Loch na h-Oidhche and Beinn an Eoin
from the summit of Beinn Dearg.
Photo: Ken Andrew

Published in 1988 by Diadem Books Limited, London

All trade enquiries to:
Cordee, 3a De Montfort Street, Leicester

Copyright © 1988 by Ken Wilson and Richard Gilbert

British Library Cataloguing and Publication Data
Wild walks : mountain, moorland & coastal
  walks in Britain & Ireland.
  1. Great Britain : Walkers' guides
  I. Wilson, Ken, *1941*– II. Gilbert,
  Richard, *1937. Nov 17*–
  914.1'04858

  ISBN 0–906371–42–2

Colour separations by
Peak Litho, Tunbridge Wells, Kent

Printed and bound in Great Britain by
W.S. Cowell, Ipswich

ACKNOWLEDGEMENTS The compilers wish to thank the following for help in producing this volume: Don Sargeant for his collection of maps;
Douglas Hughes, Janis Tetlow and Pat Leight for sundry editorial assistance; John Chambers and Roger Durban for production advice; Donald
Bennet, Hamish Brown, Irvine Butterfield and Joss Lynam for specialist advice and assistance. We are also indebted to the many photographers
who placed their slide collections at our disposal, in particular, Colin Bailey, Iain Brown, Joe Cronin, Richard and Anne Gibbens, John
Gillham, Stephen Greenwood, John Hitchings, Noel Maguire, Alan O'Brien, Muriel Soutar and Jim Teesdale, who made special efforts to
improve the photographic coverage. The photographers and essayists are credited alongside their work. A full list of contributors follows. We
owe them all (plus any we may have inadvertently overlooked) a debt of gratitude for their unstinting help in the production of this book.
  Bob Allen, John Allen, Ken Andrew, Steve Ashton, George Atkin, Chris Bailey, Chris Barber, John Beatty, David Bell, John Bevers, Donald
Bennet, Geoffrey Berry, Chris Bonington, Jean Boydell, Malcolm Boyes, Stuart Bramwell, Hamish Brown, Iain Brown, Fraser Brunton, Ken
Bryan, George Burgess, Irvine Butterfield, Phil Cooper, Joe Cronin, Trevor Croucher, John Davidson, Chris Dodd, Andy Dytch, Ian Evans,
Peter Fleming, Derek Forss, Simon Fraser, Brian Gadsby, Gordon Gadsby, Anne and Richard Gibbens, John Gillham, Fred Gordon, Philip
Gormley, Van Greaves, Stephen Greenwood, Paul Hawksworth, Neil Heaton, Charlie Herbert, Alastair Hetherington, John Hitchings, Colin
Hobday, Peter Hodgkiss, Andy Hosking, Phil Ideson, Martin Keane, Rob Kerry, Robert Jones, Sean Kelly, Joss Lynam, Ken Mackay, John
MacKenzie, Noel Maguire, Terry Marsh, Dave Mathews, Rennie McOwen, C.Douglas Milner, Martin Moran, Con Moriarty, Alan O'Brien, Roy
Peel, Stephen Poulton, Roger Putnam, Jerry Rawson, Roger Redfern, Jim Renny, Ian Reynolds, Tom Rix, Bill Ruthven, Don Sargeant, Ernest
Shepherd, Showell Styles, Patrick Simms, Gerard Simpson, Barry Smith, Dermot Somers, C.F. Soutar, Muriel Soutar, Graham Swinerd,
Maurice and Marion Teal, Jim Teesdale, John Vaughan, Varlien Viner-Brookes, David Webster, Janet and Alan Wedgwood, Pete Wells, Tony
Whilde, Ian Wild, Peter Wild, Mike Williams, John Winder, Richard Wood, Geoffrey Wright, Douglas Wiley and George Wostenholm.

CONTENTS

all uncredited chapters by Richard Gilbert

Storm in Glen Torridon.

Jerry Rawson

PREFACE

Since the publication of *Classic Walks* in 1982, the series of large format books on mountaineering which started with *Hard Rock* in 1974, has been developed on the technical climbing front, with the addition of *Cold Climbs* and *Extreme Rock*. It was therefore natural to extend the scope of the books on the hill walking side also, to the remoter regions of Great Britain and Ireland. Hence the idea of *Wild Walks* was formulated.

However *The Big Walks* and *Classic Walks* covered a tremendous range of mountain, moorland and coastal expeditions in Britain and Ireland. Having removed two layers of cream, would I find myself down to the whey? This was the question I asked myself before sitting down to commence work on *Wild Walks*. Of course I need not have worried. Our ancient land-mass, seamed and wrinkled by natural forces from the beginning of time, can provide thousands of wonderful expeditions for the adventurous walker.

Certain hills are held in high esteem on account of their height, shape, traditions or defences. Thus Snowdon, Stac Pollaidh, Great Gable and Sgurr nan Gillean are almost household names and attract hill walkers in great numbers. *Classic Walks* was directed towards such hills. Other hills have earned a reputation through their sheer individual size, or because they are linked with neighbouring hills to form a long ridge or a horseshoe. These hills provide tough expeditions, requiring skill, stamina and the utmost determination from the walker. Many of these were described in *The Big Walks*.

While such hills thoroughly deserve their popularity, an increasing number of walkers, myself included, seek to explore remote and hitherto unfashionable country. The further we can get away from roads, villages and farms the better. The length of the walk and the height of the objective is immaterial: we take particular delight in trackless moorland, lonely corries, silent tarns and broken crags.

How often have we stood beside summit cairns, happy in our success in overcoming the challenge of the ascent, casting a superior eye down to the myriads of lower hills, sweeping moors and misty valleys beneath our feet? Thus we look disdainfully from Liathach to the Flowerdale Forest, from Cader (Cadair) Idris to Waun-oer, from Ben Nevis to Ardgour and Sunart. We traverse Goat Fell and Cir Mhor without a thought for the Pirnmill Hills to the west. We roar down the A30 to the Cornish coast, crossing Bodmin Moor without a sideways glance at the rolling moors, vales and granite tors of one of the loveliest upland areas in England.

It is these less glamorous peaks, hidden valleys and undiscovered fells, the ones that we never seem to get round to exploring, that form the backbone of *Wild Walks*.

What are the conditions that must be satisfied for a walk to be classed as "wild"? I have looked for three factors: remoteness, an untamed landscape and impressive natural features. Not every walk that I have selected satisfies all of the three conditions, for I have tried to produce a mixture that will suit all tastes. Some walkers like open country with distant horizons, where they can stride out and systematically clock up the miles; others prefer the variety of a

mountain traverse with some rock scrambling included for greater challenge. But most walkers like to ring the changes.

Wild Walks offers extremes of contrast, from exposed scrambling or even mild rock climbing on the spine-tingling Blaven/Clach Glas ridge, to a twenty-five-mile leg-stretcher across the open, heather-clad moors of upper Swaledale. Between these two I have included sixty-one walks of exceptional quality, each with its own unique flavour, which will ensure a memorable experience.

Radnor Forest, and the hills which roll south to the River Wye, is virtually unknown territory, yet these high uplands and deep valleys are as remote as any in Wales and give magnificent walking. The Manifold Valley is very popular at summer weekends, but it has great charm and numerous limestone features characteristic of the White Peak; walk the dale early in the morning or on a day in winter and you will have it to yourself. Fairfield makes a popular ascent from Ambleside, but the Deepdale round from Patterdale, taking in St Sunday Crag and Gill Crag, is less well known and provides stirring views into the depths of Link Cove and Sleet Cove, two of the wildest high combes in Lakeland.

In addition to their qualities of remoteness and wild features, many wild walks have added interest from their associations with prehistoric man (Bodmin Moor, Dartmoor and Orkney), or have more recent historical significance (Minigaig Pass and the North York Moors). Much of our upland country has been used by man for living and working throughout the ages, and numerous relics remain to fascinate the wild walker.

Connoisseurs of our hills will be surprised and delighted by the new and spectacular views of well-known mountains which are made accessible through walking many of these routes. Thus the Flowerdale peaks and Beinn Dearg provide an insight into the jaws of Coire Mhic Fhearchair on Beinn Eighe, the towering northern precipices of Liathach and the hidden recesses of Beinn Alligin; Beinn Dearg Mhor holds the centre stage of the Great Wilderness and Moel Siabod's surprisingly airy ridge commands the eastern rim of Snowdonia.

As before, I have attempted to give a reasonable geographical spread to the selection of walks, but I make no excuses for the high concentration of expeditions in north-west Scotland. This region is, scenically, the most priceless asset we have in these islands, and the quality of the landscape is so great that I would be depriving the reader by not making considerable use of it. To stand by the small cairn on the summit of the Fiddler of Ben More Coigach, and to turn through three-hundred and sixty degrees bringing glorious mountains, glens, lochs, moors, sandy bays, islands and a rocky coastline into view, is as near heaven as we can ever reach.

Many Scottish Munros are wild and remote and would be strong candidates for inclusion in *Wild Walks*, but they have been well described elsewhere. However, several expeditions to the wildest parts of Scotland do involve the ascent of Munros, thus Munro-baggers will be particularly interested in the chapters on Glen

In deepest Knoydart: looking east from the summit of Ben Aden to Loch Quoich and Gleouraich.

Luibeg, Knoydart, the round of Loch Mullardoch, the traverse of the Beinn Dearg Forest and the little-known East Ridge of Mullach Coire Mhic Fhearchair.

I am often asked whether the publication of such books as *The Big Walks, Classic Walks* and *Wild Walks* will encourage so many people to come to the hills that the environment will eventually be destroyed. Obviously I hope very much that this will not be the case. I am delighted when I read about the phenomenal popularity of hill walking, for our countryside is there to be enjoyed. Provided we take sensible decisions on conservation issues our environment will stand increased pressure. The more subtle appeal of the lower hills, open moorlands and remote coastlines described in *Wild Walks* is unlikely to attract the multitudes. Nonetheless I would hope that readers of *Wild Walks* will be sufficiently conscious of the vulnerability of our uplands to be extremely circumspect. Walkers should wear the lightest foot-wear appropriate to the conditions. Too many walkers are over-booted. Not only are heavy boots tiring to wear but they cause damage to the structure of the peat, damage which leads to poor drainage, water-logged ground and erosion. If you can step on rocks rather than turf you should always do so, for rocks can withstand wear and tear whereas vegetation has but a precarious hold on the thin top-soil of the mountains, and it is extremely vulnerable to outside influences. Likewise, if you are using a path which zig-zags up the hillside, perhaps an ancient stalkers' path or a more recent track constructed by the National Park Authority or the National Trust, don't show off your fitness by cutting off the corners. You will only cause an ugly scar and hasten erosion.

May I also appeal to walkers not to build new cairns or add stones to existing ones? Our mountains are now grossly over-cairned and this can be very confusing. A single cairn marking a steep descent route from a summit plateau can serve a useful purpose but on certain hills in Snowdonia and the Lake District, cairns have been built every few yards along the popular tourist routes.

It is significant that I have enjoyed a considerably greater variety of wildlife in the preparation of this book than in *The Big Walks* and *Classic Walks*. Thus during my travels I have seen two adders, two herds of feral goats, a family of badgers, an otter, several foxes, peregrine falcons and many hundreds of deer. These have been the highlights for me but, in addition, I have enjoyed a wide selection of bird-life, together with rich and varied flora. Oyster catchers piping on lonely beaches, families of ptarmigan waddling over stony plateaux, and the flash of white as a flock of snow bunting wheels across a high corrie; all these are unforgettable experiences for the wild walker. Likewise, I treasure the memory of colonies of purple saxifrage, bravely flowering on the Donegal cliffs in April after an unseasonal weekend of blizzards.

Readers will soon notice that not all the walks have been described on days of warm sunshine and blue skies. Unpromising weather should not put off the experienced walker and the hills should be sampled in all their moods. On days of storm and racing clouds, when streaming black buttresses loom out of the mist, the wind howls round the corries and the burns roar down to the valleys in a welter of foam, even the friendly hills of Britain and Ireland become awe-inspiring and can present a real challenge.

Most of the walks are far from help and it is vitally important to take adequate safety precautions. I would never advocate carrying heavy rucksacks packed with safety gear to cope with every possible emergency, but certain items are essential. The main priorities are warm clothes, efficient waterproofs and, in winter, an ice axe. In addition, crampons should be carried onto the hills in winter and used if necessary, while emergency food, compass, whistle, first-aid kit and exposure bag should be packed as second nature. The above items do not make a daunting load and the total weight of your rucksack should not exceed fifteen pounds. Keep your map and compass in your anorak pocket and refer to them regularly. At all times you should know exactly where you are in the hills. The most important safety factor of all is to be able to assess the situation and make the necessary decisions early. In the face of threatening weather, darkness or the tiring of a member of the party, it is essential to get off the high ground and into the valley by the quickest possible route. If in doubt don't forge on hoping for the best, turn about and return to base.

In our previous books in this series we commissioned a number of authors, each a specialist in his or her particular area, to give variety to the essays. However, in *Wild Walks* I have used only nineteen external authors because the nature of this book is particularly subjective and many itineraries needed my close appraisal to ensure that they met the criteria necessary for inclusion. My descriptions, therefore, are overlaid with personal observations on what the walks actually meant to me. In spite of this I hope that the character of each walk will come through to the reader.

The search for high-quality photographs to illustrate the text has been even more exhaustive than before. It has taken three years of hard work and over 130 photographers have lent support. In the event over 10,000 photographs were submitted which were later reduced to a shortlist of 2,000. It shows great dedication to give up precious weekends to carry a camera into such places as Rannoch Moor, the Great Wilderness or the Migneint only to find, as often as not, that the view is obscured by low cloud and drizzle.

It is interesting that those photographers who contributed so willingly and prolifically to *The Big Walks* and *Classic Walks* have again provided the lion's share of the 270 photographs finally chosen for *Wild Walks*. The reason for this is probably that they have the expertise and, above all, the time and devotion to detail which are absolute prerequisites for the taking of high-class mountain pictures. Nevertheless their ranks are growing and we have been struck by the quality of the work of several new photographers, not represented in the previous volumes.

That our photographers have been enthusiastically prepared to give us their time and the benefit of their experience, to produce the all important visual accompaniment to *Wild Walks*, is very heartening. We are extremely grateful for their patience and goodwill.

I have continued the practice, used in *The Big Walks* and *Classic Walks*, of taking place names from the OS 1:50,000 maps, and omitting the accents in certain Gaelic titles. I have also used the old, familiar Scottish counties, rather than the new and uninformative regional names, like "Highland". These vast new areas may be easier to administrate, but the distinctive hill groups that are found within them are in danger of losing their old identities and traditions.

The described walks do not necessarily follow designated rights-of-way, although not once was I stopped during the preparation of the book. However, I appeal to walkers selecting any of the Scottish Highland routes to check access locally before setting out during the deer-stalking season (mid August–mid October), and on all the walks it is important to conform scrupulously to the Country Code.

My four years' work in the preparation of the book, highlighted by my walks and travels from Orkney to Bodmin, and from Kielder to Donegal, have been thrilling voyages of discovery. The fifty-nine chapters in *Wild Walks* are packed with superlatives, each one richly deserved. My active years working on the book have been a tonic and, without exception, I have arrived home from my travels brimming with enthusiasm for our hill and coastal scenery. I have climbed exciting new peaks in the Highlands, I have discovered new haunts, even in my beloved Yorkshire Dales, and I shall return many times in the future to the hitherto unknown peaceful hills and valleys of Central Wales and the Southern Uplands. No, I don't think one could ever fully explore all the nooks and crannies of Britain and Ireland in a single lifetime.

RICHARD GILBERT
Crayke, York, 1988

The view from Beinn Damh to Liathach and Beinn Eighe.

Hamish Brown

THE HOY AND ORKNEY COASTAL WALKS

Maps *O.S. 1:50,000 Sheets 6 and 7.*
Grading *Easy but exposed walking along the top of dramatic and sea-girt cliffs.*
Start / Finish *Hoy – Linksness pier (245040). Orkney Mainland – Birsay Bay (246280); Stromness (255092).*
Distance / Time *Hoy coastal walk, 13 miles/7 hours; Orkney Mainland coastal walk, 20 miles/9 hours.*
Escape Routes *None on the Hoy coastal walk. On the Orkney Mainland the walk may be conveniently terminated at the B9056 at Bay of Skaill.*
Telephones *Orgil, Rackwick, Birsay Bay, Bay of Skaill and Stromness.*
Transport *Airport at Kirkwall. Ferry services Scrabster to Stromness and John O'Groats to Burwick (summer only). Daily ferry between Stromness and Hoy. Bus: Stromness – Brough of Birsay (Mondays only).*
Accommodation *Hoy – B & B at Rackwick and Linksness. Hotels/Guest Houses at Stromness. Youth Hostels at Kirkwall, Stromness and North Hoy.*
Guidebooks *Leaflets on Hoy available at the Information Office, Stromness; 'Orkney and Shetland' by Eric Linklater (Hale); S.M.T. Guide 'The Islands of Scotland'.*

One hour out of Scrabster the P & O ferry *St Ola* approached the cliffs on the west side of Hoy. The Pentland Firth was living up to its fearsome reputation and I had to hang on to the starboard rails, stomach heaving and eyes streaming in the biting wind, to see the Old Man of Hoy. I had seen many pictures of the Old Man, and had watched the TV climbing spectacular featuring Joe and Zoe Brown, but I had not realised that the stupendous 450ft rock stack was dwarfed by the magnificence of its surroundings.

Proceeding north along the west side of Hoy there is a break in the cliffs at Rack Wick Bay, where the white surf rolls up a wide beach, then the rust coloured cliffs rise again to over 300ft on Rora Head. Next comes the Old Man, a top-heavy finger of weathered sandstone, standing out from the cliffs and precariously balanced on a plinth of granite. But when looking north, the Old Man is seen against the background of St John's Head where it plays second fiddle to gigantic cliffs, falling sheer or overhanging fully 1,140ft into the boiling sea.

As the *St Ola* rounds St John's Head and turns east to Stromness, you can glimpse the wild and rugged coastline of the Orkney Mainland running north to Marwick Head and the Brough of Birsay, a distance of seventeen miles.

When a strong westerly wind is driving Atlantic rollers against the cliff-girt coast of Orkney, columns of spray are thrown hundreds of feet into the air, the ground trembles and the roar of the waves is awesome. Under such conditions both the Hoy and the Orkney mainland coastal walks are enthralling, unforgettable experiences and you feel you are almost a part of the ceaseless battle between waves and rock which is being waged below your feet.

Stromness is a solid and rather severe little town with a Norse flavour; Orkney was pledged to Scotland by King Christian of Norway in 1468. Narrow, paved alleys run between grey stone houses, many of which are built up the hillside behind the harbour giving them wonderful views to Hoy and into Scapa Flow. Stromness is the ideal centre for the two Orkney coastal walks, accommodation is plentiful and the Hoy ferry runs several times a day.

Although it is possible to stay overnight on Hoy (at Rackwick or Linksness), most walkers will wish to return to Stromness in the evening. The schedule of ferries is such that you will only have about seven hours on Hoy, and the nagging anxiety that you might be stranded may cloud the day's expedition.

Certainly when we stepped ashore from the *Scapa Ranger* at 9 a.m., one cold and blustery day in late March, we wasted no time in watching the seals bobbing in the bay, but strode purposefully west towards Cuilags hill, *en route* for St John's Head.

With ample time you could follow the coast round to Muckle Head and then climb the hills of Lounders Fea and Enegars onto St John's Head. But the direct route, up the east ridge of Cuilags saves about two hours and allows more time to be spent on the most dramatic sections of the walk.

Cuilags was mist shrouded, snow covered, featureless and boggy,

Row Head from the south.

Although it was early in the season, several pairs had already decided their nesting sites and were sitting together, billing and cooing contentedly.

As you gaze in wonderment at this incredible rock wall, you must admire the courage and skill of Ed Drummond and Oliver Hill who climbed it direct in 1970. They spent six nights on the face sleeping in hammocks.

A muddy and very narrow path runs south along the top of the cliffs, detouring inland in several places to by-pass geos which have cut deeply into the cliffs. Sometimes you can peer hundreds of feet down between the black, dripping walls to see white foam.

Two miles south of St John's Head the cliffs curve in a wide bay and the Old Man of Hoy commands the stage. One could sit on the cliff edge for hours, mesmerised by the restless waves breaking against the cliffs, the swooping fulmars and black-

and we squelched across the high plateau towards St John's Head on a compass bearing. We startled a snipe and two mountain hares, still in their white coats, before, quite suddenly, we were at the cliff edge. The transition from heather to a deep carpet of the broad leafed greater woodrush, growing luxuriantly under the stimulation of bird droppings, and the appearance of hundreds of fulmars riding the air currents, gave us just enough warning of the approaching abyss. At that moment the clouds lifted and we marvelled at the highest sea cliffs in Britain, which dropped a horrifying 1,140ft beneath our feet.

There are precious few ledges on these cliffs of Old Red Sandstone, but those that do exist are vociferously contested by the fulmars.

backed gulls, the rafts of guillemots riding the swell and the lines of shags standing erect or spreading their wings on the off-shore skerries.

Sheep tracks lead to the very tip of Rora Head where the cliff top is riddled with the holes and burrows of rabbits or puffins. The outflowing stream from Loch of Stourdale hurtles down the cliffs into the sea in a spectacular waterfall. Beyond the fall the path climbs again to Too of the Head and then drops to the stony beach of Rack Wick Bay.

Rackwick has known better days; the village now has few permanent homes and deserted cottages and crofts are to be seen everywhere. A road runs through the hills back to the pier at

A view south-west along the Orkney sea cliffs to Marwick Head.

Beachcombing in Rack Wick Bay.

Kinnaird. If you look west to Berrie Dale, as you walk through the pass, you can see a patch of woodland containing rowan, aspen, birch and hazel; this is the most northerly natural woodland in the British Isles.

After passing Sandy Loch, which is dammed at the northern end, you meet the road which runs straight downhill back to the pier. If the tide is out you will be intrigued by a rusty hulk sticking out of the water in Burra Sound. This was sunk to prevent German U boats entering Scapa Flow following the sinking of HMS Royal Oak in 1939. Scapa Flow was the assembly point for many Atlantic convoys in the last war, and also in 1916 for the Grand Fleet under Admiral Jellicoe before the battle of Jutland. It is the resting place of the German High Seas Fleet which was scuttled there in 1919.

Orkney transport is sparse and buses only run from Stromness to the Brough of Birsay on Mondays. We found a taxi to be the answer, and didn't grudge a penny of the fare as we were dropped at Birsay Bay early one windy but brilliantly sunny morning, with the prospect of a thrilling twenty mile coastal walk ahead.

Out in the Atlantic it had been a wild night and huge combers were racing in across the sands. On the north side of the bay the causeway leading to the tidal island of Brough of Birsay was already submerged, while on the south side the combination of a high spring tide and stormy seas were producing immense breakers, which were crashing against the cliffs with frightening force.

In the bright sunshine the scene was a kaleidoscope of colour: a restless blue sea with tossing white horses, creamy surf, red cliffs

Yesnaby Castle – the impressive sea stack on the west coast of Orkney

who was drowned when the cruiser Hampshire went down off the Head in 1916.

Marwick Head is a bird sanctuary, the breeding ground for 35,000 guillemots, but we found that, as on Hoy, it was the fulmars that were out in their thousands. Down at Mar Wick Bay flocks of oyster-catchers wheeled and turned and shrieked above the roar of the waves.

There is no proper path south of Mar Wick Bay, but the walking is easy along the top of the cliffs where hundreds of rabbits have made their burrows, some-times right on the edge of a vertical drop. At our approach they scurried to the cliff edge, seemingly like lemmings rushing headlong to untimely deaths.

The sea has carved the rocks into weird and wonderful shapes: arches, stacks, caves and blow-holes where the waves drive in with a clap of thunder.

A road runs along Bay of Skaill, but this is the only contact with civilisation on this stretch of wild coastline. On the south side of the bay the ancient village of Skara Brae has been excavated and is open to the public. Skara Brae is the best preserved prehistoric village in northern Europe; it was occupied by stone-age man between 3100 and 2500BC, but was later covered and pre-served by wind-blown sand.

Climbing up from Skara Brae to Row Head the cliff top is a mass of sea pinks, but it is also littered with slivers of rock and flat stones, whirled up lethally from below by gale force winds.

The series of geos, natural arches and stacks continue as you walk south; white spume emerging from the hill-sides gives warning of the geos, their slimy but more sheltered walls making popular nesting sites for the fulmars. The stack known as Yesnaby Castle is particularly impressive; it has a large hole clean through its base through which the foam was pouring.

Breck Ness is the final headland be-fore the coastline turns east and the character of the walk changes com-pletely. Hoy Sound is relatively shel-tered and a good path runs peacefully

capped with green turf and an azure sky. From Marwick Head, the highest point on the mainland coastal walk, we could look south along the entire length of the cliffs to Hoy Sound and beyond to St John's Head. In places columns of spray were rising well above the cliff tops, reaching a height of 150ft or more, and from a distance the cliffs were veiled in a white mist. A massive stone tower has been built on Marwick Head as a memorial to Earl Kitchener of Khartoum,

above the shore passing a burial ground where the waves lap the walls, a line of old concrete bunkers, a golf course and so back to Stromness.

By now the tide was low and the beach was littered with jagged chunks of rusty metal, a legacy of the more recent history of Hoy Sound and Scapa Flow. The turbulent sea, breaking on an off-shore skerry, was the only reminder of our stimulating walk along Orkney's wild coastline.

Richard Gilbert

Cul Mor and Cul Beag seen from the south-west across Loch Lurgainn.

THE FORTRESSES OF CUL MOR AND CUL BEAG

Of the great peaks of the far North West it is Suilven and Stac Pollaidh which command the most attention. Suilven's sublime outline triggers off memories and nourishes the soul, while Stac Pollaidh's bristles have provided the first thrill of rock scrambling to countless summer visitors.

Between these two peaks lies a magnificently wild and lonely area of lochs, islands, tumbling rivers and ancient woodlands. Access from the east is guarded by Cul Mor and Cul Beag, two peaks which are considerably higher and altogether more complex than either Suilven or Stac Pollaidh. These peaks are neglected by the walker, probably because, when viewed from the A835 Ullapool to Lochinver road, they appear as rather shapeless humps.

From the south or west, however, Cul Mor is revealed as a formidable mountain. Like its neighbours it rises abruptly from the base rock, the approach is protected by badly broken ground and a linked network of lochs and rivers, while great sweeps of bare rock fall from the summit plateau. Cul Mor would be at home in the Fisherfield Forest.

Full justice to Cul Mor can only be achieved by an approach from the south-west and a determined attack on its defences. The obstacles can be overcome and the expedition provides one of Britain's great mountain days in an unsurpassed setting.

The walk described below enters the heart of the mountains from the south, climbs the steep west nose of Cul Mor, descends to the secret Lochan Dearg a'Chuil Mhoir and then traverses Cul Beag. Steep scrambling, some tricky route finding and two potentially hazardous river crossings are involved: this is a serious walk and should only be attempted by experienced mountaineers.

A stalkers' track leaves the road about a mile east of the Stac Pollaidh car-park, and winds its way under the craggy west face of Cul Beag. Just before it descends to the ancient birch wood of Doire Dhubh, a narrow cairned path branches left to a sandy bay at the west end of Loch an Doire Dhuibh. Follow this path which picks a dry route through hummocks and saturated moorland and, after passing a ruined but picturesque stone cottage with rowan trees growing out of the doorway, leads to the exit stream of Lochan Gainmheich.

The map clearly marks a bridge at this point, indeed ancient stone abutments can be seen on each bank, but there is no connecting bridge and the river must be forded. A detour to the west would

Suilven and Loch Veyatie from the summit of Cul Mor with Quinag on the distant horizon.

Looking south-west from Cul Mor to Cul Beag and Loch an Doire Dhuibh in the middle distance and the Coigach group beyond.

involve a fifteen mile circuit of Loch Sionascaig, and one to the east a distance of at least six miles, depending on the height of the Allt an Loin Duibh. On a dry day in March the water washed well over my ankles, but in any sort of wet weather the crossing would be dangerous and the use of a safety rope imperative. In flood the crossing would be impossible.

Having emptied the water out of your boots on the far bank you are now in a position to contemplate the stubby west nose of Cul Mor. Slabs and towers of Torridonian sandstone thrust up from the heather, but by keeping to the skyline ridge the angle can be lessened. Experienced walkers will have no difficulty picking a route up the rock steps, over the blocks and through the gullies, indeed they will relish the challenge. The rock is sound and the position spine tingling. Steeper than the south-west ridge of Ben More Coigach, but similar in atmosphere, the ridge provides expansive and unfolding views: the classic silhouette of Suilven across Loch Veyatie, the peaks and pinnacles of Quinag, the primeval landscape below and, out in the west, the waves breaking white on the rugged coastline and islands of Enard Bay.

Quite suddenly the difficulties are over and you are on a broad ridge with sandy pockets and deep moss underfoot. Follow the edge of Coire Gorm until it steepens to the ridge leading to the summit of Cul Mor at 2,786ft/849m. Close to this high point the weathered sandstone gives way to hard angular boulders of grey quartzite.

Cross to the splendid subsidiary peak of Creag nan Calman, 2,578ft/785m, whose cairn is perched on the edge of an abyss.

Dangerous cliffs abound on Cul Mor and extreme care must be taken when descending in poor visibility. From Creag nan Calman proceed due east until you meet the burn which rushes through a deep ravine on its way to Lochan Dearg a'Chuil Mhoir. Once through the ravine it turns sharply to the west, the glen opens out and most difficulties are over.

Lochan Dearg a'Chuil Mhoir is a beautiful, lonely, shallow loch with sandy bays, overlooked on the north by sheer cliffs, fully 500ft high. As you approach the loch these cliffs are seen in silhouette and are awe inspiring in their ferocity.

The lochan lies on a high shelf and the exit stream plunges a further 600ft into the Gleann Laoigh in a series of falls and cascades. The descent into the glen is not easy; it is best to follow the left bank

of the stream and to detour round rocky cliffs and bluffs where necessary.

Across Gleann Laoigh the northern slopes of Cul Beag rise steeply, culminating in a line of cliffs. Cross the burn and walk up the glen to Lochan Dearg, above which is the first point of weakness in the cliffs. Once on the broad ridge it is a simple walk to the 2,522ft/769m, summit of Cul Beag, passing Lochan Uaine on the way. Your eyes are drawn north to the seemingly impregnable fortress of Cul Mor, while Lochan Dearg a'Chuil Mhoir sparkles on its elevated platform under the cliffs.

The most satisfactory way off Cul Beag is straight down the steep north slopes of the peak to the bealach under Cioch a'Chuil Bhig, a

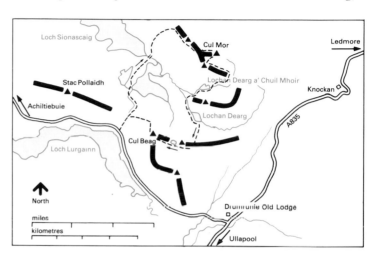

rocky subsidiary on the north side. From here the stalkers' path may be regained at Lochan Fhionnlaidh, near the starting point of the day's walk.

This direct route is easy under good conditions, but any slight deviation will lead to cliffs and serious difficulties. The correct map bearing is due north from the summit cairn but, if in doubt or in mist, it is best to play safe; head south to meet the road at the end of Loch Lurgainn. Either way you will have enjoyed a major expedition through some of the wildest and least known hill country in Britain.

Stac Pollaidh from the summit of Cul Beag.

Map O.S. 1:50,000 Sheet 15.
Grading A long and serious expedition requiring precise navigation, some rock scrambling and, in wet weather, some hazardous river crossings.
Start / Finish Loch Lurgainn (127089).
Distance / Time 11 miles/8 hours.
Escape Route From the summit of Cul Mor descend the broad east ridge to the A835 near Knockan.
Telephones Strathkanaird, Elphin and an A.A. Box at Drumrunie Junction.
Transport Railway Station at Garve, then bus to Ullapool. Daily bus service Inverness – Ullapool. Daily minibus service Ullapool to Achiltibuie and (in summer) Ullapool – Inverkirkaig – Lochinver.
Accommodation Hotels/Guest Houses and Youth Hostels at Ullapool and Achiltibuie.
Guidebooks S.M.T. Guide 'The Northern Highlands'; 'The Scottish Peaks' by W. A. Poucher (Constable).

Stephen Greenwood

BEN MORE COIGACH AND THE FIDDLER

As the sun sets and shadows lengthen, holiday visitors to Ullapool, the fishing village on the north-west coast of Scotland, often drive three miles north to Ardmair Bay. This is the best place to enjoy the breathtakingly beautiful sight of the Summer Isles floating on a mirror sea, set against a fiery red sky.

The romance of West Coast sunsets is well known, but what makes the Ardmair experience so special is the proximity of the great wall of Ben More Coigach, which frames the view on the north side of the bay.

Like so many peaks in the north-west, the ancient weathered sandstone gives the mile-long summit ridge of Ben More Coigach a saw-like appearance. On the south side the slopes fall away extremely steeply for 1,200ft and, in shadow, they look impossibly precipitous and forbidding. But when the morning sun slants onto the face, bathing the buttresses and accentuating the ledges and scree gullies, the slopes look much friendlier, indeed a competent climber could scramble up almost anywhere.

The actual summit of Ben More Coigach lies on the east side of the ridge and, at 2,438ft/743m, it is a mere pimple by Scottish standards; yet, for complexity and character, it has few rivals. Behind the great ridge, on the west side, rise numerous satellite peaks, amongst which hidden glens, corries, lochans and cliffs abound. Much of this area is not visible to the driver proceeding along the narrow, twisty road through the Inverpolly Nature Reserve, and anyway he will be enthusing about the extraordinary rock structure of Stac Pollaidh on the north side, but he gets just a peep at the plunging precipices of the Fiddler.

The Coigach range cannot satisfactorily be explored in a single day. While a whole day should be allowed for the crossing of Ben More Coigach from Culnacraig to near Drumrunie Old Lodge, the delightful outliers of the Beinn an Eoin group can be walked in half that time. Choose an afternoon following a morning's rain, when the clouds are racing away leaving the air washed and sparkling, or a long summer evening; then Beinn an Eoin will provide an unforgettable walk.

For the traverse of the main ridges of Ben More Coigach it is best to start from the road-end at Culnacraig, just beyond Achiltibuie. The Allt nan Coisiche is conveniently forded at a height of about 1,000ft before it drops into a deep ravine. Beyond the burn bear south to meet the main ridge of the mountain, where you can savour the firm rough sandstone and the ever increasing views to the west. This is peerless scrambling in an open situation, free of difficulty, yet sufficiently exposed to heighten the senses.

The ridge rises in sandstone steps so steeply from the water's edge that a bird's eye view is enjoyed of the islands, the skerries and the fishing boats. One could imagine tossing a stone straight into the sea.

If you can tear your eyes away from the Summer Isles and the white cottages dotted around Badentarbat Bay, you can see right across the Minch to the low outline of the Harris hills. Continue to gaze to the far horizons and turn your head; now the Cuillin, then Torridon, An Teallach, the twin topped Beinn Ghobhlach across Loch Broom, the peaks of the Beinn Dearg Forest and the remote Seana Bhraigh can all be recognised by their dramatic and individual shapes.

I have expounded before on the close relationship between mountains and sea which provides the unique West Highland experience. Ben More Coigach, together with Ladhar Bheinn in Knoydart and the Cuillin of Rhum and Skye are the prime examples of this particular communion.

A succession of rock towers and sandy paths make up the mile-long ridge leading to the principal summit; the towers can easily be climbed direct although sheep tracks provide easier alternatives for the timid.

The finest peak in the Ben More Coigach range is Sgurr an Fhidhleir (the Fiddler's Rock), 2,285ft/696m, which rises to a sharp point one mile along the broad north-west ridge from the principal summit. This is a detour well worth making to see sheer cliffs on three sides, the home of ravens and golden eagles, and to enjoy unsurpassed views of the Summer Isles.

Returning to the main massif, a steep descent leads west to

Map O.S. 1:50,000 Sheet 15.
Grading If the true crest of the ridges is adhered to some easy rock scrambling is involved, but all difficulties can be by-passed. Otherwise, two easy mountain walks offering unsurpassed views over the north-western seaboard.
Start / Finish Ben More Coigach – Culnacraig (064039); Drumrunie Old Lodge (166053). Beinn an Eoin – Loch Lurgainn (138066).
Distance / Time Ben More Coigach – 10 miles/6 hours; Beinn an Eoin – 6 hours/4 miles.
Escape Routes From the summit of Ben More Coigach the broad glen of the Allt nan Coisiche can be descended to Culnacraig. An easy glen leads east from the lochan under Sgorr Tuath to the shore of Loch Lurgainn.
Telephones Achiltibuie and an A.A. Box at Drumrunie Junction on the A835.
Transport Railway Station at Garve, then bus to Ullapool. Daily bus service Inverness – Ullapool. Daily minibus service Ullapool to Achiltibuie and (in summer) Ullapool – Inverkirkaig – Lochinver.
Accommodation Hotels/Guest Houses and Youth Hostels at Ullapool and Achiltibuie. No camping is allowed in the Inverpolly Nature Reserve.
Guidebooks S.M.T. Guide 'The Northern Highlands'; 'The Scottish Peaks' by W. A. Poucher (Constable).

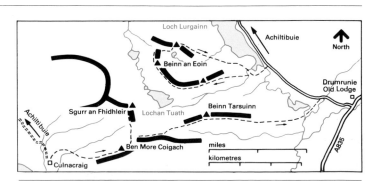

Right: Looking north from the Coigach Ridge – Stac Pollaidh framed between Sgurr an Fhidhleir and Beinn an Eoin.

Near the summit of Ben More Coigach – looking south-west to the Summer Isles.

Ben More Coigach and Sgurr an Fhidhleir seen from the summit slopes of Beinn an Eoin.

the bealach under Beinn Tarsuinn, a whale-backed ridge which descends gradually to Lochanan Dubha. The road junction by Drumrunie Old Lodge makes a convenient rendezvous for your transport, after your traverse of Coigach's most complex and rewarding mountain.

Beinn an Eoin

From the south end of Loch Lurgainn it is a wet slog across saturated moorland to the base of Cioch Beinn an Eoin. Then, quite abruptly, the layered sandstone rears up, your hands come out of your pockets, and you are scrambling up over the ledges and through the gullies, picking whichever route takes your fancy. The occasional rowan or holly tree grows out of a fissure in the rock where it has been protected from grazing, but otherwise vegetation is sparse.

Easy walking across smooth glacier-scoured slabs of sandstone leads from the Cioch, along a broad ridge, to the 2,027ft/ 617m summit of Sgorr Deas. The ridge is littered with round boulders, scattered at random and unmoved since the retreat of the ice, 10,000 years ago. Just below the summit, in a secluded hollow of the ridge, nestles a tiny lochan, its dark waters seemingly fathomless.

Across the glen the stupendous rock prow, the Fiddler, rises 1,000ft sheer above Loch Tuath, completely dominating the long north-west ridge of Ben More Coigach. Facing north, and spending most of its time in shadow, the Fiddler makes a Very Severe, exposed and intimidating rock climb; the direct line up the nose has had few ascents.

Another lonely loch is passed on the bealach under Sgorr Tuath. Set in an amphitheatre of rock buttresses its situation is perfect and, on my last visit, a pair or red breasted mergansers were peacefully swimming on its wind-ruffled surface.

From the loch, a scramble up through more gullies and rock towers leads to the short ridge of Sgorr Tuath. The summit block of this peak is split by a gash, twenty foot deep, which could be a serious hazard under snow or whiteout conditions.

The rock pinnacles of the Sgorr Tuath ridge have been sculptured into weird and fantastic shapes, providing the ideal foreground for views north to Quinag, Canisp, Suilven, Stac Pollaidh, Cul Mor, Cul Beag, Stoer Point and, on a clear day, to Foinaven and the western cliffs of Handa Island.

Under a dark sky this is Norse-God country. It engenders a sense of wonder and awe but it draws me back year after year.

The Ullapool-Stornaway ferry heads out to sea past the Summer Isles.

The Ptarmigan Ridge of Ben More Coigach.

Beinn an Eoin and the Coigach group seen from the north-west across Loch Bad a' Ghaill.

ACROSS THE BEINN DEARG FOREST: INVERLAEL TO OYKEL BRIDGE

Maps O.S. 1:50,000 Sheets 20 and 16.
Grading A long and serious walk involving the traverse of one of Scotland's remotest mountains.
Start / Finish Inverlael (182853); Oykel Bridge Hotel (385009).
Distance / Time 23 miles/10-11 hours.
Escape Routes None. Emergency shelter could be found at Coiremor bothy.
Telephones Inverlael, Oykel Bridge and Corriemulzie Lodge (emergency only).
Transport Railway Stations at Garve, Bonar Bridge and Lairg. Twice daily bus service from Inverness and Garve to Ullapool passes through Inverlael. Daily bus service Lairg to Lochinver passes through Oykel Bridge.
Accommodation Oykel Bridge Hotel. Other Hotels/Guest Houses in Ullapool and Lairg. Youth Hostels at Ullapool and Carbisdale Castle.
Guidebooks S.M.T. Guide 'The Northern Highlands'; 'The High Mountains of Britain and Ireland' by Irvine Butterfield (Diadem); 'The Munros' by Donald Bennet (S.M.T.)

The main cluster of peaks making up the Beinn Dearg Forest is reasonably accessible from the west and south, but Seana Bhraigh, the northern outlier, is distinctly remote and it poses a challenge to the Munro bagger.

From Ullapool, Oykel Bridge and Strathcarron exceptionally long glens run into the hills; these make delightful walks but I never find that *there and back* routes are entirely satisfactory. However, a traverse of the range from Inverlael on Loch Broom to Oykel Bridge combines unspoilt glens with steeply convoluted mountains; a demanding expedition across a desolate and craggy region of the Northern Highlands, as remote and unsullied as any in Britain.

Thus it was that I emerged from the dripping forest of Inverlael into Gleann na Sguaib. Torrential rain had fallen during the night and ragged clouds still hung around the precipices of Beinn Dearg, the brown river writhed down its rocky course, the path was a stream and fat, black slugs lay on the wet grass. But under any conditions Gleann na Sguaib is superb. A swift river tumbles down in a series of cascades and falls, running in places through deep, dark gorges while the south side of the glen is bounded by broken cliffs, overgrown with birch and rowan.

Just beyond the Eas Fionn waterfall I left the path and struck up to reach the west shoulder of Eididh nan Clach Geala near a lochan. The saving grace of this low and very accessible Munro is a line of crags on the south side overlooking Lochan a'Chnapaich, but today it was hidden in mist. I did not linger on the summit of Eididh nan Clach Geala but, compass in hand, picked my way carefully down steep slopes of slippery lichen-covered boulders on the north side of the mountain.

Suddenly the world was transformed; I broke out of the cloud to see the hills mottled with sunshine and a large herd of hinds grazing beside a shallow lochan on the bealach. At the same time my unexpected appearance startled four ptarmigan and a mountain hare which bolted from the rocks.

With great relief I looked out across two-and-a-half miles of desolate wasteland to the west facing crags of Seana Bhraigh; pocketing the compass I strode out purposefully. Poor visibility saps the hill walker's spirit as well as presenting problems of route finding. This high expanse of flattish ground, which is a maze of bogs, burns, peat hags, lochans, hillocks and crags, would have caused difficulties had the clouds been any lower.

On the north side of the plateau the ground falls away precipitously to Cadha Dearg, the corrie of upper Glen Douchary, and the most interesting traverse route follows the lip of the cliffs. To the south, rough boggy ground, interspersed with rock outcrops, gradually falls away to Gleann Beag which drains into the Dornoch Firth at Bonar Bridge. Since the Douchary river runs into the Atlantic Ocean, the plateau is a true watershed of Scotland.

Seana Bhraigh throws down wet, mossy cliffs into Cadha Dearg. Streams cascade down these cliffs which are composed of seamed and shattered schists producing terraces, chasms and fissures. The

Heading west to Seana Bhraigh from Creag an [L...

Creag an Duine from Seana Bhraigh.

Cul Beag, Cul Mor and Suilven in the distance.

summit of the mountain bears a stump of an OS pillar surrounded by a low circular wall of stones. Not only is it one of Scotland's remotest tops but it is also one of its finest. Only feet away a wall of black rock plunges down over a thousand feet towards Loch Luchd Choire. This loch is enclosed by a cirque of vegetated cliffs rising to An Sgurr, a subsidiary summit of spiky rock on the northern end of Creag an Duine on the north-east side of the great amphitheatre. Today, alas, an icy squall of rain swept the mountain top; the cliffs were mere shadows and the corrie a gaping void.

Heading north down the ridge I emerged into sunshine at a tiny lochan, and the full extent of Strath Mulzie could be seen running away into the far distance, eight miles to the forestry plantation below Duag Bridge. Four miles beyond Duag Bridge stands the Oykel Bridge hotel, a haven of civilisation and comfort and the end of the walk.

Strath Mulzie is wide and desolate, only narrowing at the upper end where Loch a'Choire Mhoir is enclosed between craggy slopes. The north ridge of Seana Bhraigh allows an enticing peep into the upper corrie where the lonely grey-stone cottage of Coiremor sits beside the loch. Coiremor is an open bothy maintained by the Mountain Bothies Association.

Although exceptionally long, I found the walk-out through Strath Mulzie to be very pleasant. The river was lively after the night's rain, rumbling the boulders on its bed and sparkling in the sunshine. A good track follows the river bank, but sizeable tributary burns, particularly the Allt a'Choire Bhuidhe, must be forded.

At Corriemulzie Lodge the track passes through a collection of half-a-dozen low, whitewashed buildings, several let as holiday cottages. Power is provided by a thumping diesel generator. I spoke to the keeper at the lodge, receiving a friendly welcome. He is quite happy for walkers to enjoy the hills of the Beinn Dearg Forest, and he enthused over their wild beauty. His one proviso was a clear six weeks starting in early September for the deer stalking, the major source of income from the estate. A reasonable request from an enlightened and tolerant man.

Beyond the lodge the glen becomes more enclosed and the river runs faster; birch, hazel and rowan trees grow on the banks and in places ravines have been carved through the rock.

On the hillsides above Duag Bridge considerable areas of ancient birch forest are thriving. They provide an essential ingredient to this very beautiful and very Scottish scene. This is more than can be said for the square blocks of fir plantations that begin just below Duag Bridge and continue almost to the road at Oykel Bridge.

Nevertheless, this is a magnificent walk and it will leave lasting memories of the rich Northern Highlands' scenery, a perfect combination of hill, crag and glen.

Top left: On the summit of Seana Bhraigh.

Centre left: Creag an Duine and Loch a' Choire Mhoir from Coiremor bothy.

Lower left: The Seana Bhraigh massif from Strath Mulzie.

A view across Strath na Sealga to Beinn Dearg Mhor from Shenavall.

BEINN DEARG MHOR FROM SHENAVALL

The stalkers' path from Corrie Hallie leading south into the heart of the Fisherfield Forest is the start of many of Scotland's greatest walks. It passes through woods of birch and hazel with wild roses, contouring below the rough eastern slopes of An Teallach, where deep heather and slabs of red sandstone lead up to the pinnacles and buttresses of Coire an Lochain. On either side of the corrie, the colossal conical peaks of Glas Mheall Liath and Sail Liath send down wide fans of bruising quartzite screes.

After fording the Allt Chaorachain the path zig-zags up to a plateau at 1,300ft, where a breathtaking panorama of peaks bursts into view: Beinn Dearg and its satellites, the Fannichs, the Sgurr Ban ridge, Beinn Tarsuinn, Slioch and Ruadh Stac Mor.

Opposite Loch Coire Chaorachain a narrow cairned path branches off to the right, while the main track continues south to Achneigie. This small path crosses the shoulder of Sail Liath at 1,400ft and then gradually descends to Shenavall bothy in Strath na Sealga, the last 200ft running down beside a leafy ravine. Across the strath, beyond the head of the loch, rise Beinn Dearg Mhor and Beinn Dearg Bheag, the day's objectives. The green oasis of the strath is surrounded by some of Scotland's mightiest Munros, yet Beinn Dearg Mhor, at only 2,974ft/906m, holds the centre of the stage.

The summit of the mountain forms the apex of a semi-circle of cliffs, ringing a high corrie. The symmetry is perfect and is reminiscent of the north corrie of Ben Lui, except that the scene is grander with deep gullies, seamed buttresses and rock towers.

Two unbridged rivers guard the base of Beinn Dearg Mhor and great care must be taken in fording them. In any sort of spate a safety rope should be used. The first river, the Abhainn Strath na Sealga, can usually be crossed just downstream of Shenavall where it divides round an island. Although the map indicates a bridge across the second river, the Abhainn Gleann na Muice, just upstream of

[25]

Preparing to ford the Abhainn Strath (Srath) na Sealga.

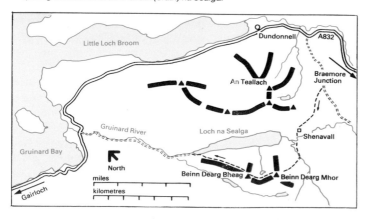

Larachantivore, only a single strand of cable remains. Unfortunately this cable is useless because it spans the river at a deep and narrow part. Again, under normal conditions the river can be crossed just above the collapsed bridge. On my last visit I was able to cross both rivers dryshod but, in the past, I have stayed at Shenavall during torrential rain when both rivers had burst their banks and were quite unfordable.

A shallow green depression rises from the rough slopes behind Larachantivore and leads to a band of rocks high up on Beinn Dearg Mhor; this is a steep but direct route to the summit. An easier, but longer way, is to follow the track for half-a-mile up Gleann na Muice Beag and then strike northwards up a wide corrie which leads to the summit ridge. In good conditions the direct route is the more

An Teallach and the summit buttress of Beinn Dearg Mhor.

enjoyable one with an ever increasing bird's-eye view of Loch na Sealga, bordered on the north side by the jagged ridge of An Teallach. The rock outcrops below the summit ridge can be scrambled over or turned quite easily, and the exposure adds spice to the ascent.

A great fang of rock overhangs the top of the corrie and, just beyond, the cairn is built at the end of a short spur. Whatever the conditions it is a thrilling summit: in good weather the view extends south right across the wilderness of the Fisherfield Forest with rank after rank of rugged mountains, when cloudy the mists swirl up between black, dripping cliffs of bare rock, the abyss below your feet seemingly fathomless and like the gateway to hell.

A 1,000ft descent of steep and rocky slopes bring you to the bealach under Beinn Dearg Bheag. In the shallow corrie below the bealach lies a kidney shaped lochan, and beyond that the grey waters of Loch na Sealga can be seen to stretch away endlessly on either side.

Beinn Dearg Bheag is a revelation, and it adds an unexpected bonus to the day. Its summit ridge is long and knife-edged, and it includes four rock turrets. Broken cliffs, blocks and towers of sandstone must be scrambled over in a manner worthy of the Torridonian giants to the south. Scorning the poor soil and the exposure to the elements, tormentil and purple mountain saxifrage thrive between the sandstone rocks.

As you walk westwards along this exciting ridge, the line of the Gruinard river, which drains Loch na Sealga, can be traced six miles

The summit ridge of Beinn Dearg Mhor with An Teallach towering above Loch na Sealga in the background.

Looking north from Ruadh Stac Mor to Beinn Dearg Bheag and Beinn Dearg Mhor with the western summits of An Teallach beyond.

to its estuary in Gruinard Bay. The massive hump of Sail Mhor sits like a Christmas pudding west of An Teallach; beyond lies the mouth of Little Loch Broom, Cailleach Head and the Summer Islands. Twin-topped Priest Island (Eilean a' Chleirich) is the furthest west of these islands; now uninhabited and a bird sanctuary it was once the temporary home of the naturalist Fraser Darling, and his life there is fascinatingly described in his book *Island Years*. Gruinard Island, just off the coast, has far less pleasant associations. During the war it was contaminated with anthrax spores which only now are being neutralised by government scientists.

There is no path, or indication of the best route to take along this airy and switchback ridge, and the descent of the rocky west end needs careful negotiation.

Once on lower ground, cross the tussocky moor to Loch na Sealga. There is no proper track alongside the loch and the going is hard; in some places cliffs fall straight into the loch and high detours are necessary, but in others the flat stones on the shore make the best route. In summer, watch out for salmon leaping clean out of the water. When you reach the two boat-houses at the west end of the loch, all difficulties are over because a good Land Rover track runs for six miles beside the river to the A832 near Gruinard House.

Strolling down the long glen to Gruinard Bay makes a pleasant end to the day. The track follows the west bank of the river, passing through remnants of ancient birch forest, and fording the fast flowing tributary, Allt Loch Ghuibhsachain. The Gruinard river has many moods and is always a delight; sparkling over its stony bed, roaring along a tempestuous course over cataracts and through ravines, and running deep with its still, black water flecked with foam.

At Gruinard Bay, with the weariness of a long walk behind you, it is satisfying to look back to the abrupt end of the Beinn Dearg Bheag ridge, the *pièce de résistance* of this magnificently wild and rugged expedition.

Alan O'Brien

Descending Beinn Dearg Mhor on the route to Beinn Dearg Bheag.

Map O.S. 1:50,000 Sheet 19.
Grading A long expedition over remote and rugged mountain country. Some rock scrambling is involved and in wet weather river crossings could prove troublesome.
Start / Finish Corrie Hallie (114852); Gruinard Bay (962912).
Distance / Time 18 miles/10-11 hours.
Escape Routes None. Emergency shelter can be found at Shenavall bothy and at the boat houses at the west end of Loch na Sealga.
Telephones Roadside near Gruinard House and Dundonnell.
Transport Gairloch – Inverness bus on Mon, Wed and Sat passes through Gruinard and Dundonnell. Ullapool – Gairloch bus on Wed, June to September.
Accommodation Dundonnell Hotel. Hotels/Guest Houses at Ullapool, Poolewe, Gairloch and Aultbea. Youth Hostels at Aultbea and Ullapool. J.M.C.S. Hut, The Smiddy, Dundonnell.
Guidebook S.M.T. Guide 'The Northern Highlands'.

BEINN LAIR AND THE LOCH MAREE TRAVERSE

Map O.S. 1:50,000 Sheet 19.
Grading A long and tough walk across a remote and inhospitable region. In winter this itinerary should only be attempted by an experienced and fully equipped party.
Start / Finish Poolewe (857808); Kinlochewe (028619).
Distance / Time 26 miles/10-11 hours.
Escape Routes None. Emergency shelter can be sought at Carnmore and Letterewe.
Telephones Poolewe and Kinlochewe.
Transport Railway Station at Achnasheen. Daily bus service Gairloch – Achnasheen runs through Kinlochewe. Poolewe – Inverness bus service on Tues, Thurs and Fri.
Accommodation Hotels/B & B at Poolewe and Kinlochewe. Youth Hostels at Torridon, Aultbea and Carn Dearg near Gairloch.
Guidebook S.M.T. Guide 'The Northern Highlands'.

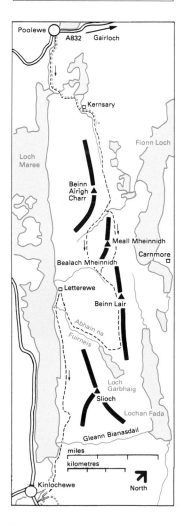

Slioch, Beinn Lair, Meall Mheinnidh and Beinn Airigh Charr form a high wall of mountains running all the way along the north side of Loch Maree from Kinlochewe to Poolewe. They delineate the southern boundary of the 'Great Wilderness' containing the Strath-nasheallag and Fisherfield Forests. Not until An Teallach is passed and Dundonnell on Little Loch Broom is reached is there a permanent dwelling; 19 miles as the crow flies.

From the south, Slioch, rising like a fortress above the eastern end of Loch Maree, provides one of the classic mountain views in Britain. However, when seen from the remote peaks north of Lochan Fada, Mullach Coire Mhic Fhearchair, Beinn Tarsuinn and A'Mhaighdean, it is the long line of plunging cliffs on Beinn Lair that draws the eye. An early guide book to Scotland reported: 'Beinn Lair possesses, for a distance of two-and-a-half miles, what is possible the grandest inland line of cliffs to be found in Scotland'.

Beinn Lair is a rewarding but tough objective for the hill walker. It can offer spectacular views over the tree studded islands of Loch Maree to Beinn Eighe and the Flowerdale Forest, as well as across the wonderfully complex and rugged Fisherfield Forest, but it is extremely remote of access.

Because it is roughly equidistant from Poolewe and Kinlochewe, Beinn Lair's ascent is best included in a long west–east traverse linking the two villages.

The route into the mountains from Poolewe takes the private road along the north bank of the river Ewe to Inveran; it then bears away north-east to the cottage at Kernsary. This is a right-of-way and walkers should not be put off by the locked gates and threatening notices: 'Private Estate. Strictly No Admittance Between September 1st and February 15th'.

Beyond Kernsary the path runs pleasantly through some birch and oak woods but it soon enters a forestry plantation. Where the forestry track turns off north, carry straight on, along the Carnmore path which keeps close beside the Allt na Creige.

Stalkers and estate workers go into Carnmore by boat across the Fionn Loch, and only the feet of walkers and climbers keep the path open. Although the path is narrow, boggy and indistinct it is vastly preferable to ploughing through coarse grass, heather and hags. This is true of the Fisherfield Forest as a whole; a network of well constructed paths exists and these are well worth taking, even if the routes are circuitous and result in extra miles having to be covered.

As I walked under Beinn Airigh Charr sheets of bare, dripping rock rose up into a steely-grey, scudding sky. Before long I was being lashed by icy rain squalls moving in curtains off the Atlantic. With difficulty I waded the sizeable burn rushing down the Srathan Buidhe, only to find it bridged higher up. Rivulets of rain were running down inside my collar and I wallowed in self-pity. However, a return along the Carnmore quagmire, into the teeth of the gale, was unthinkable; I tightened my anorak hood and pressed on.

The stalkers' path through the Srathan Buidhe to Letterewe on Loch Mareeside is beautifully made; the larger burns are bridged

Beinn Lair seen from the slopes of A' Mhaighde

Beinn Mheinnidh and Beinn Lair seen from the

Beinn Tharsuinn Chaol and Gorm Loch Mor in the middle distance, on the
approach.

Fionn Loch from the summit of Beinn Lair.

[31]

Abhainn Fuirness from the Letterewe woods.

and tree trunks have been laid across the boggiest sections. Just beyond the bridge over the Allt Folais another path is met; this runs north over the Bealach Mheinnidh, under the west ridge of Beinn Lair, to the Dubh Loch causeway and Carnmore. Reluctant to miss out Beinn Lair, my principal objective, I persuaded myself that the clouds were lifting, turned my back on the pastures of Letterewe and headed up to the bealach.

Bealach Mheinnidh, at 1,600ft/487m, is a natural pass between the rocky peaks of Meall Mheinnidh and Beinn Lair. An alternative route to the bealach is from the Dubh Loch causeway on the north side, via a steep and winding path.

The gale was howling through the bealach as I set off up the broad, west ridge of Beinn Lair, hugging the edge of the great north-facing cliffs for over a mile. In spite of the weather it was dramatic walking and my pulse quickened. Below the cliffs the clouds were boiling like a witch's cauldron and buffets of wind roared and echoed around the rock towers and buttresses, sending plumes of vapour racing and swirling up the gullies. The highest point on the cliff edge is marked by a low cairn but the true summit of Beinn Lair, 2,817ft/860m, lies a short way back, at the top of a gently contoured mound. The broad summit plateau has been scoured smooth by the wind and rain and it is strewn with flat slabs of gneiss. I was surprised to discover a large conical cairn, painstakingly constructed of boulders and topped with white quartzite.

The rain stopped and the wind tore holes in the cloud cover as I continued walking eastwards over the subsidiary summit of Sgurr Dubh. At two lochans, high on the ridge, I turned south and made my way down very rough slopes to the west end of Loch Garbhaig. Quite suddenly

the sun came out and I was in a different world. Loch Garbhaig glinted, the path steamed, grey woolly clouds rolled away from Slioch's massive shoulders and rainbows played in the spray of the myriads of tumbling burns and rivulets.

To my delight I saw a herd of wild goats with long curved horns, shaggy grey and black mottled coats and long beards. Several herds are known to live in the 'Great Wilderness' and I have been lucky to see them on previous occasions in Gleann Bianasdail and on the summit of Sail Mhor.

The Abhainn na Fuirness descends to Loch Maree in a series of spectacular cascades and waterfalls. Unfortunately though, it was unfordable and I was forced to forgo a planned short cut and follow the west bank all the way down to the bridge at Furnace, by Loch Maree.

In the early eighteenth century, iron ore was smelted with charcoal at Furnace for the manufacture of cannons, and much of the ancient oak forest was felled. Nevertheless, the oak woods that remain on the north side of Loch Maree are some of the finest in the Highlands.

The Letterewe Estate is now supplied by boat from across Loch Maree, and the once heavily used footpath, running for nine miles from Kinlochewe, has sadly fallen into disrepair. Along most of its length the path runs close to the upper boundary of the woods and, although indistinct, it can still be detected through the bracken and heather.

This delightful switchback path beside the cool woods of oak, hazel, birch and holly makes the ideal contrast to the severe crags of Beinn Lair. Loch Maree, looking its most majestic, stretches away to the west for twelve miles, waves lap the shores of tiny bays and inlets while cascades of white water streak down from the upper slopes of Slioch.

The gorge of the Abhainn an Fhasargh which runs through Gleann Bianasdail is spanned by a wooden bridge. This marks the beginning of the Slioch-Kinlochewe trade-route, the path is patterned by vibram prints and, inevitably, it was here that I met my first human being since leaving Poolewe.

The western slopes of Slioch seen from the western shore of Loch Maree.

THE GREAT WILDERNESS: MULLACH COIRE MHIC FHEARCHAIR'S EAST RIDGE

by DAVE MATHEWS

Finding this excellent and remote walk, like many of our best discoveries, came about by an involuntary change of plan.

The petrol supply crisis of the 1970s caused particular anxiety to Scottish hill lovers dwelling south of the border. My own plan to minimise the effect of restricted car travel was to visit the more inaccessible regions whilst I could, and rely on rail and bicycle transport when the petrol dried up (back to the pioneering days!). As a result, I concentrated my holidays on the Northern Highlands and in June 1970 stood on Conival, my last 3,000ft top in the area. The mist and freezing rain did little to dampen my spirits as I celebrated this event in the Inchnadamph Hotel, and reflected on the great days I had spent in the Northern Hills.

It is an amazing fact of life that Scottish Hills have a habit of changing height year by year and that tops rise and fall in accordance with seasons. Visiting all the interesting looking summits in an area, however, tends to protect one against the vagaries of the Tables and completeness should be assured. But the 1981 revision of Munro's Tables caught me out with two unnoticed separate tops on Mullach Coire Mhic Fhearchair on the east side of the Great Wilderness; one of them, Sgurr Dubh, was hidden down the East Ridge, whilst the second, East Top, was quite close to the summit.

These new tops gave me the stimulus needed to revisit the area and, as a further incentive, I recalled my excitement at seeing these hills from the summit of A' Chailleach in the Fannichs, some years before. I was particularly attracted by the sight of vast slabs descending from the summit of Sgurr Ban. By studying the maps I now devised a route that would take in the two rogue tops, and allow me a closer look at the impressive rock architecture of the region.

In contrast to my ascent of Conival in foul weather I set out in glorious sunshine along the north bank of Loch a' Bhraoin. The path is rough in places and occasionally gets lost in the shale at the water's edge, but after four miles arrives at the bothy at Lochivraon. This bothy is still in good repair and is a wonderful place to linger, watching the many varieties of birds that make their home by the edge of the loch.

As the path continues west, the rocky aspect of the east face of Mullach Coire Mhic Fhearchair increasingly fills the view ahead. One soon arrives at the ruined bothy of Feinasheen, which gives perspective to the hills and cliffs looming ahead. A short distance beyond the bothy the path swings north and it is then possible to cross boggy, lumpy ground to the streams falling east from the ridge. The rock scenery here surpassed my expectations from the Fannichs view, with steep cliffs on the left, and enormous sheets of slabby rock falling from Sgurr Ban on the right.

Some care is needed to get on to the East Ridge safely. Firstly, one must ascend between slab and cliffs. The cliffs on the left gradually become shorter and more broken and a way is found onto the ridge either up a grassy break, or up one of the easy gullies.

The ridge top is wide and grassy, but becomes increasingly narrower and more rocky until the first top, Sgurr Dubh, is reached.

Beyond this lies a section of moderate but airy scrambling until the ridge levels out and the East Top is ascended without difficulty. From this East Top, it is just a short step to the main summit of Coire Mhic Fhearchair at 3326ft/1019 m.

After the uncertainty of finding a way through the cliffs I was glad to relax on the summit and take in the tremendous view. On this beautiful hot day I could clearly see from An Teallach and Beinn Dearg Mhor in the north to Slioch and Beinn Eighe in the south. The feeling of isolation on this summit was enhanced by the nearness of normally distant hills; Beinn Tarsuinn to the south and A' Mhaighdean to the west. I enjoyed a pleasant half-hour lying back against the summit cairn retracing my previous visit to this unique area.

I headed north over the long and switchback ridge running over Sgurr Ban and Beinn a' Chlaidheimh. Memories here are of walking and sliding over mounds of greasy quartzite blocks before the long drop to Loch a' Bhrisidh on the bealach. A further ascent of 1,000ft

---

Maps O.S. 1:50,000 Sheets 19 and 20.

Grading A long and serious expedition over rough mountainous country, involving some rock scrambling and a potentially dangerous river crossing towards the end of the day.

Start / Finish Loch a' Bhraoin roadhead (162760); Corrie Hallie (114852).

Distance / Time 22 miles/10-11 hours.

Escape Routes From Sgurr Dubh a way can be found S to meet the Gleann na Muice track leading to Kinlochewe. Emergency shelter at Lochivraon cottage or Shenavall bothy.

Telephones Braemore Junction, Dundonnell and Kinlochewe.

Transport Gairloch-Inverness bus on Mon, Wed and Sat passes through Dundonnell and Braemore. Ullapool-Gairloch bus on Wed, June to September.

Accommodation Dundonnell Hotel. Hotels/Guest Houses and B & B at Ullapool, Poolewe, Gairloch and Aultbea. Youth Hostels at Aultbea and Ullapool. J.M.C.S. Hut, The Smiddy, Dundonnell.

Guidebooks S.M.T. Guide 'The Northern Highlands'; 'The High Mountains of Britain and Ireland' by Irvine Butterfield (Diadem); 'The Munros' by Donald Bennet (S.M.T.).

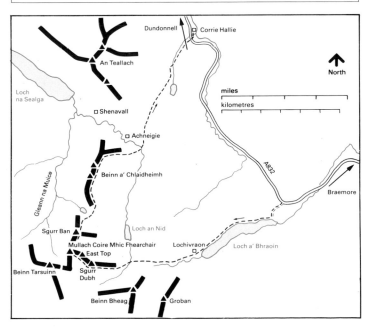

A photomontage of Mullach Coire Mhic Fhearchair seen from Sgurr Ban. The East Top and Sgurr Dubh are on the left and Beinn Tarsuinn is on the right.

A view along the East Ridge of Mullach Coire Mhic Fhearchair from Sgurr Dubh.

Dave Mathews

Sgurr Ban and An Teallach from Mullach Coire Mhic Fhearchair.

Tom Rix

put me on the narrow, multi-topped summit of Beinn a' Chlaidheimh, its grass a welcome relief after the quartzite toil around Sgurr Ban. An easy descent north-east leads to the glen near the Achneigie-Dundonnell track.

The Abhainn Strath na Sealga is forded here, which can be tricky even on a dry day. On a wet day this river can become impassable, a fact which must be borne in mind when planning this walk as there are no obvious escape routes. Such a river crossing, late in the day, adds a serious dimension to this expedition; a safety rope should be carried and used without hesitation if the need arises.

Once over the river a wide track leads firstly over moorland, and then down through the beautiful wooded Gleann Chaorachain to Corrie Hallie a short distance from Dundonnell.

The Great Wilderness had yielded another fine and challenging walk through some of the remotest and ruggedest hills in Britain.

Beinn Tarsuinn and Slioch from Mullach Coire Mhic Fhearchair. The peaks of the Flowerdale Forest are seen in the distance.

THE PEAKS OF THE FLOWERDALE FOREST

Maps O.S. 1:25,000 Outdoor Leisure Map – 'The Cuillin and Torridon Hills'; O.S. 1:50,000 Sheet 19.
Grading A long mountain walk in a very remote area. Some scrambling is involved on the ridge of Beinn Dearg.
Start / Finish Am Feur Loch on the Kinlochewe – Gairloch road (856720).
Distance / Time 24 miles/10-11 hours.
Escape Routes There are no quick ways out of the Flowerdale Forest, although from the E summit of Beinn Dearg a descent could be made S to Coire Dubh or Coire Mhic Nobuil. The bothy Poca Buidhe is often locked, but the boat shed at the N end of Loch na h-Oidhche could provide emergency shelter.
Telephones Gairloch pier and Talladale.
Transport Railway Station at Achnasheen. Daily bus service Gairloch – Achnasheen. Gairloch – Inverness bus service on Tues, Thurs and Fri.
Accommodation Hotels at Kinlochewe, Loch Maree and Gairloch. B & B at Gairloch and Badachro. Youth Hostels at Torridon, Carn Dearg near Gairloch, Craig and Aultbea.
Guidebook S.M.T. Guide 'The Northern Highlands'.

Flowerdale Forest: the name alone should be sufficiently emotive to entice walkers to this remote region of Ross-shire. Yet few visitors venture west of the Torridon giants. Having traversed Beinn Eighe, Liathach and Beinn Alligin they return home sated with superlatives, or make for sandy coves at Gairloch and Gruinard to relax.

When viewed from the lofty heights of Liathach's Spidean a'Choire Leith or Beinn Eighe's Ruadh-stac Mor, much of the Flowerdale Forest appears flat and boggy, a desolate area criss-crossed by rivulets and patterned with a mosaic of tiny lochans. A bleak and watery world, not unlike Coigach to the north. But the quality of the landscape is transformed by three superb individual peaks which rear up from the sandstone bedrock to a height of nearly 3,000ft. Baosbheinn, Beinn an Eoin and Beinn Dearg have fine ridges linking their principal summits which throw down steep, gully seamed, shoulders enclosing wild corries and dark lochans.

I shall never forget the view of Flowerdale from Coire Mhic Fhearchair one sparkling March day, when the peaks were plastered in snow, the sun glinted on the ice-covered lochans and Loch na h-Oidhche reflected the arctic-blue of the sky. The scene was so beautiful that it made a greater impression on me than Coire Mhic Fhearchair's famous triple buttresses themselves.

The Flowerdale Forest peaks are not easily won. A stalkers' path runs in for six miles from the Gairloch–Loch Maree road to a boat house at the northern end of Loch na h-Oidhche, but from there onwards the going is trackless. You must pick your own route up the steep, rough slopes of heather and boulders and negotiate your own way through the crags and along the ridges which, on Beinn Dearg, are exposed and require some scrambling ability. But this is what high quality Scottish hill walking is all about; paths should be confined to the glens leaving the uplands untamed and unscarred.

The stalkers' path starts from Am Feur Loch and winds its way into the heart of Flowerdale. For much of the way it follows the Abhainn a'Gharbh Choire which, in late autumn after a night of torrential rain, we found to be brown and foaming, while clouds raced overhead. The gale-force southerly wind came in buffets, catching us unawares and driving us off the path into the bog.

After two hours we reached Loch na h-Oidhche and took shelter in the squat, robust boat-house for some chocolate, while wind-driven spume dashed against the corrugated iron roof.

It was a steep scramble to the Beinn an Eoin ridge, the last 100ft through a fringe of weathered sandstone outcrops. Although the rocks provided some shelter from the worst of the gale, the scene below was dramatic. At the end of the loch water spouts, raised by the tremendous gusts of wind, were racing over the surface and spending their energy on the flanks of Baosbheinn. First a curtain of spray, blown up by the wind, would speed down the loch; then it would contract into a spiralling column of white foam, 50ft high, and roar away towards the shore.

Once on the broad saddle of the ridge, we paused for breath and feasted our eyes on the view. Far away on the northern horizon An

Beinn Alligin from the summit ridge of Beinn Dea[rg]

A view from Liathach to Beinn Dearg and Carn n[...]

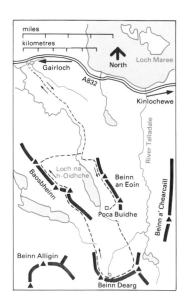

a with Beinn an Eoin beyond.

Baosbheinn from Poca Buidhe.

Carn na Feola and Beinn an Eoin
seen beyond the one of Fasarinen
Pinnacles of Liathach.

Jim Teesdale

The Baosbheinn chain from Beinn Alligin.

Teallach was basking in bright sunshine, perhaps the last before the coming of the winter snow. Closer at hand shafts of sunlight were playing on the islets and bays of Loch Maree, catching the white horses on the loch's surface and burnishing the leaves of the oak woodlands at Letterewe. Slioch however was brooding in the shade, seemingly as impregnable as a fortress. We could have dawdled all day, watching the deer grazing Coire na Ciche on the north side of the ridge, but daylight was limited and we had far to go.

Approaching the summit of Beinn an Eoin, 2,801ft/855m, the ridge narrows suddenly and we had to cling to the rocks to prevent the wind plucking us off and whirling us into Strath Lungard. A rapid descent of the broken slopes on the west side took us straight to the estate-owned cottage of Poca Buidhe. This low, stone-built bothy nestles amongst huge boulders, merging almost invisibly into the background.

Beinn Dearg lies two-and-a-half miles south of Poca Buidhe across a barren wilderness, liberally sprinkled with boulders and shallow pools. From the heights of Beinn an Eoin the going looked tough but, to our delight, we found large areas of glacier-scoured sandstone enabling us to make good speed.

A green gully provided a simple route from Coire Beag to Carn na Feola, the eastern summit of Beinn Dearg. Here we ate a late lunch, gazing right into the jaws of Liathach. The northern pinnacles, the Am Fasarinen pinnacles and the plunging cliffs of Coire na Caime make up the dark side of Liathach, and underline the serious nature of the traverse of Torridon's mightiest peak.

Before Beinn Dearg's main summit, 2,995ft/914m, is reached, the ridge steepens and rock buttresses seemingly block the way ahead. Broken cliffs fall away to a shallow corrie containing a picturesque lochan, Loch a' Choire Mhoir. Taken directly the rock scrambling is reminiscent of the Corrag Bhuidhe but-

tresses of An Teallach, but most of the difficulties can be bypassed on the south side.

The afternoon was well advanced as we climbed through the sandstone formations on Ceann Beag, the southern summit of Baosbheinn and the largest of the Flowerdale Forest mountains. Beinn Alligin and the Horns rose cheerlessly across Loch a' Bhealaich as black clouds rolled up, but, with the gale now at our backs, we sped north.

A stag bellowed in a hidden corrie and a flock of snow bunting flashed across the ridge like leaves caught in a flurry of wind; otherwise we were in our own world. Beyond the 2,869ft/875m, top of Baosbheinn the ridge continues in a series of rocky turrets before descending to a broad grassy shoulder. From this point, with the sky now dark except for an amber glow in the west, we ran down An Reidh-choire, waded the burn and regained the path.

The torch-lit walk back to the car was no penance for stealing such a day; nourished by our high spirits the miles slipped by.

Approaching the summit of Baosbheinn from the north with Beinn Alligin on the right.

BEINN DAMH

Maps O.S. 1:50,000 Sheets 24 and 25.
Grading An exhilarating mountain walk along a stony but broad ridge, giving fine views of the Torridon peaks. The descent to Drochaid Coire Roill from the principal summit is a very steep scramble, and inexperienced parties should return by the route of ascent.
Start / Finish Loch Torridon Hotel (887542).
Distance / Time 9 miles/6-7 hours.
Escape Routes The low bealach between Beinn Damh and Sgurr na Bana Mhoraire provides an easy descent into Coire Roill.
Telephones Annat and Loch Torridon Hotel.
Transport Railway Stations at Lochcarron and Achnasheen. Daily bus service Lochcarron Station – Torridon (Mon, Wed, Fri in winter). Daily bus service Kinlochewe – Torridon, connecting with the Achnasheen – Kinlochewe service.
Accommodation Hotels at Loch Torridon and Shieldaig. B & B locally. Youth Hostel at Torridon.
Guidebooks S.M.T. Guide 'The Northern Highlands'; 'The Scottish Peaks' by W. A. Poucher (Constable).

Just forty-three feet protect the individual and shapely peak of Beinn Damh from the relentless tread of the Munro-baggers. While its illustrious neighbours, Beinn Alligin, Liathach, Beinn Eighe and Maol Chean-dearg syphon off most of the active hill walkers to their lofty crests, Beinn Damh is left undisturbed. Yet from its northern outlier, Sgurr na Bana Mhoraire, a high, broad and stony ridge runs over two miles south to its principal summit at 2,957ft/902m. This ridge provides an inspiring mountain walk, worthy of Beinn Damh's position amongst the giants of Torridon.

In its heyday, the Ben-Damph estate was thriving deer forest, and one of the most superbly situated in Scotland. Ben-damph House on the south shore of Loch Torridon enjoyed unsurpassed views of Beinn Alligin and Beinn Dearg, while the adjacent craggy mountains, giving way to well wooded lower slopes, ravines and waterfalls combined to make a romantic Highland scene.

Ben-damph House has now become the Loch Torridon Hotel, and only a neon sign announcing 'Ben-damph Bar' acknowledges this most traditional of lodges. However, the great days of the estate have left a legacy of beautifully constructed stalkers' paths, which make for easy walking into the heart of the mountains.

It was a cold night in Glen Torridon and we woke to find two inches of fresh snow on the tent. But a strong wind was tearing holes in the cloud-cover and exposing patches of blue sky, while even a few rays of sunshine reflected off the white shoulders of Beinn Alligin.

About twenty yards to the west of the road bridge over the Allt Coire Roill, a narrow gate gives access to a path running up through the trees towards Beinn Damh. This path makes a perfect start to the day, for it is well drained, gently contoured and carpeted with a soft bed of pine needles. The trees of larch and Caledonian pine are well spaced giving green glades of moss covered boulders and tangled rhododendrons, while the branches are festooned with lichen, indicative of the clean air. Gaps in the trees allow views down to some magnificent cascades and falls, as the burn thunders through a ravine.

Once above the shelter of the trees the snow squeaked underfoot and an icy wind from the north pinched our faces. The rock buttresses of Creag na h-Iolaire on the northern spur of Beinn Damh, topped with icing sugar and outlined against a blue sky, looked daunting; it was November 2nd and winter had arrived overnight.

Even through the snow we were able to follow the line of the path, zig-zagging up to the wide bealach under the north-west ridge of Beinn Damh. By a stroke of luck our arrival at the bealach coincided with a lull in the weather. Away out to the west we could see squalls of snow and hail racing in across the Sound of Raasay. Further south the clouds were just touching the top of the Applecross Hills, but light was flooding into the corries of Beinn Bhan and Sgurr a'Chaorachain, where the mantle of snow emphasised the horizontally striated sandstone buttresses. Although the clouds were streaming off Maol Chean-dearg exposing its cliff-girt, sugar-loaf

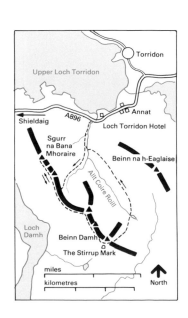

On the Beinn Damh ridge – heading south to the main summit.

A photomontage showing the view to the north from the main summit of Beinn Damh showing the north top, Loch Torridon, Beinn Alligin, Baosbheinn and Beinn Dearg.

summit, Liathach was suffering a day of almost continuous blizzard.

Turning north, the ridge rises to a subsidiary summit where it narrows and runs along the top of a line of crags overlooking Loch Damh. It then descends to a second bealach under the rocky turret of Sgurr na Bana Mhoraire, 2,251ft/686m. From the bealach the direct ascent of Sgurr na Bana Mhoraire is a steep scramble, but we discovered a cairned path which traverses the rocks to the north-west side, where the angle eases. Sadly we were allowed only a brief glimpse west towards Skye, and north to Beinn Alligin and the Flowerdale Forest, before a squall hit us, obscuring the view with blinding snowflakes.

With heads hooded and gloved hands grasping the compass we turned south, regained the main bealach, and struck up the boulder fields to the main massif of Beinn Damh.

There are three tops on the long, broad ridge of Beinn Damh, the principal summit being the furthest south. It is an easy ridge walk, although rather rugged underfoot where the rounded sandstone gives way to angular blocks of quartzite. Height may be saved by following a cairned path which skirts the first two tops on the west side, returning to the ridge at the bealach under the summit.

The cairn is perched above an impressive line of cliffs and the north-east ridge, with a covering of fresh snow on the rocks and several crags to be negotiated, looked intimidating. Likewise the south-east ridge appeared anything but easy, descending 300ft to a gap under a vertical rock tooth. Below the summit, on the southern slopes, light coloured rocks form a strange stirrup-shaped mark, clearly seen from the Kishorn road and the Applecross Hills.

The thought of returning down the main ridge, facing into the wind and driving snow, was not to be entertained, so we scrambled down the south-east ridge to the gap, and then managed to continue the descent into the corrie. It was an unpleasant route over frozen, snow-covered grass and scree but, in good conditions, both the north-east and south-east ridges are perfectly straightforward.

A short climb back over the Drochaid Coire Roill, passing under sandstone cliffs, grey with hanging ice, took us to a tiny lochan and an excellent stalkers path.

Floods and frosts have made little impression on this superbly constructed path. Built to take the pressure of hooves of ponies, heavily laden with the carcasses of deer, the path is shored up, paved, bridged and drained with runnels of natural stone. Most of Scotland's great estates have such paths, skilfully constructed with picks and shovels and using only rough boulders as building materials. It is a pity that such talent exists no more; many of our eroded hill paths would benefit from the attentions of such craftsmen.

The stalkers' path gives a close-up view of the line of east-facing cliffs dropping from the summit ridge of Beinn Damh. Towering up in tiers of black rock, and seamed by snow-filled gullies, the cliffs looked very fierce in the fading light of the late afternoon.

Little snow had melted during the day and we were easily able to cross the Allt Coire Roill at the treeline, and so regain the path of the morning's ascent.

Across Loch Torridon a snowplough was at work on the Diabaig road, its blue stroboscopic light penetrating the gloom. The clouds descended, flurries of snow swirled down the road; we hastened into dry socks, jumped into the car and drove off in search of tea.

Looking east from Beinn Damh to Maol Chean-dearg and An Ruadh-stac.

Alan O'Brien

Heading north along the Red Cuillin ridge (Beinn Dearg Mhor) towards Glamaig.

THE RED CUILLIN TRAVERSE

Hill walkers give scant attention to the Red Cuillin of Skye. Speeding away from the ferry at Kyleakin they hasten to Glen Brittle, Sligachan or Loch Slapin, eyes firmly set on the black, jagged rocks of the main Cuillin ridge, Bla Bheinn (Blaven) or Clach Glas. If anything, the huge, bulky, scree covered hills of Glamaig and Beinn Dearg are mere frustrations, since they deny the visitor the classic view of Sgurr nan Gillean and the Bhasteir Tooth until he has reached the head of Loch Sligachan.

But look down Glen Sligachan towards Bla Bheinn, and the beautiful conical peak of Marsco commands the middle distance. Marsco belies its modest 2,414ft/735m by rising straight up from sea level, its sharp summit supported by dramatic rock buttresses and towers which throw down fans of scree. Set amidst the grandest mountain scenery in the British Isles, Marsco still holds its own, and I liken its appearance to that of Great Gable seen dominating the head of Wasdale in the Lake District.

In Tertiary times gabbro, a black igneous rock, welled up through the earth's crust and arched up the surface layer of basaltic lava to form the hills of the Black Cuillin and Bla Bheinn. Subsequent intrusions of dykes and sills of dolerite, followed by weathering, producing the serrated ridges which we see today. In the same era, a major intrusion of granite through the gabbro formed the Red Cuillin which, in the absence of dykes and sills, have weathered into more rounded hills.

Since most of the walking on the Red Cuillin traverse is easy, you have a wonderful opportunity to appreciate the unique surroundings, better perhaps than from a day spent on the careful negotiation of a section of the main ridge itself. A traverse from Glamaig over Beinn Dearg to Marsco leads you into the very heart of the Cuillin, giving unsurpassed and ever changing views of Bla Bheinn and the entire main ridge from Sgurr nan Gillean to Gars-bheinn.

From Sligachan a stubby ridge of heather, scree and boulders leads straight to Sgurr Mhairi, the 2,537ft/775m, summit of Glamaig. A more interesting, but less direct, approach is from Sconser where

The view from Glamaig, across Bealach na Sgairde to Beinn Dearg Mhor, Beinn Dearg Mheadhonach and Marsco (right) with Bla Bheinn (Blaven) in the background.

easier angled slopes rise to An Coileach, whence a fine ridge runs south-west to Sgurr Mhairi.

It is worth spending a few minutes on the summit of Glamaig to look around. As you gaze north across Portree and the Storr to the distant hills of Harris, and then turn clockwise; Dun Caan on Raasay, the Applecross Hills, the Five Sisters of Kintail, Bla Bheinn, neighbouring Beinn Dearg, the Pinnacle Ridge of Sgurr nan Gillean, the thrusting ridge of Druim nan Ramh and McLeod's Tables all come into view.

On my traverse in late March the snow level was 1,500ft and the saw-toothed ridge of the Black Cuillin, outlined against the bluest of skies, looked truly formidable. I could imagine the climbers inching their way along the ridge on the finest winter challenge our mountains can offer; a traverse first completed by Patey, MacInnes, Robertson and Crabb in 1965.

The snow, which was curled into cornices over the northern slopes, vastly increased the stature of our more rounded hills and it sparkled and crunched under our feet as we strode along the ridge of Glamaig, our enthusiasm knowing no bounds.

A steep and loose descent to Bealach na Sgairde now follows, and a further halt will be called to empty the pebbles out of your boots. This is the first of many such descents on the switchback traverse of

the Red Cuillin. However, with many different descent-lines on offer, each of equal merit, paths have not yet been worn and it is still possible to find tongues of runnable scree.

Beinn Dearg is a huge, hump-backed whale of a mountain, divided into the two distinct peaks of Beinn Dearg Mhor and Beinn Dearg Mheadhonach by a low col, Bealach Mosgaraidh at 1,500ft. It is a much more interesting mountain than appears from below: broken cliffs, corries, gullies and spurs abound, and the close proximity of the Inner Sound on the east side with its sprinkling of islands – Scalpay, Longay, Pabay and the Crowlins – gives an enhanced sense of space and freedom.

Out of the wind the sun was warm: a day for dawdling, enjoying the thermos of coffee by the summit cairns, and trying to identify all the west coast peaks strung out from Ben Cruachan to Liathach.

Walking south down the Red Cuillin it is the individual peak of Marsco that wins respect as the dominant peak of the range. Its rocky shoulders are steeper, its summit sharper and it appears an altogether haughtier mountain than its more mundane neighbours.

To reach the Mam a' Phobuill under Marsco's north facing Coire nan Laogh, it is possible to scree-run from the south ridge of Beinn Dearg Mheadhonach. But a far better way is to continue along the ridge, to the subsidiary top of Ciche na Beinne Deirge, and then

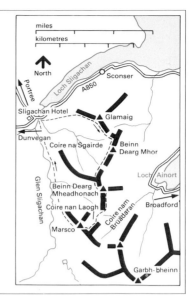

Maps O.S. 1:50,000 Sheet 32; O.S.
1:25,000 Outdoor Leisure Map – 'The
Cuillin and Torridon Hills'; S.M.T.
Special map of the Cuillin, about
3 inches to a mile, outline contour.
Grading The hills are mainly rounded
and scree covered, and the going is
easy apart from a steep scramble
down the north ridge of Marsco.
Start / Finish at Sligachan Hotel
(486298).
Distance / Time 10 miles/8-9 hours.
Escape Routes Easy routes may be
taken from any of the low bealachs
between the hills, back to Glen
Sligachan.
Telephone Sligachan Hotel.
Transport The Glasgow – Portree long
distance bus passes through Sligachan.
Daily bus service from Kyleakin to
Sligachan, Carbost and Portree.
Accommodation Slighachan Hotel.
Hotels/Guest Houses at Portree and
Broadford. Youth Hostels at Glen Brittle,
Broadford and Kyle of Lochalsh.
Guidebooks S.M.T. Guide 'Island
of Skye'; 'The Magic of Skye' by
W. A. Poucher (Constable).

descend firmer slopes to the Mam. Now walk up into Coire nan Laogh, cross the burn and scramble up the shoulder on the east side, this leads to the narrow summit ridge of Marsco.

Throughout your ascent you will be transfixed by the walls of black rock falling sheer on the west side of the Bla Bheinn – Clach Glas ridge, which confronts you across Am Fraoch choire. South of Garbh-bheinn the crooked teeth of Clach Glas lead to a vee in the ridge (the 'putting green') beyond which shattered rock buttresses rise to the twin summits of Bla Bheinn. This is one of the most exciting views in the Cuillin and I hope it will entice you to try the magnificently exposed scramble of the Bla Bheinn–Clach Glas ridge, described by John MacKenzie in the next chapter.

The summit ridge of Marsco is a revelation. A short, but extremely narrow ridge snakes up to a tiny cairn, while plunging slopes on either side provide a degree of exposure, particularly under snow, reminiscent of sections of the Mamores' ridges or the Carn Mor Dearg arête.

Marsco is sufficiently far south to give views right up Harta Corrie

Glamaig, Bealach na Sgairde and Beinn Dearg Mhor from the west.

to the fearsome overlapping slabs on Bidein Druim nan Ramh. Further south, above Coruisg, the Inaccessible Pinnacle of Sgurr Dearg, An Stac and the spires of Alasdair and Sgumain are conspicuous features of the Cuillin main ridge.

Proceeding north, Marsco's sharp ridge soon gives way to a broad spur which dips steeply on three sides. Five hundred feet of broken cliffs must be negotiated to reach the heather and grass slopes of Glen Sligachan. Care must be exercised when descending north from Marsco; it may be necessary to retrace your steps to find an easier way through the crags. In general gullies should be avoided. If in doubt descend easier slopes on the north side of Coire nan Laogh and regain the Mam a' Phobuill.

A three mile stroll along the boggy track through Glen Sligachan returns you to your starting point, at the welcoming Sligachan Hotel.

THE BLAVEN – CLACH GLAS RIDGE

by JOHN MacKENZIE

The traverse of Clach Glas and Bla Bheinn (Blaven) on a fine summer's day probably cannot be surpassed by any other mountain group in Britain. In full winter conditions it gives problems not usually associated with this country, and this provides the theme of this essay, blacks and whites, summer and winter. First however a warning: this is not just a rough walk over optional difficulties, but a precipitous mountain traverse where rope handling, the competence to lead up to a Difficult standard and route-finding are all essential skills. If uncertain, do easier traverses such as An Teallach, Liathach and the Aonach Eagach ridge first. In fact the Clach Glas section is more precipitous than anything on the main Cuillin Ridge itself, so a head for heights is also a prerequisite.

The road from Broadford suddenly reveals the group as you near Loch Slapin, a fantastic serrated outline of black gabbro isolated from the main Cuillin, so preserving its unique majesty set above the waters of the loch. Rounding the bend and crossing over the Allt na Dunaiche you can park at an oxbow layby, a rarity on single track roads. Cross to the north bank of the burn and plough through the dismal swamps where once a track lay, now ruined by water and feet. This wet mile is fortunately offset by the wall of rock ahead and, where the track crosses the burn, strike out right by any dry means you can to reach Choire a'Caise and drier ground.

Steep scree slopes lead to the narrow col immediately north of Clach Glas, hemmed in by vertiginous rock walls on the left and the friendlier slopes of Sgurr nan Each on the right. Already you realise that this is something different from the usual British hill. The col is stopped by a wall of rock, easily turned by a left traverse into a shallow gully which is climbed to a platform. Ahead lies a formidable tower. This thin wedge of inhospitality is the edge-on view of Clach Glas and fortunately is a bit of an imposter.

Keeping to the ridge, an exposed arête is climbed to a crest and then descended steeply leftwards by grooves to a full stop just short of a little col. Features of this mountain are seductive lines terminated by vertical drops, in this case turned by another left groove. This section is exhilaratingly narrow but ahead the buttressed ridge broadens. Now go up right and traverse slabs to reach a stone shoot which ends at an exposed narrow col. Ahead lies a vertical wall, about Severe in standard, but you will have noticed a slanting gully inset into the right wall of the shoot and a little lower. This leads over Moderate bumps and humps and takes you to a narrow neck. Above lies the terminal tower of Clach Glas, and an ascent up steep slabs leads shortly to the thin crest itself. The ridge is now exposed, the free fall potential being considerable. Where difficulties on the way up were turned on the right, now they are best avoided on the left. To descend, a crack is followed down a slab for 30ft followed by a narrow and rather rotten arête which, when viewed from below, impressed the pioneers greatly. This arête,

'Pilkington's Imposter', leads down to another little col and a rather steep tower beyond.

A vertical wall is scaled on generous holds for a few feet before a traverse and another drop is reached. The haven of the Clach Glas-Bla Bheinn bealach is near, and some judicious route finding soon leads to it. By now you will be getting the general drift of these mountains, up a bit, down a bit, along a bit more, back again and so on, all very satisfying. An escape for the weary can be made down the great scree run to the east of the bealach, but make sure that you have reached it first for the gullies you have crossed previously are not feasible descents.

Ahead lies Bla Bheinn, its steep ridge towering above. To the west the Main Ridge lies in a splendid arc, your height above sea level greatly exaggerated by the sheerness of all that surrounds you. The grassy hollow of the bealach, the 'Putting Green', so named by the Victorians, leads to a steep wall avoided on the left where an easy 12ft section gains scree which is crossed to the right. The second chimney along is a stone shoot, above which is another scree platform at the eastern end of which is Naismith's imposing 'Half Crown Pinnacle'. Going left along the platform for a few yards leads to a 60ft chimney, climbed by its fine right wall on good holds. Difficulties now ended, cross over some big stones to descend into a large stone shoot which is ascended leftwards to the skyline above the Bla Bheinn precipices.

The North Top is the summit at 3,044ft/927m, the South Top being a little lower and separated by a scree-filled gully, which drops eastwards to the Fionna-choire. This makes a jarring descent so continue to the South Top, admire the tremendous view and descend the easy south ridge for a short while before steep grassy slopes lead down to the col above Fionna-choire. The lochan of the same name gives the hardy or over-heated a swim, before the track

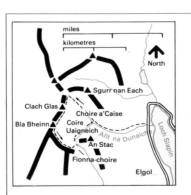

Maps O.S. 1:50,000 Sheet 32; O.S. 1:25,000 Outdoor Leisure Map – 'The Cuillin and Torridon Hills'.

Grading An exceptionally exposed but delightful traverse of a rocky arete. A rope will be needed to safeguard certain sections of the route, and climbers should be competent up to 'difficult' standard. In conditions of snow, high wind or heavy rain the ridge should be left to the experts.

Start / Finish N end of Loch Slapin (561216).

Distance / Time 6 miles/7 hours.

Escape Route Descend E into Choire a'Caise from the Clach Glas – Bla Bheinn bealach.

Telephones Torrin, Strathaird House and Elgol.

Transport Daily bus service from Kyleakin to Broadford. Weekday bus service Broadford to Elgol passes the start of the walk.

Accommodation Hotels in Broadford, B & B in Torrin and Elgol. B.M.C. Climbing Hut in Glen Brittle. Youth Hostels in Glen Brittle, Broadford and Kyle of Lochalsh.

Guidebooks S.M.T. Guide 'Island of Skye'; 'The High Mountains of Britain and Ireland' by Irvine Butterfield (Diadem); 'Scottish Climbs' Vol 2 by Hamish MacInnes (Constable); 'The Munros' by Donald Bennet (S.M.T.).

Left: The south side of Clach Glas in a view from Bla Bheinn (Blaven). Two climbers can just be seen on the face below the left-hand ridge.

Richard Gibbens

Gordon Gadsby

Left and above: The spectacular rock scenery near the summit of Clach Glas.

left of the burn descends to Coire Uaigneich. The Allt na Dunaiche is now followed back over the bogs to the car. A splendid day if the weather is clear, but if the mist is down and the way not sure then to quote an early guide, 'many strangers who tackle the two peaks in thick mist fail to carry out their programme'.

The winter traverse of Clach Glas is a truly magnificent expedition requiring considerable expertise in snow and ice climbing.

On the last day of 1986 Bob Brown and I approached Clach Glas through deep unconsolidated snow on a perfect winter's day. Its white fang looked impossibly big and awesomely impressive with cloud pluming off the summit. That day it would have graced the Karakoram, and was perhaps the single most arresting peak I had seen in many years winter climbing.

The summer pitches were well buried under the snow and they provided sustained and exposed climbing. Several abseils were necessary to descend vertical ice walls.

The negotiation of Clach Glas under such conditions gave us a day made unforgettable by the complex route finding, perhaps a fitting end to the year amidst the wildest, grandest mountains in all Britain.

Bla Bheinn (Blaven), Clach Glas and Sgurr na Each from the eastern shore of Loch Slapin.

A view north-west to the Black Cuillin Ridge from the Blaven-Clach Glas ridge. Ruadh Stac and Marsco are the peaks in the middle distance.

ACROSS KNOYDART TO BEN ADEN

It was early November and the winding road alongside Loch Arkaig was slippery with fallen leaves and pine needles, while the vivid colours of the larch, oak, alder and birch trees shone even through the curtains of rain which swept down the glen beneath a leaden sky.

We were bound for Knoydart, the wettest, roughest, remotest and wildest peninsula in these islands, and we shivered at the thought of the walk ahead: nine tough and boggy miles to the open bothy of Sourlies at the head of Loch Nevis.

The motor road ends at Strathan and a Land Rover track continues west to serve the shooting lodge of Glendessarry and a cottage at Upper Glendessarry. Recent planting by Fountain Forestry has left Glen Dessarry even more dreary than before; a new access road has been built on the south side of the glen, passing above A'Chuil bothy, but no advantage can be obtained by taking it.

Beyond Upper Glendessarry the path to Loch Nevis is purgatory; at best it is a stream and at worst a quagmire and our progress against the westerly gale seemed imperceptible. In such conditions our Goretex suits offered only token resistance to the icy rain, and we shuddered as the cold penetrated to the bones. Over four hours passed before we squelched over the wet seaweed and burst into the haven of Sourlies, a primitive but dry bothy kept in first class order by the Mountain Bothies Association in collaboration with the Knoydart estate.

A big river foams down from the Mam na Cloich Airde pass and enters Loch Nevis near the ruins of Finiskaig. A recent flood had deposited branches of trees and logs of wood on high ground well above the river bank, and this provided ample firewood for the evening. Wet wood mixed with broken plastic from old fish boxes burnt well, and as circulation was restored so our spirits rose.

Overnight the gale blew itself out and we awoke to a still and frosty morning with the sun burnishing the moor grass on the upper slopes of Beinn Bhuidhe across the loch. Traversing round into Glen Carnach we were confronted by the rocky wedge of Ben Aden dominating the head of the glen and now dusted white with new snow. On the west of the glen the path to Inverie zig-zagged up under Meall Buidhe, while on the east side the summit cone of Sgurr na Ciche rose white and aloof against the blue sky, seemingly impossibly high and impregnable.

Our hearts leapt at the beauty of the scene, we had struck a day in a thousand and our step was light as we strode across the sea-washed turf to the ruins of Carnach, and the splendid new suspension bridge over the notoriously dangerous river.

The present bridge was built in 1982 by Phil Gribbon and members of the SMC, with help from the Knoydart estate. It replaces an old bridge long since washed away by floods. Rivers in Knoydart are particularly dangerous and a few years ago a man was drowned while attempting to cross the nearby Allt Coire na Ciche. Nevertheless, the Carnach bridge has been criticised by some people who think that a wilderness area should be free of man-made safety aids, and parties venturing into the hills should be prepared to deal with any emergencies.

Above: Nearing the summit of Ben Aden with Ladhar Bheinn prominent in the background.

Map O.S. 1:50,000 Sheet 33.
Grading A serious expedition over rugged and remote mountains where help is far away.
Start / Finish Sourlies bothy at the head of Loch Nevis (869950).
Distance / Time 10 miles/8-9 hours.
Escape Route From Bealach na h-Eangair, between Ben Aden and Meall a' Choire Dhuibh, an easy descent may be made W to reach Glen Carnach.
Telephone Inverie, 9 miles away across the Mam Meadail pass.
Transport Railway Stations at Fort William and Spean Bridge. Bus service on school days from Fort William Station to Achnacarry at the east end of Loch Arkaig. There is no bus service along Loch Arkaig to Murlaggan.
Accommodation Hotels/Guest Houses at Fort William, Spean Bridge and Gairlochy. B & B at Gairlochy. Youth Hostel at Glen Nevis.

Guidebooks S.M.T. Guide 'The Western Highlands'; S.M.T. Guide 'The Munros'; 'The Big Walks' by Ken Wilson and Richard Gilbert (Diadem); 'The High Mountains of Britain and Ireland' by Irvine Butterfield (Diadem).

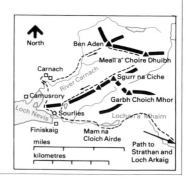

Ben Aden from Loch Nevis.

The flood which had supplied us with firewood had left its mark on the Carnach bridge. The wooden slats, fully ten feet above the present water level, were thick with tangled grass and twigs, and I was reminded of my terrifying experience of flooded rivers in Knoydart in March 1963, described in *The Big Walks*.

Ben Aden, a prominent rocky peak rising to 2,905ft/887m, at the upper end of Glen Carnach was our first objective of the day. The peak is in the heart of Knoydart and, missing Munro status, it is seldom climbed but has gained the reputation of posing a real threat to Ladhar Bheinn and Sgurr na Ciche as the finest hill in the district.

An indistinct path runs along the west bank of the Carnach river and we followed this for two miles until, at a ruined croft, the Allt Achadh a'Ghlinne runs in from the north side of Sgurr na Ciche. Shortly above the junction we crossed the river and tackled the steep south face of Ben Aden direct, and succeeded in finding a scrambling route beside the conspicuous gully which splits the face

Richard Gilbert

Ben Aden from Sgurr na Ciche; the Carnach approach takes the slopes on the left.

between the twin summits. An easier alternative route follows the west ridge, which ascends from upper Glen Carnach in a series of rocky steps.

As we breasted the summit ridge, and crunched through the frozen snow to the small cairn set on a pile of huge rocks, the sun hit us for the first time and we entered fairyland. The frost feathers and

Route-planning in Sourlies bothy.

Anne Gibbens

ice crystals sparkled like diamonds in the clear, sharp air, and the long arms of Loch Hourn and Loch Nevis drew our eyes west to Ladhar Bheinn, Ben Sgriol, Skye, Rhum, Eigg and beyond to the long line of the Outer Hebrides. We turned slowly through 360°, bringing almost every peak in the Northern and Western Highlands into view from An Teallach and Ben Wyvis in the north, through Sgurr nan Ceathreamhnan, Mam Soul and Kintail, down to the blue waters of Loch Quoich and on to Sgurr Mor, Sgurr Thuilm, Beinn Resipol and Ben More on Mull.

The shadowy north face of Sgurr na Ciche looked grim, white and wintry, rising steeply in great bluffs of rock from the deep glen to the south. This peak was our next objective and we picked our way down the very rocky east ridge of Ben Aden towards the Bealach na h-Eangair. It required a good deal of weaving and back-tracking to avoid crags and gain the bealach which divides Ben Aden from Meall a' Choire Dhuibh. Stags were belling continuously from the wild and desolate glen which runs west from Meall a' Choire Dhuibh, under the north face of Sgurr na Ciche, to Glen Carnach. By contouring round the head of this glen onto the north-east ridge of Sgurr na Ciche we were able to save some height.

It was chill in the shadow of Sgurr na

Ciche and we glanced longingly at the sun-drenched south face of Ben Aden, but the climb over verglassed rocks and through powder snow took most of our attention. The north-east ridge is the most challenging ascent route on Sgurr na Ciche and it is infinitely preferable to the long approach from the east over Sgurr nan Coireachan and Garbh Chioch Mhor. Scrambling up the rocks below the summit ridge, looking down on all the neighbouring peaks, gives a thrill of exposure.

Late afternoon found us basking in the thin sunshine on the pointed summit of Sgurr na Ciche. The cylindrical OS pillar lay a few yards away, uprooted from its plinth by a bolt of lightning some years ago. A fishing boat was rippling the mirror waters of Loch Nevis as it headed through the narrows of Kylesknoydart back to Mallaig. Stags were still belling in the glens and a ptarmigan croaked in the rocks nearby, otherwise we were left in peace to enjoy a spell of high elation on one of Scotland's greatest peaks. Such times are rare but they nourish the mind and provide treasured memories for us all.

We ambled down the long south-west ridge of Sgurr na Ciche as the sun dipped and reddened the western sky. The cliffs of Ladhar Bheinn's Coire Dhorrcail suddenly appeared black and threatening,

Garbh Chioch Mhor and Sgurr na Ciche, viewed across Coire nan Gall from Druim Buidhe.

grey clouds rolled over the peaks of Glenfinnan and our thoughts switched to the bothy fire and the evening meal.

The weather window had been brief but kind, and we laughed at the wind and rain that drove us back across the Mam na Cloich Airde the following day. Our high spirits could not be dampened.

A rest stop during the descent of the south-west ridge of Sgurr na Ciche; Garbh Chioch Mhor is the peak on the right.

BACKPACKING IN THE WESTERN HIGHLANDS: THE LOCH MULLARDOCH CIRCUIT

The vast tract of wild mountainous country running north from Kintail to Achnasheen is almost uninhabited. It is the abode of arctic hares, deer, foxes, ptarmigan and eagles, and the high ridges are only visited by the occasional stalker and a few intrepid hill walkers.

Although the great glens of Affric, Cannich and Strathfarrar penetrate deeply into the mountains from the east, no road bisects the region, and the area is therefore particularly remote, offering the hill walker many unforgettable days on a scale rarely paralleled elsewhere.

It is ironic that since the building of hydro-electric dams in the 1930s, which raised water levels in the lochs, access is more difficult.

In the nineteenth century Sir Hugh Munro would drive by dog-cart along a carriage-way from Cannich to the Benula shooting lodge west of Loch Mullardoch. This gave him enviably easy access to Beinn Fhionnlaidh, now perhaps the thorniest Munro of all.

Twelve proud Munros overlook the pencil-thin Loch Mullardoch and these include plums such as Sgurr na Lapaich, An Riabhachan, Sgurr nan Ceathreamhnan, Mam Sodhail and Carn Eige, the latter at 3,880ft/1,183m claiming the crown as the highest peak north of the Caledonian Canal. Most of these peaks can only be reached after hours of arduous walking but difficulty of access is inspiration to the wild walker, who will relish a backpacking expedition of several days round the circuit of the Mullardoch hills taking in all the peaks in one go.

In winter or early spring this major expedition can provide a test of stamina, all-round mountaineering ability and commitment unrivalled in Britain. High mountain camping or bivouacking in snow always demands expertise, first-class equipment and a cool head, but the Mullardoch hills are exceptionally isolated and exposed; help is far away and in the face of a fierce blizzard survival rather than progress may be paramount.

Many years ago, while still students, Alan Wedgwood and I tackled the circuit in mid-March. Carrying large packs, which included a heavy storm-proof tent and several bottles of whisky, it took us four long days. I remember Alan, influenced by the writings of Messrs Douglas, Raeburn and Inglis-Clark, insisted on wearing an old tweed jacket throughout. We experienced extremes of weather from blizzard and whiteout to warm sunshine, while conditions underfoot

ranged from hard ice and névé to soft snow and deep heather. Such contrasts make for the ideal Scottish expedition, and our venture gave us a lasting love of the Highlands in winter.

A car may be left conveniently at the Mullardoch dam, 8 miles west of Cannich, and the north shore of the loch followed round to the Allt Mullardoch which drains Coire an t-Sith. The ugly concrete dam and Hydro-Board debris are soon out of sight and the upper reaches of the corrie quickly gained by the use of an old stalkers' path. Just below the snow-line at 1,500ft, and looking across the loch to Toll Creagach, was the site of our first camp. I wrote in my diary, '9.30 p.m. in duvet jacket and sleeping bag. It is a cold, clear night with a haloed moon. Dying embers of the fire outside and Vat 69 and pipe smoke within. Life at its best.'

Easy grassy slopes run up to the broad bealach east of Carn nan Gobhar and thence to the summit of the mountain itself; but ahead lies Sgurr na Lapaich, a most complex peak with many subsidiary tops and corries, the traverse of which constitutes, perhaps, the crux of the entire circuit.

The east ridge rises gently at first but then it narrows, becomes rocky and a scrambling section must be negotiated before you suddenly arrive at the cairn and OS pillar (3,775ft/1,150m) perched on the sharp summit.

Continuing to An Riabhachan it is essential to descend Lapaich's boulder slopes in a southerly direction for 600ft before working westward to gain the bealach under the north-east top of An Riabhachan. This whole area abounds in cliffs and bluffs and is extremely confusing in mist. In spite of careful compass work Alan and I strayed too far west, onto treacherous ice-bound ground overlooking Loch Mor. Our predicament actually entailed the use of the rope for protection.

Once you have located the long ridge which runs up to the outlying east top (3,696ft/1,129m) of An Riabhachan, route-finding problems are over, for the ridge hugs the precipitous edge of the deep corrie containing Lochs Mor and Beag. For three miles the summit ridge of An Riabhachan twists and turns and rises and falls, but it imparts a feeling of absolute freedom and spaciousness. To the south, beyond the grey, foam-flecked waters of Loch Mullardoch,

Map O.S. 1:50,000 Sheet 25.
Grading A long and serious backpacking expedition over some of the largest and loneliest mountains in the Scottish Highlands. In winter conditions this is a major undertaking which should only be attempted by a thoroughly fit, experienced and well equipped party.
Start / Finish Mullardoch dam (220317).
Distance / Time 38 miles/3-4 days.
Escape Routes From Carnach a good track leads to Killilan and Dornie. From bealach E of Sgurr nan Ceathreamhnan head S to Alltbeithe Youth Hostel.
Telephones Cannich, Killilan and Cluanie Inn.
Transport Daily bus service Beauly to Cannich. Regular connections Beauly to Inverness.
Accommodation Hotels/B & B at Cannich. Youth Hostels at Cannich, Ratagan and Alltbeithe (Glen Affric).
Guidebooks S.M.T. Guide 'The Western Highlands'; 'The Big Walks' by Ken Wilson and Richard Gilbert (Diadem); 'The High Mountains of Britain and Ireland' by Irvine Butterfield (Diadem); 'The Munros' by Donald Bennet (S.M.T.).

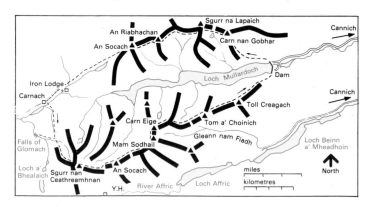

The view along the Mullardoch ridge from the summit of Sgurr na Lapaich to An Riabhachan.

The western end of the ridge – An Riabhachan to An Socach.

The southern slopes of Sgurr na Lapaich with Sgurr nan Clachan Geala and the Affric ridge in the background.

Looking back west along the Affric ridge to Mam Sodhail, Carn Eige and Stob a' Choire Dhomhain.

Approaching Sgurr nan Ceathreamhnan along Creag a' Choire Aird. The route continues along the left skyline ridge.

On the gendarmed section of the Affric ridge east of Stob a' Choire Dhomhain.

Richard Gilbert

Mam Sodhail and Carn Eige from Toll Creagach, the final summit of the Mullardoch circuit.

In thick mist route-finding along these wide and rather featureless ridges is tricky, particularly so on the intricate and twisty section over Mam Sodhail and Carn Eige. Both these peaks have satellites, Ciste Dhubh and Stob a' Choire Dhomain respectively, and all four mountains have subsidiary ridges down which it is very easy to stray. However, the OS pillar on Carn Eige makes a foolproof reference point and, provided you head east, you will soon gain the more prominent ridge leading, in three miles, to Tom a' Choinich. This is a most delightful ridge where crazy pinnacles and gendarmes sprout from the rocks in several places, while to the south glimpses may be caught of Loch Affric, set amongst ancient Caledonian pines in the most traditional and romantic of settings.

The tenth and last Munro of the circuit is Toll Creagach, a broad-ridged, flat-topped mountain lying two miles east of Tom a' Choinich. It presents no difficulty and the north-east ridge brings you conveniently down to Mullardoch Dam.

rises the great wall of the Affric peaks, while to the north-west range upon range of hills roll away to the distant horizon; Bidean a' Choire Sheasgaich and the West Monar Forest, Applecross, the Coulin Forest, Torridon and the Fannichs.

The flat-topped separate Munro of An Socach marks the turning point of the walk; the pressure eases temporarily and grassy slopes run down to Loch Mhoicean, where you pick up a Land Rover track to Iron Lodge and Carnach.

You are now under the shadow of Sgurr nan Ceathreamhnan, one of Scotland's most mysterious and beautifully-proportioned peaks. Rising to 3,771ft/1,151m in a gracious cone with twin summits, it throws down ridges in all directions and holds five distinct corries. Before embarking on this fine mountain, which leads naturally to the long ridge of Affric, it is worth spending a comfortable night in a sheltered glen. There is no better spot than beside Loch Lon Mhurchaidh, just below the north-west ridge of Sgurr nan Ceathreamhnan and close to the celebrated Falls of Glomach which should not be missed from the itinerary.

The Glomach river, which rises on Ben Fhada, falls 475ft in three steps, one of which is nearly 300ft, making the Falls Scotland's highest. It is the quantity of water in the fall, the clouds of spray and the deafening roar which echoes round the rocky chasm which make this cataract so impressive.

The north-west ridge of Sgurr nan Ceathreamhnan leads easily up to the little saddle between the twin summits, where the view to the south is suddenly revealed: Ben Fhada, the Kintail and Cluanie ridges, the Loch Quoich peaks, Knoydart and Ben Nevis. Of more immediate interest is the way ahead; steeply down the curved east ridge to another An Socach and then up to and across the massive head and shoulders of Mam Sodhail and Carn Eige.

From Bealach Coire Ghadheil (2,350ft/716m) a long pull of 1,500ft over two miles takes you to the broad summit of Mam Sodhail, where there are a few rocky outcrops and a ruined stone shelter. Mam Sodhail, another wonderful viewpoint, was used as a principal sighting station during one of the early surveys of Scotland.

Given good weather, a strong party could complete the homeward stretch of nineteen switchback miles from the Falls to Mullardoch Dam in a single day. But, bowed down with heavy rucksacks, it may not be the best policy to rush headlong along this magnificent mountainous ridge. The walk is of such quality that it should be savoured over two days. In many places it is quite easy to drop down a short way off the ridge and find a sheltered nook for the night, in idyllic surroundings. It is one of life's greatest experiences to camp or bivvy above the 3,000ft contour, with the silhouette of familiar and much-loved hills outlined against a pale green evening sky, sipping pure malt whisky from a plastic mug and listening to the mountain foxes barking from their bouldery lairs.

It was early in the morning of our fifth day when Alan and I exuberantly ran down through soft snow to the shore of Loch Mullardoch which was reflecting the blue sky, while the hills we had conquered gleamed white in the spring sunshine.

Happy as sandboys we sat on a rock, peeled off our jerseys and drained the last drops of the whisky.

Alan Wedgwood stops for a celebratory dram during the descent of Toll Creagach.

Richard Gilbert

The ancient pine forests of Glen Derry in the vicinity of Derry Lodge.

BEN MACDUI AND THE GLEN LUIBEG CIRCUIT

Mountain walkers consider the Cairngorms to be Britain's most precious asset. This huge massif of rounded granite hills may look unimpressive when viewed from afar, but the adventurous walker can unravel its secrets and explore with delight the magnificent corries, cliffs, lochans, glens and sanctuaries.

To walk across the barren wastes of the Cairngorm plateau under a pale blue winter sky, with a Siberian wind whipping up snow-devils and nipping your ears and nose, is one of life's most exhilarating experiences. Likewise in early summer, the snow patches recede, families of ptarmigan emerge from the safety of the boulder fields, flocks of snow bunting skim over the screes, the least willow, three fingered rush and woolly hair moss creep across the beds of decayed granite; then the lonely and desolate plateau takes on a fragile beauty that is reminiscent of the arctic.

Unfortunately, ugly and distasteful ski developments on Cairn Gorm preclude an approach to the mountains from the north, but the long glens running south to the Dee are majestic. Live rivers rush through gorges and down twisting beds, while the hillsides above carry sizeable remnants of the old Caledonian pine forest. The natural beauty of the Scottish scene is immeasurably enhanced by these proud trees, and Glens Luibeg, Derry and Quoich contain some of the most notable areas of natural forest in Scotland.

It would take a lifetime to explore every crag and gully in the Cairngorms, but a wide variety of contrasts and experiences can be enjoyed by a day's walk over the hills enclosing the Luibeg burn: Derry Cairngorm, Ben Macdui and Carn a' Mhaim. This is a long expedition over wild and remote mountain country and a word of

warning is appropriate. The scale of the Cairngorms is immense and distances are easy to underestimate. The weather and conditions underfoot can quickly deteriorate, and walkers attempting this route should be fit, experienced and thoroughly equipped.

Park the car at Linn of Dee, peer over the old stone bridge at the boiling cauldron of white water and marvel at the audacity of

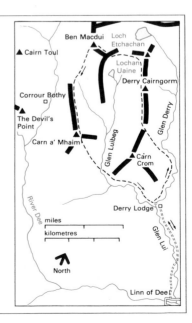

Maps O.S. 1:50,000 Sheets 43 and 36; O.S. 1:25,000 Outdoor Leisure Map – 'The Cairngorms'.
Grading A long and serious expedition to Britain's second highest mountain. Only experienced parties should attempt this walk in winter.
Start / Finish Linn of Dee (062897).
Distance / Time 20 miles/10-11 hours.
Escape Routes None. Emergency shelter could be sought at the Hutchinson Memorial Hut in Glen Etchachan or Corrour Bothy in the Lairig Ghru.
Telephones Derry Lodge and Inverey.
Transport Railway Station at Aberdeen. Daily bus service Aberdeen – Braemar.
Accommodation Hotels/Guest Houses at Braemar. Youth Hostels at Braemar and Inverey.
Guidebooks S.M.T. Guide 'The Cairngorms'; 'The Cairngorms' by D. Nethersole – Thompson and Adam Watson (Melven Press); 'The High Mountains of Britain and Ireland' by Irvine Butterfield (Diadem); 'The Munros' by Donald Bennet (S.M.T.); 'The Scottish Peaks' by W. A. Poucher (Constable).

The view down Glen Luibeg from Derry Cairngorm with Cairn a' Mhaim in the distance.

Looking north from Derry Cairngorm to Beinn Mheadhoin.

Ben Macdui and Loch Etchachan from Beinn Mheadhoin.

Fraser Brunton

Menlove Edwards who swam through the gorge in 1933. A short way beyond the Linn a locked gate marks the entrance to Glen Lui and easy walking along a track leads, in three miles, to Derry Lodge.

The lodge stands amongst ancient pine trees near the junction of the Derry and Luibeg burns, and in the nineteenth century it was the home of the head stalker who offered warm hospitality to visiting mountaineers. Sadly it has now been vandalised and is rapidly decaying; perhaps in a few years it will have collapsed into a ruin, like Papadil Lodge on the Isle of Rhum.

Cross the footbridge and walk up through the trees into Glen Derry. The lower stretch of the glen is paradise at any time of the year. In the summer the sweet smell of pine needles pervades the air, ants scurry underfoot and birds chatter in the branches; you may be lucky enough to see a crossbill, crested tit, siskin or goldcrest. In winter all is silent and even the river may be stilled. Deer stand in small herds seeking the shelter of the trees and nuzzling for moss under the snow.

It is possible to proceed straight up through the trees to reach the end of the ridge at Carn Crom, but Glen Derry is such a joy that it is worth following the path north for a mile and then striking west to reach the bealach.

The broad, stony ridge continues north over two subsidiary summits to the main top of Derry Cairngorm, 3,788ft/1,155m. My first ascent of this mountain, from Coire Etchachan in January 1968, coincided with hurricane-force winds which caused the deaths of eighteen people in Glasgow and forced us to crawl from rock to rock, clinging on for dear life. But in normal conditions the summit is a fine viewpoint for the eastern Cairngorms.

In early June cornices still rimmed the cliffs of Coire Sputan Dearg, the gullies held ribbons of snow and Lochan Uaine, at 3,142 feet one of the highest lochs in Scotland, was still frozen and snow covered. To the north Beinn Mheadhoin is made conspicuous by its granite tors, and the swelling mound of Cairn Gorm rises beyond. The two enormous outliers, Beinn a' Bhuird and Ben Avon, can be seen away to the east above the high plateau connecting Beinn Bhreac and Beinn a' Chaorruinn, while further to the south Lochnagar and its satellites dominate the horizon.

Easy walking leads round the head of Glen Luibeg and then you can follow the edge of the Coire Sputan Dearg cliffs to their high point. This is exciting walking amidst typical Cairngorm scenery. Vertical walls of weathered granite plunge down to fans of scree, ravens ride the upcurrents and, from your 4,000ft perch, you feel in a different world from the thread-like river and green patches of pines far below in Glen Luibeg.

Turning west, a desolate boulder field rises to a ruined stone shelter and the summit of Ben Macdui, at 4,296ft/1,309m, the second highest mountain in Britain. The view west now opens up and your eye will be held by the perfectly proportioned high corrie under the summit of Cairn Toul and the wild Garbh Choire of Braeriach holding snow until late in the season. A large plinth of stones supports the ugly white concrete OS pillar and you are quite likely to meet large parties of day trippers, who have ascended Cairn Gorm by chairlift and have walked or skied five miles across the plateau to bag Ben Macdui.

It is a relief to set off south-east down a wide boulder field into the upper reaches of Coire Clach nan Taillear. Rounding the head of the corrie a spur leads to the low bealach under the north ridge of Carn a' Mhaim. Don't be enticed by the footpath which runs out to the subsidiary top of Sron Riach.

The north ridge of Carn a' Mhaim is nearly two miles long and it snakes down stepwise from the summit, providing an airy route of ascent. The black, glistening, overlapping, boiler-plate slabs on the Devil's Point, seen directly across the Dee, make the direct ascent of this peak from the Lairig Ghru look appropriately fearsome.

Easy boulder-strewn slopes, which are popular nesting sites for ptarmigan, descend to Glen Luibeg where an iron bridge, built by the Cairngorm Club in 1956, crosses the burn.

The walk back on the north side of the river to Derry Lodge is sheer delight, for again the scene is set by the magnificent stands of Caledonian pines on the surrounding hills. Within the Cairngorm National Nature Reserve the trees are safe; certain areas have been fenced to allow for regeneration and others have been replanted. Between Derry Lodge and Linn of Dee, however, much clear-felling has recently taken place and, although the Mar Estate is replanting with mixed conifers, it will be many years before the landscape is restored.

THE FUNGLE AND THE CLASH OF WIRREN

In Aberdeenshire the Indian summer was lingering on well into October. The clear still nights were followed by frosty dawns when low banks of white mist hung in the glens; yet, by mid-morning, the air was shimmering with heat-haze as the sun beat down fiercely.

I leant over the parapet of the old stone bridge at Aboyne, watching the river Dee flowing black and sluggishly under the arches. For once the Dee was in sombre mood. A cloudburst was desperately needed on the Cairngorm plateau to provide a transfusion to the Dee, to rejuvenate its cascades and falls and to rumble its boulders, thereby restoring its pride. Nevertheless, the well wooded banks made an idyllic setting, for the early frosts had hastened the autumn tints and the colours of the leaves and berries were rampant.

Just south of the bridge a sign, erected by the Scottish Rights-of-Way Society, points the way 'To Tarfside by the Fungle'. This Mounth path links Deeside with Glen Esk, and in this chapter I have extended the walk over the Clash of Wirren by the Whisky Road.

The vast range of mountains extending south-west from Aberdeenshire is known loosely as the Grampians. But the ancient name of these mountains was Mounth, from the Gaelic *Monadh* meaning mountain. Nowadays, Mounth is used to describe old rights-of-way across these mountains, for there were no roads as such in the Highlands before the arrival of General Wade in 1726. The routes of the Mounth paths were chosen for their drainage and firmness and, because they are now only used by shepherds and occasional walkers, they provide wonderfully wild walks over lonely hills and moors, linking villages and glens in the Grampians.

The path from the Dee ascends the broad valley of the Allt Dinnie, passing through woods of sweet chestnut, birch, beech, sycamore, hazel and maple. It was a golden morning and I kicked through the carpet of fallen leaves with a full heart; a red squirrel scurried across the path and a skein of geese honked by overhead, heading south to warmer climes.

High above the valley, and overlooking Aboyne and the Dee, a viewpoint known as The Seat was constructed, by Victorian romantics, on a plinth of granite blocks bearing the inscription 'Ye Mountains and Waters Praise Ye the Lord'. Beyond The Seat the valley floor levels out and the path narrows and becomes rather indistinct, but generally it follows the burn, winding through stands of Caledonian pines, deep heather and bilberry shrubs bearing fruit the size and

sweetness of cherries. I disturbed a herd of young hinds who made off like lightning through the heather, leaping a six-foot fence with the utmost ease and grace.

Soon after crossing the burn the path meets a Land Rover track running south from Birse, and this is followed past a gaunt stone shooting lodge towards Birse Castle and Water of Feugh.

Birse Castle is set in a protective belt of trees overlooking the Feugh, but it still appears stark, grey and forbidding. However, the Fungle is waymarked well to the west of both the castle and the farm at Ballochan and it soon climbs back up into wild and rolling hills.

It is three miles from the Feugh to the bealach at 2,000ft between Tampie and Mudlee Bracks and the path becomes ever fainter, finally petering out in an evil area of hags and bogs at the watershed. But the walking is majestic and the sense of space and freedom profound. As far as the eye can see, the purple heather-clad hills of the eastern Grampians sweep on to distant horizons. These are rounded, folded hills where rushing burns have carved seams and gorges out of the bedrock; only here can flourish ribbons of scrub trees and shrubs where the sheep are unable to graze.

By keeping well above the Burn of Clearach on the bare, broad shoulder of Tampie, the going becomes much easier and the path falls gently southwards towards Glen Esk. Here the Fungle meets the line of the Firmounth Road, another of the Grampians' ancient Mounth roads, which runs from Dinnie to Tarfside.

I was disheartened to see that several new estate roads had been bulldozed up into the hills, leaving ugly scars running down to the once lonely cottages at Glentennet and Shinfur in the wide strath of Glen Esk. In addition, a virulent strain of myxomatosis was rife in Glen Esk, killing rabbits in their thousands. The path through the meadows was littered with rotting corpses, a sickening smell hung in the still air and I had to step around dying animals which were too feeble to move.

I lunched in warm sunshine beside the wooden footbridge over the North Esk at Tarfside. Like the Dee to the north, the river was torpid and clouds of mosquitoes were dancing over the pools of oily water, but the scene was enhanced by the rowans, heavy with brilliantly red berries, lining the banks.

The path which runs south from Glen Esk to the West Water valley, Bridgend and Glen Lethnot is known as the Whisky Road. It was used by smugglers with ponies, laden with illicit spirits, bound for the lucrative markets in the city of Brechin. A delightful path zig-zags up through the heather from Buskhead to join the Whisky Road at the bealach between Cowie Hill and Garlet, it then crosses the Burn of Berryhill, skirts East Knock and descends through the Clash of Wirren to Tillybardine. The Clash of Wirren is one of the secret hollows of the Grampians; a spring rises in an area of lush green grass and boulders below a craggy outlier of West Wirren hill. I scrambled down to the spring for a drink and was surprised to find foxgloves still in flower and another herd of hinds grazing.

The path hugs the hillside above Tillybardine and meets the farm road at Stonyford. It is a further three miles to Bridgend but, as the sun dipped, the temperature dropped and the shadows of the trees on the river bank lengthened, I found the West Water valley to be a haven of serenity, an appropriate finale to this most peaceful and beautiful walk through the foothills of the Grampians.

Note that if transport cannot be arranged at Bridgend it is a further five miles walk to Edzell.

Map O.S. 1:50,000 Sheet 44.
Grading The walk follows an ancient path over rolling, heather clad hills.
Start / Finish Aboyne (523980); Bridgend (536684).
Distance / Time 23 miles/8-9 hours.
Escape Routes Motor roads are crossed at Birse Castle and Tarfside.
Telephones Aboyne, Tarfside and Bridgend.
Transport Regular daily bus service from Aberdeen to Aboyne and Ballater. No public transport to Bridgend but good connections from Edzell (5 miles) to Brechin and Aberdeen.
Accommodation Hotels/Guest Houses at Aboyne and Edzell. Youth Hostels at Banchory and Kirriemuir.
Guidebooks 'Scottish Hill Tracks' by D. G. Moir (Bartholomew); 'Grampian Ways' by Robert Smith (Melven); S.M.T Guide 'The Cairngorms'.

Looking north from the Fungle to Birse Castle and Aboyne.

The Clash of Wirren.

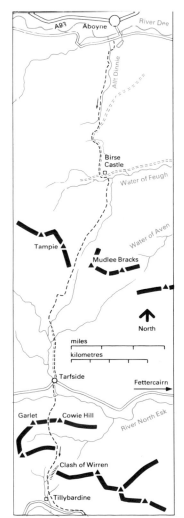

THE MINIGAIG PASS

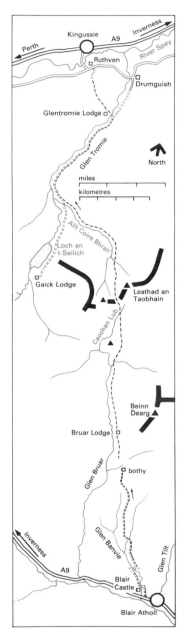

The Drumochter Pass now bears the full brunt of the south-north communication and service network between Perth and Inverness. The rot started in 1728 when General Wade built the military road over the pass and this has been followed by the railway, power lines, water pipes and the A9 trunk road. Yet before General Wade's arrival the only road north between Blair Atholl and Kingussie was the Mounth path known as the Minigaig, which is shown on maps of 1689 and 1725. Other archives indicate that the Minigaig replaced a much earlier pass constructed in the thirteenth century by the Comyns of Ruthven castle near Kingussie.

General Wade's road through Drumochter measures thirty six miles between Blair Atholl and Kingussie, but travellers taking the Minigaig can save themselves ten miles. This saving, however, is at the expense of having to climb to a high point of 2,750ft/838m against 1,485ft/452m on Drumochter: hardly a bargain during the winter snows.

Even over high ground the original line of the Minigaig can still be discerned through the heather, and it is rewarding to discover a few ditches, culverts, walls and paving stones that have survived over 250 years of neglect. Today the Minigaig offers a long walk through some remote, little known and extremely beautiful glens and across a high, exposed and barren plateau. In spite of its historic interest and importance, complete crossings of the Minigaig are rare for the walk is a considerable challenge which is not for the faint-hearted. Snow lies deep on the plateau until late spring, navigation would be very difficult in mist and bad weather and there are no satisfactory escape routes.

The walk starts in style as you pass confidently through the massive, decorated wrought iron gates, and march along an avenue

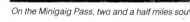

On the Minigaig Pass, two and a half miles sou

Upper Glen Bruar.

Richard Gilbert

Sheicheachan bothy.

Heading north after the Allt Sheicheachan bothy.

of elms to Blair Castle, the home of the Duke of Atholl. The path continues through woods of exotic fir trees which were planted in the early eighteenth century and contain some of the most spectacular species in Britain. Beyond Old Blair the track runs through woods of beech, sycamore and oak, with rhododendrons and broom adding extra colour, while the Banvie burn roars down a deep and rocky gorge far below.

Once through the trees you cross the burn and start climbing up to Carn Dearg Beag on the north side of Glen Banvie. Here the Minigaig is a wide track and you can make rapid progress over the rounded heather-clad hills. From the broad bealach at 1,700ft you can look down to Glen Bruar with its fast river and private motor road running from Calvine to Bruar Lodge. But the Minigaig traverses the hills high up on the east side of the river, passing the lonely cottage known as the Allt Sheicheachan bothy. The bothy is maintained by the Mountain Bothies Association and is open to all comers: it is beautifully situated by the burn and is popular with Munroists bound for Beinn Dearg and the Tarf.

A cairn on the north bank of the burn marks the continuation of the Minigaig which, for the next two miles, nearly disappears under

The view north to Allt Coire Bhran from the head of the Minigaig Pass – the old drovers' route through the Grampians before General Wade established the more circuitous Drumochter Pass ro[a...]

Looking east to the Glen Feshie hills from above Glentromie Lodge.

the heather, bilberries, cloudberries and boulders. However, the twin tracks made by cart wheels have left distinct grooves in the hillside, and paving stones can still be seen on the boggy sections.

Bruar Lodge is one of Scotland's largest and most impressive shooting lodges with a full range of outbuildings. The estate have maintained a Land Rover track which runs for three miles to the head of the glen. This is one of the pleasantest stretches of the Minigaig: a small loch just above the lodge has extensive reed-beds where I saw heron, waders and red throated divers, then, as the glen narrows, the cliffs of Creag na-h-Iolair Mhor overlook the path. Beside the path the burn rushes down from the hills in cascades and falls producing deep, clear, trout pools overhung by birch, rowan and alder.

The burn divides at a grassy platform which would make an idyllic camp site, and the Minigaig climbs quite steeply for 700ft to the plateau. This is another rather indistinct section, but once the plateau is reached a line of white quartzite boulders set at intervals in the heather marks the route over the eastern shoulder of Uchd a'Chlarsair.

Running through these gently undulating heathery hills is the Caochan Lub burn. This swift stream of pure water flows between banks of lush grass; an extraordinary feature at a height of 2,500ft

and one which made the Minigaig a popular route with cattle drovers. Nowadays the whole area is prolific deer country and I could see their silhouettes on the skyline as they watched my progress from a safe distance. The deer frequent the Caochan Lub in particular, and I startled a large herd which was too engrossed in feeding from the succulent grass to notice my approach.

The high point of the Minigaig Pass is the 2,750ft/838m bealach south of Leathad an Taobhain, which is marked by a quartzite cairn. From the bealach a whole new landscape bursts into view: the Allt Coire Bhran falls away steeply, broadening into a wide glen which merges with the northern end of the defile containing Loch an t-Seilich and Gaick Lodge to become Glen Tromie. In the far distance the massive wall of the Monadh Liath rises behind the Spey valley.

A wide green strip of turf, which descends the corrie keeping well to the west of the Allt Coire Bhran, marks the line of the Minigaig, but the path remains indistinct for nearly six miles until it reaches the Land Rover track from Gaick. Gaick Lodge lies out of sight in its gloomy setting beneath steep hillsides. Near the lodge a granite monument commemorates five men who were overwhelmed and killed by an avalanche in January 1800 whilst sheltering in a hut.

Glen Tromie provides a welcome contrast to the bare corrie of the Allt Bhran. The river sparkles between banks of alder, Caledonian pines, gorse, broom and juniper while remnants of ancient birch forest grow on the hillsides. If it were not for the line of poles and power cables running up to Gaick Lodge, and the disastrous modern lodge at Lynaberack (which looks like a Glasgow tenement), Tromie would be a perfect example of the romantic Scottish glen.

It is possible to continue down the full length of Glen Tromie to Drumguish, but the original Minigaig crossed the river at Glentromie Lodge and cut across the slopes of Beinn Bhuidhe to Ruthven Barracks outside Kingussie. The track over Beinn Bhuidhe is very clear and it provides an excellent view of the old barracks, built by the English after the 1715 rising on the same grassy mound that once carried the fortress of the Comyns, rivals of Robert the Bruce in the early fourteenth century. The barracks are now gaunt and roofless and little changed since Prince Charlie's Highlanders fired it in 1746.

Ruthven Barracks with the Feshie hills in the background.

Maps O.S. 1:50,000 Sheets 35 and 43.
Grading A long expedition through very remote hills. A serious undertaking in winter or early spring when the snow lies deep.
Start / Finish Blair Atholl (870652); Kingussie (757005).
Distance / Time 27 miles / 11-12 hours.
Escape Routes From Bruar Lodge along the estate road to Calvine. Emergency shelter could be found at Allt Sheicheachan bothy or Bruar Lodge.
Telephones Blair Atholl, Calvine, Drumguish, Ruthven Barracks and Kingussie.
Transport Railway Stations at Kingussie and Blair Atholl. Express bus services between Edinburgh, Glasgow and Inverness will stop at Blair Atholl and Kingussie.
Accommodation Hotels/B & B at Blair Atholl and Kingussie. Youth Hostels at Perth and Kingussie.
Guidebooks 'Scottish Hill Tracks' by D. G. Moir (Bartholomew); 'Grampian Ways' by Robert Smith (Melven); S.M.T Guide 'The Cairngorms'.

Donald Bennet

BEINN RESIPOL

by JANET and ALAN WEDGWOOD

What a classic view greets you when you reach the seaward end of Glen Coe and look west across the waters of Loch Leven and Loch Linnhe towards the Ardgour hills. But it is not until you climb much higher up, on the Aonach Eagach or on Beinn a'Bheithir, that you see a peak even further out to the west: the shapely blue cone of Beinn Resipol peeping over the shoulder of Garbh Bheinn. Distance adds height to the mountain, and its remoteness is compelling.

Once over in Ardnamurchan, Beinn Resipol tends to dominate not only the landscape but also one's own immediate ambitions, so that a single break in the clouds was enough to tempt us out to traverse the mountain after rain-washed days of frustration. Our starting point was the summit of the road leading north out of Strontian to Polloch and from here we struck west across relatively gentle slopes. The going was trackless and very wet, and I was reminded of advice meted out during my earliest excursions into the hills: 'Get your feet good and wet right at the start, and then you won't waste all that energy trying to keep them dry.' So we splashed nonchalantly across the undulating bog, with the magnificent backdrop of the Ardgour hills quite making up for the rather featureless nature of the country. Here and there we came across traces of old mine workings, small leats and overgrown dams. An intrusion by the industrial world into this splendid isolation? Or a romantic link with the past? Lapse of time dictated the latter, for the mines which were opened for lead in 1722 were already drifting into disuse by the end of the eighteenth century, although they were still active enough to provide most of the bullets fired by the English at the Battle of Waterloo. Armed with this knowledge, and the fact that the element strontium was first discovered here in 1764, it seemed safe to designate these remains firmly as Heritage. Certainly we were glad of the fairly robust dam at Lochan Dubh which provided a rare patch of dry turf on which to lunch.

By now we were rewarded with a forward view of Beinn Resipol, still three miles away, rising loftily between Loch Sunart to the south and Loch Shiel to the north, and extending its heathery east ridge in our direction. But before getting to grips with the mountain itself one more descent took us to the Bealach nan Carn (798652) where some well weathered cairns provide evidence of an ancient coffin track, one of several that once led from Sunartside to Loch Shiel. These date from the time of St. Finan's occupation of the Loch Shiel island of Eilean Uaine in the sixth century, after which this site became regarded as such a sacred burial place that for many centuries funeral processions from Sunart would toil over the rugged slopes of Beinn Resipol to reach it. This particular route came up from Ardnastang, and is now more or less followed by the old miner's track (also accessible from Ariundle) which affords a good alternative approach to the mountain from this side.

Beyond the Bealach nan Carn we launched on to Resipol's east ridge and our route became much better defined. So, unfortunately, did the worsening weather. At first the summit cone had fended off

the rainstorms that came rolling in from behind us, sending some scudding down Loch Sunart and some down Loch Shiel, but eventually the onslaught became too intense. The clouds descended and one tantalising glimpse of Rhum and Eigg was all there was to remind us that we were approaching the finest vantage point for miles around. Even the relentless rain, however, could not spoil the enjoyment of the final section of the ridge where a series of rugged prominences were separated by grassy scoops, perfect bivouac sites which demanded a return in fairer weather. Then will be the time to linger over the magnificent panorama stretching beyond Rhum and Skye to the Outer Hebrides and round the great arc of mainland mountains, perhaps Sgurr na Ciche, certainly Ben Nevis, the Mamores and the mountains of Appin and south to Ben More on Mull. Then we will watch the sun set out over the Atlantic and stay to watch it rise again ...

Just now there was absolutely no incentive to linger on the 2,774ft/ 845m summit. Eager to escape the rising wind we plunged with precipitate haste down the steep south face towards Lochan Bac an Lochain. This was perhaps unwise in such poor visibility and we blundered and slithered for an age through a maze of crags and grass terraces before at last emerging out of the mist at the lochan a thousand feet below. On a clear day the descent would be straightforward and the steep-sided lochan an enchanting place, but it was grim and forbidding today. Here we were crossing another coffin route, one that ascended from Camuschoirk by the boggy looking Allt Camas a'Choirce and crossed the western slopes of Resipol even

Map O.S. 1:50,000 Sheet 40.
Grading A straightforward walk in good conditions although some steep ground and broken cliffs must be avoided, particularly on the N and E sides of the mountain.
Start / Finish The highest point on the Strontian to Polloch road (838666); Resipole Farm (722640).
Distance / Time 10 miles/6-7 hours.
Escape Routes Descents may be made almost anywhere on the S side of the mountain, leading to the main road on Loch Sunart-side.
Telephones Strontian, Camuschoirk and Ariundle.
Transport Weekday bus service Ardgour – Kilchoan passes through Strontian and Resipole.
Accommodation Hotel at Strontian. B & B locally. Youth Hostels at Glencoe and Fort William.
Guidebook S.M.T. Guide 'The Western Highlands'.

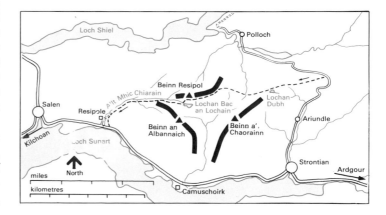

Left: The western slopes of Beinn Resipol from the Allt Mhic Chiarain.

Beinn Resipol from the southern shores of Loch Sunart.

higher than the Bealach nan Carn track to the east, but we saw no sign of it as we skirted the lochan and set off down the outflowing stream.

Soon our stream joined the main Allt Mhic Chiarain which rises only a few hundred feet below the summit of Beinn Resipol on the north side and would give a surer way down to this point. From the junction the going was much easier and the remaining three miles

down to Resipole Farm provided a pleasant walk along the south bank of the stream. For the latter part there was even a good path, the first we had used all day, following the stream as it descended through the woods in a series of deep gorges, and leading finally to a gate at the roadside by Loch Sunart, 200 yards east of Resipole Farm.

There remained only the problem of the fourteen miles of road that separated us from our car, still parked on the road to Polloch.

The view east from the summit of Beinn Resipol to Sgurr Dhomhnuill and other Ardgour peaks.

THE EXPLORATION OF GARBH BHEINN

by DONALD BENNET

Despite the exorbitant fare, I always enjoy the short sail on the Corran ferry to Ardgour. There is a sense of pleasure and anticipation at the prospect of crossing Loch Linnhe to reach the far western part of the Highlands, an area more akin to the islands than to the rest of the mainland. In Ardgour and its neighbouring districts of Sunart and Moidart there is the feeling of having left the mainland behind on the eastern side of the Great Glen, and of having reached the westernmost peninsula of Scotland, there to follow the long winding lochs of Shiel and Sunart to the rocky point of Ardnamurchan, battered by Atlantic storms.

For the climber Ardgour means one mountain above all others, Garbh Bheinn, whose bold outline of ridge and buttress is so compelling when seen from the foot of Glen Coe or from Ballachulish. No wonder we are drawn westwards across Loch Linnhe to reach it. Of course, there is more to Ardgour than this one mountain; there is a tangle of lonely glens and rocky peaks that make this one of the wildest parts of the Highlands, but whereas most of these peaks can only be glimpsed in the hinterland far beyond their surrounding foothills, Garbh Bheinn rises above Loch Linnhe with few intervening heights, clear for all to see and admire.

Usually a visit to Garbh Bheinn starts with a walk up the well trodden and often muddy path in Coire an Iubhair to the foot of the north-east face, followed by a climb up one of the ridges or buttresses which give the mountain its character. On this occasion, however, we were planning a longer approach to the summit, the circuit of the ridge above Coire an Iubhair followed by the ascent of the steep north face above the Bealach Feith'n Amean. By this way we hoped to extend our knowledge of this grand mountain, exploring parts which in previous visits had been neglected in our preoccupation with the more obviously imposing features such as Leac Mhor and the Great Ridge. I knew too that given good weather there would be great views of Garbh Bheinn across the head of Coire an Iubhair, but the day was starting with overcast skies, and it seemed that in this respect we might be disappointed.

We started up the broad grassy ridge, the Druim an Iubhair, on the east side of the corrie. After the first steep climb the ridge is more level, though hummocky, and in such a lonely place I hoped to see some signs of the wild goats that inhabit the hillsides above Loch Linnhe, or possibly a pair of divers on Lochan Druim an Iubhair, but no such luck came our way. To the west Garbh Bheinn was shrouded in slowly swirling clouds which only occasionally parted to reveal Loch Linnhe in sunshine far below.

On days such as this, when the spectacular aspects of the mountains are hidden from us as we climb in a grey world of cloud and mist, our thoughts range far beyond the immediate surroundings. From the top of Sgor Mhic Eacharna, the first summit along the ridge, we looked down through parting clouds to the green flats of Glen Gour, utterly deserted but showing here and there the traces of earlier cultivation and signs that once this place was home for a few hardy highlanders. Now this glen, like so many others in the western

highlands, is uninhabited and desolate, regarded by some as wilderness and worthy of being preserved as such. To others it is a matter of regret that now, because of the depopulation of the last two centuries, glens where once there were homes and people have come to be regarded in this way, and for them it is no cause for pride that the Scottish highlands are regarded as one of the last remaining wilderness areas in western Europe.

From Sgor Mhic Eacharna the ridge drops steeply, then rises again over rock and scree to the next top, Beinn Bheag. Considering its name, the little hill, I found this a long climb, unexpectedly so, and was glad to reach the cairn, beyond which a more level ridge led in a further half mile to the west top. At last the clouds were parting high up, and across the head of Coire an Iubhair the great North-East Buttress of Garbh Bheinn appeared for a few minutes as a huge dark tower, criss-crossed by grassy ledges and streaked with dark patches of wet rock and waterslides. At our feet the slabs of Beinn Bheag dropped steeply towards the corrie, and it was in that direction that we had to go.

I seemed to remember that there was an easy gully leading down to the pass, the Bealach Feith'n Amean, at the head of Coire an Iubhair, and sure enough a hundred yards further on we arrived at its top. There were even a few old iron fence posts and a faint track to show the way down to the tiny lochan that lies in the defile of the pass. It is a lonely and impressive spot, with the steep northern crags of Garbh Bheinn rising a thousand feet directly above the lochan.

Deliberately avoiding the easiest line of ascent, we moved towards the east where the dark rocks of the north face are at their steepest, and for a few hundred feet we enjoyed a good scramble from grassy ledge to ledge by steep walls and slabs, one of which was worthy of a much more distinguished route. No one would

Maps O.S. 1:50,000 Sheets 40 and 49; O.S. 1:63,360 Tourist Map 'Ben Nevis and Glen Coe'.
Grading A superb mountain circuit including the traverse of one of Scotland's finest and rockiest peaks. Steep slopes and cliffs abound and great care with route finding must be taken in misty weather.
Start / Finish The road junction at Inversanda (933593).
Distance / Time 9 miles/7-8 hours.
Escape Route If time is short or the weather deteriorating, a descent from the bealach Feith 'n Amean, between Beinn Bheag and Garbh Bheinn, can be made easily down into Coire an Iubhair.
Telephone Inversanda.
Transport Corran Ferry daily throughout the year. Weekday bus service Ardgour – Kilchoan passes through Inversanda.
Accommodation Hotel at Corran. B & B locally. Youth Hostels at Glencoe and Fort William.
Guidebooks S.M.T Guide 'The Western Highlands'; 'The Scottish Peaks' by W. A. Poucher (Constable).

The magnificent East Face of Garbh Bheinn viewed from Sgor Mhic Eacharna. The Great Ridge is on the left with Great Gully to its right. The Pinnacle Ridge (centre) and North East Buttress (right) are the other principle bastions.

The view up Coire an Iubhair.

Above the north face we came to the summit ridge, an undulating crest of rough rocky outcrops, befitting a mountain called Garbh Bheinn, the rough hill. On the east side steep crags and gullies plunge into Coire an Iubhair. We scrambled on, up and down and up again until at last the cairn, at 2,903ft/867m, appeared through the mist, and a few steps beyond it we stopped abruptly on the brink of the precipitous south face. On a good summer day one would expect to see climbers on this steep wall, but on this occasion we could see nothing down there, and no sounds came up through the mists. We had the mountain to ourselves, but there was no temptation to linger so down we went by the rocky path and slabs to the col below the south face.

There one has a choice of routes, either down steeply into Coire an Iubhair, scrambling among the huge fallen boulders at the foot of the Great Ridge, or up again for a short distance to reach the top of Sron a' Gharbh Choire Bhig. This is my favourite way, despite the extra effort, for the mountain day is prolonged and for another hour we walked down this long easy ridge, dropping below the clouds and revelling in the pale sunshine that filtered through, casting dappled lights on the Morvern hillsides and sparkling on the waters of Loch Sunart.

pretend that this is the easiest way up the northern end of Garbh Bheinn, but on that day it was a route that suited our spirit of exploration. An easier and more obvious route from the pass is straight up the steep grassy gully directly above the lochan, but even this is not always simple as we discovered on another day in spring when, axeless, we had to kick steps up hard snow, finding occasional handholds on the side wall to help progress.

A view down Coire an Iubhair and across Loch Linnhe to the Appin and Benderloch tops.

The Garbh Bheinn group from Beinn Cille to the east, with Sgor Mhic Eacharna and Beinn Beag the obvious tops on the intervening ridge.

The south-eastern slopes of Garbh Bheinn.

Buachaille Etive Mor from the western side of Rannoch Moor.

The northern shore of Loch Laidon.

ACROSS RANNOCH MOOR

by HAMISH BROWN

'An immense vacuity, with nothing in it to contemplate, unless numberless mis-shapen blocks of stone rising hideously above the surface of the earth, would be said to contradict the inanity of our prospects'. So wrote a Sussex rector in the eighteenth century about Rannoch Moor, one of the most fascinating of wild places, which modern walkers have happily explored.

Most people are aware of the Moor from motoring over it to Glen Coe or from climbing the Munros and Corbetts that ring it round, but it also deserves to be explored for itself. The English Lake District would fit neatly into its vastness and only in Sutherland are there empty quarters of such character. In its heart you can walk for 'ten miles in a straight line without gaining or losing more than 50 feet' (W. H. Murray), but the straight line is more metaphorical than accurate on a landscape of eroded blanket bog, granite boulders, moraine bumps, peaty lochans and all kinds of ambushing challenges. It is this utter wildness that is its great attraction.

The Moor has a split-level plan and a curious plumbing system. Though almost on the western seaboard the waters of the Black Mount drain eastwards across the middle of the moor to reach the North Sea as the Tay Estuary. Its lower southward slopes drain to Loch Tulla and the river Orchy to Loch Awe and the western sea. The waters from Kingshouse and the Buachailles escape down Glen Etive to the same destination. Glen Coe does not drain the Moor at all. For most of the walk described you are above the 1,000ft contour.

In ancient times all communications were made from the sea and Rannoch Moor's geography kept it out of the mainstream of history. The eighteenth century military road had to bridge the River Orchy and swing round Loch Tulla to cross the Black Mount to Kingshouse and on over the Devil's Staircase to Loch Leven and Fort William. The road we use was only built in the 1930s. The railway to Fort William flanked the Moor to the east, its creation quite an epic tale. In places there was just no solid ground and the track is 'floated' on brushwood. An old route through to Loch Lyon was a suggested road and rail line and Kingshouse to Rannoch is another old way. Neither of these was ever made a proper road and the bold A82 over the Black Mount and the railway caterpillaring round the east only emphasise the desolation of the Moor.

Very little is written about the Moor, apart from giving warnings that it is a fearsome place and best avoided – which means it must be good! It is not to be treated casually and in bad weather the going can be laborious and sometimes dangerous, but in a dry summer spell or in crisp winter conditions walking into the Moor can be magical. It has a great deal of wildlife, an ever-changing horizon of mountains, and plenty of fascinating detail. Sandy bays lure the swimmer and I have skied and skated, canoed and tramped all over it without diminishing the lure. To pin this huge area down in one walk is hardly fair but if you tramp the following I'm sure you will be back for more.

Bridge of Orchy is a good base. The hotel welcomes outdoor enthusiasts (bunkhouse, camping available) and the railway can be

Maps O.S. 1:50,000 Sheets 41, 50 and 51.
Grading A long and strenuous walk with additional hazards in adverse weather conditions.
Start / Finish Bridge of Orchy (298397), with train to Rannoch Station to commence walking.
Distance / Time 22 miles/9-10 hours.
Escape Route From Loch Laidon via Black Corries to Kingshouse.
Telephones Rannoch Station, Kingshouse and Inveroran.
Transport Bridge of Orchy is on the Glasgow – Fort William bus and train routes.
Accommodation Hotel/Bunkhouse accommodation at Bridge of Orchy and Kingshouse. Hotel at Rannoch Station. Youth Hostels at Glencoe, Loch Ossian and Crianlarich.
Guidebooks S.M.T Guide 'The Central Highlands'; 'Companion Guide to the West Highlands of Scotland' by W. H. Murray (Collins); 'The Rannoch Line' (Famedram); 'Mountaineering in Scotland/Undiscovered Scotland' by W. H. Murray (Diadem).

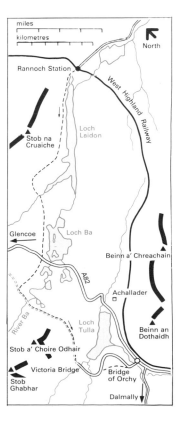

Looking south across Rannoch Moor to Beinn a' Chreachain.

A north-bound train at Rannoch Station.

used to start the day. Catch the 8.10 from Bridge of Orchy to arrive at Rannoch Station at 8.36: a journey on which I can never remain seated – there are good things to see on both sides. As the view over Loch Tulla drops behind, the line passes above Achallader Farm and Castle (the latter an early Campbell tower) and then runs through Crannach Wood, a beautiful remnant of the old forest that once covered the Moor. (During the day you will see plenty of the flaring skeletons of tree roots out in the bogs.) Gorton Halt has been abandoned but the gap above leads to Glen Lyon by Gleann Meran, 'The Robbers' Pass'. For many miles the eastern fringes have been planted with a blanketing spread of plantations, a sad substitute for the ancient forest of Caledon.

The 'Soldiers' Trenches' on the map are now merely some scar-rings where a post-Culloden attempt was made to try and reclaim part of a forfeited estate. It did not work out and the five trenches can

easily be overlooked from the trundling train.

The train rattles over a viaduct above the Garbh Ghaoir, which drains Loch Laidon, to reach lonely Rannoch Station. There is a hotel (and little else!) and with more time you could walk there in a day rather than reach it by train in half an hour and stay overnight. Likewise the next day you could cross to Kingshouse (hotel, bunk-house, camping) and back to Bridge of Orchy on the third day by the old military road, now saddled with the West Highland Way. A train once lost its guard's van near Corrour Station and it ran back over the viaduct at Rannoch and on over the Moor to finally halt at Bridge of Orchy. The story of surveying the railway route is worth reading in Alastair Borthwick's *Always a Little Further* and he also says something about the Blackwater dam construction. Patrick McGill's *Children of the Dead End* is based on this fringe-of-the-Moor saga.

Loch Laidon reaches away to the south-west and our walk follows

The Black Mount peaks from Loch Ba.

its northern shores. There is a track past the plantation but it becomes less well-defined thereafter until the Black Corries estate road is joined. In some ways keeping by the shore gives more enjoyable tramping. On a good day however there are just too many tempting spots to swim and brew and swim and brew and ...

From Tigh na Cruaiche it is worth flanking higher up as the lower ground is even worse than usual, then cut down to round the western arm of Loch Laidon to Tom Dubh-mor, a wee bump with a big view. The going on the Moor in fact varies and is often not bad at all. In the remoter corners rickles of stone and green swards show people once lived there. Divers and waders haunt the Moor with their lonesome cries and whinchats, ducks, larks, gulls all add their voices. The mosses and lichens can be a tapestry of colour. Grass of Parnassus, louse-wort, thyme, lady's mantle, clubmosses, cranberry, even waterlilies are among the floral delights. There are plenty of deer and you might just spot an otter.

Head south to the Abhainn Ba. Unless in spate this presents no problems in crossing (canoeists should go when there is plenty of water) and the south shore of Loch Ba is followed to the A82 where the River Ba enters it. Eilean Molach has trees (pines, rowan, birch, holly) because it is safe from the teeth of the deer. Two hundred metres of the A82 is enough, then a path leads off west towards Ba Cottage (ruin) and Ba Bridge. The view ahead is as grand as any in the country and a walk up the Ba into the huge Black Mount Corries can be listed for 'next time'. You are now on the old road (*The New Road* of Neil Munro's classic novel) and this is followed down to the Moor's basement at Victoria Bridge. The West Highland Way goes over by Mam Carraigh, a tiring pull at the end of a hard day, or you

Rannoch Moor seen beyond the Abhainn Shira at Victoria Bridge.

can tramp the road through Doire Darach (another good forest remnant) to return to Bridge of Orchy.

There is no short-cut across that western arm of Loch Laidon and if the Abhainn Ba could be in spate then keep north of Loch Ba to the A82. Once across the Abhainn Ba an alternative tramp is by Leathad Beag (or even Leathad Mor for its bigger view) to Gorton. The saddle of the Dubh Lochain is very wet so keep on the slopes above. Gorton has a bothy available outwith the stalking season when the Moor is best avoided. The walk from Gorton by Crannach and Achallader

back to Bridge of Orchy is pleasant but not as spectacular as the Black Mount.

Years ago we spent a week on Rannoch Moor trying to find a rush which grows there and only in one other place on earth. We never did find it but a friend joining us at the weekend brought the astonishing news of John Kennedy's assassination, four days before. We must have been some of the last people in the world to have heard that news. And that too is typical of the great, wild solitudes of the marvellous Moor of Rannoch.

A typical Rannoch landscape in the vicinity of Black Corries.

THE OCHILS: ROUND-OF-THE-NINE

by RENNIE McOWEN

The ancient Celts called these lovely, green hills Uchel, the high ground, and they are mainly rounded, grassy hills, split by chattering burns which in past centuries turned the millwheels in the villages at their southern foot, and which processed the wool from sheep which have dotted their flanks for many centuries.

The hills soar spectacularly up from the plain of the Forth, the so-called Ochils Fault which excites geologists, and silver, copper and calcite have all been extracted in past times.

With the fertile farmland and moors of Strathearn to the north and the silver links of the river Forth to the south, on land once covered by the sea and swamp, the Ochils have an island-like situation which can provide beautiful all-round views over a wide variety of terrain.

They were barrier hills, blocking the way north between Stirling and Perth, and round their sides, and occasionally over them or through the passes, swirled the tide of Scottish history. The Celtic saints, soldiers, clansmen, royalty, packmen, the famed cattled drovers, local people accused in the seventeenth century of being witches and warlocks, and modern hunters for semi-precious stones all knew these hills.

They were beloved of the literati: Sir Walter Scott and Burns praised them and Robert Louis Stevenson and his family climbed the shapely, rocky peak of Dumyat at the Ochils western end and, some scholars believe, brought it into the map of *Treasure Island*.

To get an initial feel of these intimate hills an ideal plan is to do the Round-of-the-Nine, a traverse of the Donald-defined 2,000ft tops.

My own preference is to leave one's car in Stirling or in the Hillfoots' village of Menstrie and catch a bus to Dollar. One can then return directly to the vehicle at the end of the day.

Walk from Dollar up the gorge of Dollar Glen to picturesque Castle Campbell, whose roots go back to the fifteenth century. There is a clear path through the gorge, walkways and bridges, and the burn in spate and the gloominess are impressive.

From the castle walk round to the entrance to Glen Quey, now affected by creeping forestry, where there is a track and you soon get onto the north-east side of the burn and are walking through a clear defile, a route once used by the cattle drovers to dodge toll gates elsewhere. Keep an eye out on the left for the tiny, falling cascades of the Maiden's Well, but don't go to sleep beside it because Ochils' legend has it that you will never return to this earth if you do.

About a quarter of the way along the Glenquey Reservoir turn sharply north-west up the hillside and grind away until you reach Innerdownie where you can flop down, muttering. The views to the eastern Ochils and across to Loch Leven and the Lomond, Cleish and Saline hills are attractive.

Turn south-west and follow the obvious ridge back to Whitewisp, keeping a look out for a little shelter beside the drystone dyke on Innerdownie where the dykebuilders lived last century.

Whitewisp is so called because it holds snow late on. You are still bounded by forestry plantations on the north slopes at this point and also on the easy walk on grassy turf to Tarmangie (the mound-of-the-goats) to the west.

The summit cairns on these hills are tiny and care is needed with navigation in mist.

Then comes a wide sweep west and south and a pull up to the summit of King's Seat above Dollar, a big 'un for the Ochils at 2,111ft/643m and another good place for a breather. You can see below the farms, villages, towns, disused pits and minor industry on the flat ground where the sea once lapped against forest-clad hills and the remains of oysters and other sea creatures have been found.

Then it's back again and heading north until one turns down to the upper reaches of the Gannel burn; at this point you are crossing the line of the old hill-crossing from Tillicoultry to Blackford where weavers took tartan and other cloth across the Ochils to be sold.

The small rocky top of Andrew Gannel hill, not named on the present Ordnance Survey map, is easily found: it is the mound immediately to the west of the crest of the pass and is on the south-east side of the fence which crosses the hill from Ben Cleuch.

Some Ochils buffs feel Andrew Gannel sounds like a character out

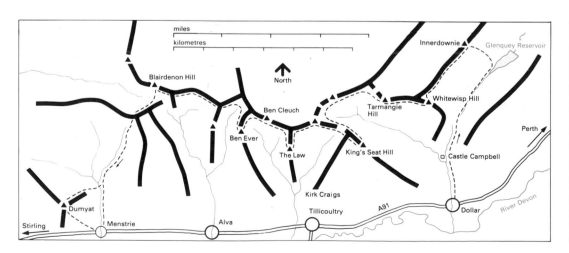

Maps O.S. 1:50,000 Sheets 57 and 58.
Grading A long walk over easy terrain: mainly undulating hills with grass and some heather.
Start / Finish Dollar Glen (964985); Menstrie (849971).
Distance / Time 19 miles/10-11 hours.
Escape Routes It is easy to turn down any of the glens running south to Dollar, Tillicoultry or Alva.
Telephones Dollar, Tillicoultry, Alva and Menstrie.
Transport Railway Stations at Stirling and Dunblane. Bus services from Alloa and Stirling to Dollar and Menstrie.
Accommodation Hotels in Dollar, Alva, Stirling and Alloa. B & B in all of the Hillfoots villages. Youth Hostels at Stirling and Glendevon.
Guidebooks S.M.T Guide 'The Southern Highlands'; 'Discovering the Ochils' by Rennie McOwen (John Donald).

Castle Campbell and the Ochils.

The view north from Ben Cleuch to the Crianlarich and Ben Vorlich hills.

On the southern slopes of Ben Ever looking across the Alva Glen to Kirk Craigs.

of a John Buchan yarn but it is a corruption of the Gaelic for a sandy-bottomed burn (*an sruth gainmhail*).

At this point the highest top, 2,363ft/721m, Ben Cleuch (*cliotach*, a slope) is just ahead, but you have first to swing south to the prominent top of The Law which means The Hill and the modern tendency to say the Law Hill is, in fact, to say the Hill Hill!

Turn and toil back up the long slopes to the top of Ben Cleuch where there is a battered viewpoint indicator, a trig. point and a surrounding 'wall'. The views can be superb. The Cairngorms can be picked out and Ben Nevis and the Galloway Hills.

On again and round to another grassy swelling, Ben Ever (*eibhr*, granite) and with one to go the hills change character a little. Just under three miles away lies the last 2,000 footer, Blairdenon Hill, which has no cairn. The summit is near the junction of some fences.

First you have to cross The Moss, a series of peat hags and rough moorland, a little bit of Highland scenery set down in Lowland hills. It is not difficult, but it slows one a little. On your way up to Blairdenon you pass a small cross, memorial to a student pilot who was killed when his training plane crashed in the Ochils.

The blue hills of the Grampians are ahead of you, another great

The Ochils from the north, viewed across the Upper Glendevon Reservoir.

Ben Ever and Ben Buck from the south.

sight, and it is worth flopping on the top of Blairdenon for an orgy of peak identification.

Blair means a plain, but it can also mean a battle and down below lies Sheriffmuir and its 1715 battlefield and the site of guerilla clashes in William Wallace's time. Contour carefully off Blairdenon Hill until you get on to the east side of the Second Inchna burn, with Colsnaur Hill on your left (east) and descend into Menstrie glen. Forestry planting is rearing its monstrous head on some of the higher slopes. And that's the Nine!

An exhilarating tailpiece for those with puff and time left is to cross the Menstrie burn and toil up steep slopes to the top of 1,276ft Dumyat, one of the outstanding viewpoint small-hills in Scotland. Its name derives from the dun (or fort) of the Pictish tribe, the Maeatae or Miathi and it is pronounced Dum-eye-at.

An old rhyme says:

'What hills are like the Ochils hills?
There's nane sae green, tho' grander.
What rills are like the Ochils rills?
Nane, nane on earth that wander.'

Ben Ledi seen across the River Tieth at Callander.

THE LOCH LUBNAIG HILLS: BEN LEDI AND BENVANE

Now that the motorway has extended to Stirling, the winding road through Callander and alongside Loch Lubnaig has become a trade-route for climbers making for Glen Coe and the North West Highlands. Ben Ledi is the first real mountain which is seen on the drive north. It towers above Loch Lubnaig to a height of 2,873ft/ 879m, presenting a high, wild corrie and a craggy face to the east, and the fact that it does not even win Munro status has caused many a heart to flutter with dismay at the thought of the relative monsters that must lie ahead.

Wild walkers will find it particularly satisfying to spend a day on the lonely hills west of Loch Lubnaig, far above the tourist high-spots of Callander, the Falls of Leny and the Trossachs.

This is country rich in folk-lore and legend, the setting for Sir Walter Scott's epic poem *The Lady of the Lake*, published in 1810, and where Rob Roy outwitted the Duke of Montrose in the early part of the eighteenth century.

More recently the television series *Dr Finlay's Casebook*, whose Tannochbrae was based on the town of Callander, has swelled the number of visitors, and picnic sites, holiday lodges and jetties have sprung up beside Loch Lubnaig. Yet the region is so inherently beautiful that it does not need promotion: lochs, islands, woods, crags, corries, ravines, tumbling burns, waterfalls and purple heather

are all to be found; in fact everything that is romantic in the highland scene is contained in this small area.

Near the south end of Loch Lubnaig a bridge crosses the outflowing river and leads to a car-park. The tourist route up Ben Ledi is waymarked from here, but it follows a not very inspiring route up the south-east ridge and it is much better to walk north for a mile and climb through Stank Glen.

Maps O.S. 1:50,000 Sheet 57; O.S. 1:63,630 Tourist Map 'Loch Lomond and the Trossachs'.
Grading An easy walk over mainly grassy hills.
Start / Finish Ben Ledi car-park (587092).
Distance / Time 14 miles/7 hours.
Escape Route From Lochan nan Corp a waymarked path descends the Stank Glen to Loch Lubnaig.
Telephones Strathyre, Kilmahog and Callander.
Transport Railway Station at Stirling. Regular daily bus service Stirling to Callander.
Accommodation Hotel/Guest Houses at Callander. Youth Hostels at Stirling, Trossachs, Loch Ard and Killin.
Guidebooks S.M.T Guide 'The Southern Highlands'; 'The Trossachs' by Campbell Nairne (Oliver and Boyd); 'Walks in the Trossachs' by Rennie McOwen (St. Andrew Press).

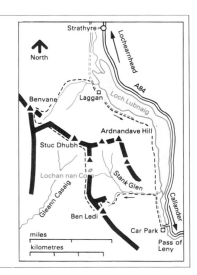

Left: The descent to Loch Lubnaig from the south-east ridge of Ben Ledi.

Approaching Ben Ledi up Stank Glen.

A narrow path runs up through the forest, keeping close to the burn which rushes headlong down the hillside in a series of cascades and falls. Where the block of forestry ends you turn south-west and climb the open slopes beside a small stream. After passing a few enormous detached blocks of rock the slope steepens and makes for an extraordinary collection of chaotic, splintered boulders set at crazy angles, as if cast on the hillside by a giant.

The stream drains a small corrie high under the summit ridge of Ben Ledi, and a narrow spur on the north side provides an airy route of ascent.

Ben Ledi commands views extending to Ben Cruachan, Beinn Laoigh, Ben More, Stob Binnein, Ben Lawers and Ben Vorlich. Nearer at hand it looks over Loch Venachar, Loch Katrine, Ben Venue and the beautiful country of the Trossachs, visited by William and Dorothy Wordsworth and Samuel Taylor Coleridge in 1803. Dorothy wrote ecstatically about the trees growing in profusion on the rocks, knolls and hills.

A narrow but grassy ridge leads north from the summit trig. point of Ben Ledi to a bealach and tiny lochan, Lochan nan Corp (loch of the bodies). Legend has it that a funeral party, crossing from Gleann Casaig to St Bride's chapel in the Pass of Leny, fell through the ice on the lochan and were drowned.

A line of rusty iron fence posts are followed over a group of rocky hummocks on the west side of Ardnandave Hill, while the green mound of Benvane beckons across Gleann Casaig.

It is an easy two hour walk round the head of Gleann Casaig from Ben Ledi to Benvane. A path of sorts runs beside the stakes, but you may prefer to pick your own way across the broad shoulder of rough grass enjoying expansive views of the Southern Highlands. A stream of clear water running through a grassy gully provides a refreshing drink before the final haul up the summit cone.

Benvane is a lonely hill and you should have time, on this modest expedition, to stretch out beside the cairn and enjoy absolute peace and solitude. Far below, the fields of Glen Buckie and the busy village of Strathyre are in another world.

Retrace your steps down the south-east ridge and scramble down beside a gorge containing a splendid waterfall. Follow the stream to the edge of the plantation and take the forestry road which zig-zags through the trees to the farm at Laggan beside Loch Lubnaig.

Forestry roads are always confusing, but if you keep losing height you will eventually reach the lochside and the line of the old Callander-Strathyre railway which fell under Beeching's axe. In the eighteenth century, under the instructions of General Wade, a military road was constructed along the west side of Loch Lubnaig, but now only a footpath remains. This was the route taken by the bearers of the 'Fiery Cross' in Scott's poem, the cross being carried by a relay of runners to call the clansmen to arms.

'Benledi saw the Cross of Fire,
It glanced like lighting up Strath-Ire.'

It is a delightful four-mile walk back to the car-park. The track is overgrown with hawthorn, broom, gorse, wild roses and raspberries; and in early June I found almost the entire length of the embankment to be a mass of bluebells, whose fragrance hung in the still air. On the other side of the track alder and hazel trees lean out over the loch, their roots lapped by the waves.

The track passes under the eastern spur of Ardnandave Hill, where a massive, knuckle-shaped wall of rock thrusts out towards the loch, and it then passes a group of log cabins before reaching the Ben Ledi car-park.

Top right: Looking south from Lochan nan Corp to Ben Ledi.

Lower right: Benvane from Ardnandave Hill with the Crianlarich summits Cruach Ardrain, Stob Binnein and Ben More prominent in the background.

THE PAPS OF JURA

by GORDON GADSBY

To visit the Hebridean island of Jura is to journey back in time on one of the wildest islands off the Scottish coast. Twenty eight miles long by eight miles wide, Jura lies north-east of Islay and is named after the Norse for Deer Island. Our ancestors hunted deer and wild boar on the island at the close of the Great Ice Age; flint arrowheads found on Jura are the earliest evidence of man in Scotland. Deer still abound and George Orwell, who lived on Jura in 1948 whilst writing *Nineteen Eighty Four*, commented: 'The crofters would be comfortable if they could get the landlords off their backs and get rid of the deer'.

The main features on Jura are the three cone-shaped peaks called the Paps, and the traverse of all three is a hard day's work involving over 5,000ft of ascent.

My first real look at Jura came a few years ago in early April when we had just completed a walk on the Islay hills. All day the winds and rolling grey clouds had assailed us, but then, on the final rocks, it became strangely calm and a white clammy mist enveloped us. Suddenly a blast of wind removed the mist and exposed us to the evening sun above a heaving sea of cloud. We looked on enthralled as the curving sunlit crest of Beinn an Oir, 2,571ft/784m, (Hill of Gold), the highest peak on Jura, emerged from the cauldron of clouds. Within a few seconds it was again engulfed in a grey shroud but, brief though it was, the invitation had been received and two days later we crossed to Jura.

As we left the Jura Ferry the sun's rays were already trapped by leaden clouds with more than a hint of rain. The ferryman was concerned, and as we walked away from the boat he jokingly offered us the ferry's lifebelts. 'If it rains you'll need them for the bogs,' he yelled.

Map O.S. 1:50,000 Sheet 61.
Grading A tough walk over exposed and stony hills with no recognised tracks.
Start / Finish Craighouse (527672).
Distance / Time 18 miles/9 hours.
Escape Routes An easy descent to the glen may be made from either of the two bealachs separating the three peaks.
Telephone Craighouse.
Transport Steamer from Kennacraig to Port Askaig (Islay). Daily ferry Port Askaig to Feolin (Jura). Feolin to Craighouse by Charlie's bus.
Accommodation Hotel/B & B at Craighouse.
Guidebook S.M.T Guide 'The Islands of Scotland'.

The Paps of Jura seen from near Craighouse. The peaks in view are (left to right) Beinn a' Chaola

Charlie's bus took us to the main village of Craighouse and from there we headed north along the coast road to the bridge across the Corran river. As we walked, slanting rays of sunlight broke through the massed clouds and hit the distant hills of Knapdale and Kintyre across the Sound of Jura. With the wind strong in our faces we followed a rough track steadily upwards towards Loch an t-Siob and the sombre shapes of Beinn an Oir, Beinn Shiantaidh and Beinn a'Chaolais; each peak composed of fine-grained quartzite.

An hour later we reached the wind-splattered waters of the loch, leaning into the gale to make progress towards the protecting flank of Beinn Shiantaidh. After a brief rest we moved up gently rising ground to reach a string of small lochans on the col between Shiantaidh and the small hill Corra Bheinn. From the col we worked our way up the east flank of the mountain avoiding the steeper parts. Views were non-existent as the clouds swirled amongst us and, on reaching the large summit cairn, we met the full force of the westerly gale. It was not a place to linger, the wind seemed to be increasing in velocity, tearing at the cairn and at our anoraks.

We descended north-west on a compass bearing, carefully picking our way down the steep screes towards a small lochan below the east flank of Cnoc an Oir. It cleared here and we saw several groups of red deer in the sunshine at the bottom of the north ridge of Beinn an Oir. The ridge was rocky in places and looked as if it would provide an interesting route to the summit. We contoured round to gain the ridge, but now were exposed to the full force of a strong cross wind which rocked us from side to side; the view disappeared completely and it started to rain. We were lashed incessantly and were thankful to find shelter in a grassy hollow beside some large rocks.

A few minutes later the weather cleared and excitedly we scrambled up the dripping crags, enjoying fantastic views. The north end of Jura, Colonsay and parts of Islay were bathed in sunshine with Loch Tarbet dominating the view north, its flashing blue waters

Oir and Beinn Shiantaidh.

almost cutting Jura in half, save for a small spit of land near the Standing Stones, Tarbert. Beyond the loch we could see across miles of barren moorland to the cliffs of Carraig Mhor and the Gulf of Corryvreckan, the most formidable tide-race in Britain.

Above us the north ridge curled up towards the summit, making a delightful route as we followed it to the top and the welcome shelter of a large circular cairn. Just before reaching Beinn an Oir's highest rocks we passed the strange ruins of two substantial buildings and a rough causeway, about which there has been much conjecture.

We had a late lunch by the cairn, pausing now and again to jump

Beinn a' Chaolais from Beinn an Oir.

up and take in the splendid views of the uninhabited west coast of Jura and the golden beaches of Gruinart Bay on North Islay.

To continue our traverse we had a choice of two routes of descent: one an easy scree and grass slope down the north-west ridge from the dip by the ruined buildings, the other by the spectacular 1,500ft scree gully that splits the south face of Beinn an Oir and is well seen from Feolin. We chose the latter which was steep and interesting but not hard and, within forty minutes, we were again in sunshine beside the Na Garbh-Lochanan.

We walked round the west edge of the largest lochan over boggy ground, disturbing several wild fowl on the way, and then made an ascending traverse of the west flank of Beinn a'Chaolais to reach the south-west ridge; this led easily to the cairn on the rather flat summit.

The wind had now abated and, gazing across the sunlit U-shaped valley towards Loch an t-Siob, it was hard to realise that, during the Ice Age, Jura laid claim to no fewer than nineteen glaciers.

Time was pressing, so we descended southwards into the wide and beautiful Gleann Astaile, crossing the glen at the east end of Lochan Gleann Astaile and continuing up the gentle slopes of Aonach-bheinn. From here a broad, wet escarpment led past several small lochans on Glas Bheinn, and then easily down the eastern flanks of the hill to the ancient settlement of Keils, the village of Craighouse and Charlie's bus.

THE PIRNMILL HILLS OF ARRAN

by ALASTAIR HETHERINGTON

Conventional wisdom says that the Pirnmill Hills, on the west of Arran, are just big round boring lumps, Quite wrong: for although they are part of a granite dome they have pleasing ridges and they include the island's finest high-level lochan. Red deer, red-throated divers, and a golden eagle (if you are lucky) are all to be seen. Above the coastal crofts, these hills have stood unchanged for thousands of years – and you won't meet many people on them.

Whether they qualify as a wilderness is arguable. With a westerly gale blowing off the Atlantic or when the cloud is down and careful compass work is required on the ridges, they are not easy. Eastwards there are neither tracks nor habitation for many miles. Only in a small sector to the south-west has man intruded, with forestry plantations. Even the sheep are few once you are above 1,000ft.

For years an uncle of mine had a cottage at Pirnmill, and it was the base for many expeditions. In high summer he thought nothing of going up Beinn Bharrain ('Varren') or Beinn Bhreac ('Vrack') before breakfast – three hours or so up and down. But to cover the whole stretch, south to north or north to south, is an all-day task. In winter the tops can be snow-covered for weeks on end, crisp or icy under-foot. In bad weather a crossing west-east to Catacol Glen or Glen Easan Biorach provided – and still provides – a rewarding day. And, of course, if you want a really long walk you can start from Lochranza and tackle Beinn Bhiorach and Beinn Tarsuinn (the lesser of two Arran hills with that name) before crossing over to the Pirnmill group – a round of over twenty miles.

The best day, in my view, is to leave Pirnmill by the path on the north side of the Gobhlach ('Go-lach') burn. Note the birch and hazel coppices as you go – good cover for birds – and the surviving beech hedges probably planted about 1850 on the orders of the eleventh Duke of Hamilton, one of Arran's few creative landlords. Higher up the Gobhlach burn you will see a sequence of fine little waterfalls as you climb to the open moorland.

There, cross the burn and head south-south-east, not for the prominent westerly ridge of Beinn Bharrain (though it will give you a good walk another day, leading to the rocky Casteal na h'Iolaire) but to the shorter and steeper middle ridge, leading almost directly to Bharrain's main peak. It provides some good, airy rock scrambling. It is steep at first, with easy slabs, but becomes narrower and more broken later. It is a miniature A'Chir, requiring care in places. If you wish, however, all the awkward places can be bypassed on the west side.

At the main top, only 2,368ft/721m above the sea but likely to feel higher, look west to the Atlantic. This is the greatest panorama of the day. On the Antrim coast of Ireland you can pick out Fair Head, and further to the west the mouth of Loch Foyle. Then to your west the islands of Islay and Jura, and to the north-west the summit of Ben More, Mull. In the foreground are Kintyre and the Kilbrannan Sound, with the Caradale fishing fleet at work and possibly a sub-

Looking north from Meall Donn to Coire Fhionn Lochan.

Ken Andrew

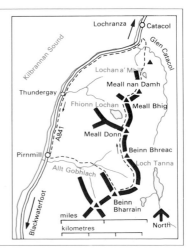

The main Arran Ridge seen from Beinn Bhreac with Glen Catacol in the middle distance.

marine or two in training.

Having viewed and rested, keep north-east and then north along the broad ridge to the second summit, Beinn Bhreac, 2,333ft/711m. It is here, or just beyond, that you stand the best chance of seeing a golden eagle, for they are thought to like the far side of Catacol Glen. Keep on northwards to a lesser hump with a prominent cairn, and from just beyond it you can look down past granite cliffs to Coire Fhionn Lochan, or colloquially Corrie Lochan to most Arran people, with a sandy beach and a dramatic setting which make it a popular walk from the clachan of Thundergay. The red-throated diver nests beside the loch; and in spring-time groups of geologists can also be seen on its shore (some of both sexes even swimming in the icy water).

If by now you have had enough, the descent by the lochan and the path to Thundergay is always pleasing. The ardent, however, will keep going northwards – past Meall Bhig to the day's final top, Meall nan Damh, which is no more than 1,870ft/570m but has an unbroken view northwards up Loch Fyne and to the Southern Highlands. Its north-eastern shoulder is adorned by another small stretch of silver water, Lochan a' Mhill, which you will almost certainly have to your-selves. Not sandy, but good for swimming on a hot day. You are, however, getting down into the territory of the midge, so in July and August prepare to be bitten.

Beware, finally, of the descent to Catacol village through the bracken. The birch woods are lovely and the bracken vile. Find a sheep track and follow it, for in summer the bracken can be as much as five feet high and exceedingly tiresome. The beach at Catacol is stony, so not good for swimming, but about one-and-a-half miles down the road back to Pirnmill there is a little sandy stretch just south of Rubha Airigh Bheirg. For campers there is good grass here too, but no amenities.

Map O.S. 1:50,000 Sheet 69.
Grading A straightforward mountain traverse over a fine granite ridge with superb sea and coastal views. Some rock scrambling is involved on Beinn Bharrain.
Start / Finish Pirnmill (872442).
Distance / Time 12 miles/6-7 hours.
Escape Routes The mountain ridge may be descended easily to the A841 on the W side from many of the bealachs.
Telephones Pirnmill and Catacol.
Transport Regular steamer service from Ardrossan to Brodick. Summer service from Claonaig to Lochranza. Bus service: Brodick – Lochranza – Pirnmill.
Accommodation Hotels in Lochranza. B & B in Pirnmill. Youth Hostel at Lochranza.
Guidebooks S.M.T Guide 'The Islands of Scotland'; 'Hill Walking in Arran' by Ronald L. Meek (Arran Tourist Association).

Coire Fhionn Lochan.

A historic footnote: though the country inland is wild and empty, the thin strip of crofting land along the coast has long antecedents. From Beinn Bharrain and Beinn Bhreac you can see the Irish coast, not so very far away, and it was from Dalriada in the north of Ireland that the first 'Scots' came to colonise south-west Scotland. Feargus, one of three brothers, became the ruler of Kintyre, Arran, Bute and other islands in the Clyde, while one of his brothers ruled Islay and Jura and another held Lorne and Mull. All that was in the sixth century, and all three owed loyalty to the Irish Dalriada. The main settlements were round Blackwaterfoot, Lochranza, Brodick and Lamlash.

In the seventh century a grandson of Feargus, Aiden MacGabhran, united the Scottish Dalriada into one kingdom, secured its separation from Ireland, and extended it as far as Stirling and Perth on the mainland. He is a lineal ancestor of the present royal family, and he was the first British monarch to be consecrated at his crowning (by Columba, in Iona). Think of him as you walk these hills. It is highly probable that he walked them too. Suidhe Fhearghas ('the seat of Feargus') above Glen Sannox takes its name from his grandfather.

The rocky north-west ridge of Beinn Bharrain.

THE ETTRICK HILLS

Ettrick was in the iron grip of winter. I stood on the old stone bridge over Ettrick Water and gazed down at the ribs of snow stretching in places from bank to bank and sculptured into curls and whorls by the wind. Through the translucent green ice the water was still visible, bubbling and gurgling on its way into the Tweed at Melrose.

Outlined against the bluest of skies, gleaming white from top to toe and carrying banners of wind-blown powder snow the hills were magnificent.

For seven miles the Ettrick valley runs deep into the hills, served by a narrow road which ends at the farm at Potburn, and a snow-plough had cut a channel through the drifts to maintain access to the lonely homesteads.

The community at Ettrick is as isolated as any in Britain south of the Highlands, and only a post office, which doubles as village store, and an inn at Tushielaw on the Selkirk road cater for the needs of visitors. A Tibetan settlement complete with pagoda has been established at neighbouring Eskdalemuir, and the inhabitants must feel very much at home amongst these beautiful hills and glens.

Yet in the early part of the nineteenth century James Hogg, the Ettrick Shepherd, brought fame to the area. Hogg was born in Ettrick and worked as a shepherd at Yarrow near St Mary's Loch. He spent his spare time writing poetry, was discovered and taken under the wing of Sir Walter Scott and introduced to Edinburgh society. His best known poem, *The Queen's Wake*, was published in 1813.

Ettrick typifies the grand walking country of the Southern Uplands. The hills are rounded and bald, bracken is creeping up from the valley, while coarse moor-grass and heather on the upper slopes provide a meagre bite for a scant population of sheep. In places broken crags and grey, lichen-encrusted boulders emerge from the turf, and eroded gullies and seams carry tumbling burns down to the valley.

A few patches of deciduous woodlands remain in the valley bottom and on the banks of Ettrick water, but extensive planting of conifers on the south side is rapidly altering the landscape. Nevertheless most of the principal summits, including the rounded dome of Ettrick Pen, the highest hill in the region at 2,270ft/692m rise well above the trees.

The unbroken horseshoe of hills which encloses the valley can be traversed in a single day's walk of twenty two miles. This is an energetic, switchback course over rough, trackless and at times boggy hills, but the spaciousness, freedom, solitude and lack of a single road or dwelling will prove irresistible to the wild walker.

On my winter visit to Ettrick the beauty of the scene belied the true conditions on the hills. From the picturesque church set amongst trees I struggled to reach the stone cairn on Craig Hill. The piercing wind and ice spicules rasped my cheeks but it was the deep, crusted, powder snow which defeated me. Three miles in as many hours was the rate, with boots breaking through the glazed surface into knee-deep icing sugar at every step. Having reached the ice-festooned boundary fence on Peniestone Knowe, and marvelled at

the winter view of White Coomb and Loch Skeen across the Yarrow valley, (it could have been the Beardmore Glacier) I turned for home.

Ettrick on a sunny May morning was a different world. The tiny church was ringed with daffodils, the roadside verges were bright with cowslips, and primroses and violets decorated the banks of every rill.

But rain was forecast for mid-morning and, knowing that the idyll would not last, we hastened over Craig Hill to Peniestone Knowe. At the head of the Scabcleugh Burn we crossed the line of the Southern Uplands Way and I was pleased to see that the waymarked path was still free from erosion and as narrow as a sheep trod.

The hills on the north side of the Ettrick valley run parallel to the Hart Fell, Firthhope Rig, Broad Law range, described in the Peebles to Moffat chapter of *The Big Walks*. Thus our eyes were drawn west to Loch of the Lowes, St Mary's Loch and the lingering snow patches on White Coomb.

The walking is easy and the boundary fence is followed over

> *Map* O.S. 1:50,000 Sheet 79.
> *Grading* A long switchback walk over trackless hills of coarse grass, heather and peat.
> *Start / Finish* Ettrick Church (260144).
> *Distance / Time* 22 miles/10 hours.
> *Escape Routes* From the low col S of Bodesbeck Law tracks lead to Potburn and to the Moffat road. From almost all points on the walk easy slopes lead down to the Ettrick valley.
> *Telephones* Ettrick and Shorthope.
> *Transport* None to Ettrick. The nearest towns are Hawick, Selkirk, Moffat, Langholm and Lockerbie.
> *Accommodation* Hotels at Tushielaw and Buccleuch. B & B at Ettrick. Youth Hostels at Roberton and Broadmeadows near Selkirk.
> *Guidebooks* S.M.T Guide 'The Southern Uplands'; 'Guide to Walks and Climbs in Dumfries and Galloway' by R. D. Walton (T. C. Farries).

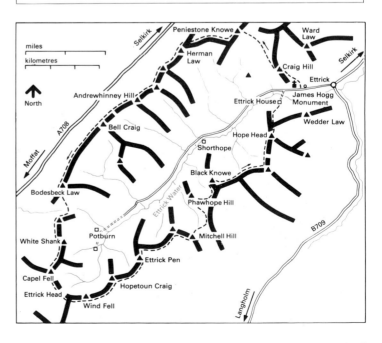

The view south-west from Ettrick Head to Selcoth Burn.

Capel Fell and Selcoth Burn from Ettrick Head.

Looking north-west from Andrewhinney Hill to the Moffat Hills, Loch Skeen and the Grey Mare's Tail.

Two views on the northern Ettrick Ridge – approaching Bodesbeck Law from Bell Craig.

Herman Law, Trowgrain Middle, Mid Rig and Andrewhinney Hill. From the latter you can peep over the corrie lip to see Loch Skeen, that most austere of lochs which nestles under the eastern crags of Firthybrig Head. I felt a twinge of guilt at invading the privacy of this secret place, even from a distance of three miles.

As clouds gathered and the wind rose, the thin silver thread of the Grey Mare's Tail became more distinct and the outline of Saddle Yoke and Raven Craig darker and more menacing. An old wall gave some protection from the wind as we climbed to the rock outcrop on the shapely hill of Bodesbeck Law, but big icy drops heralded the onset of the depression and heavy rain set in for the rest of the day.

The descent south from Bodesbeck Law leads to a col at 1,550ft/ 472m where a track crosses the hills from Moffat Water to Potburn farm. A steep climb over White Shank and Capel Fell follows before another descent leads to the watershed at Ettrick Head.

This is the wildest area of the entire walk, where bottomless ravines disappear down to the valleys and steep hillsides rise up into the mists. An evil black bog must be crossed before the fence leads you up again to Wind Fell and Hopetoun Craig.

An extraordinary collection of elegant stone cairns has been built on the south-west ridge of Ettrick Pen, which announces its supremacy over the neighbouring hills with a massive pile of stones and a gate in the fence. Ettrick Pen provides a view over almost the whole of the southern lowlands of Scotland, the Eildons and the Cheviots, but we could see little save the fence marching away into the swirling mists; besides which, the driving rain had penetrated every stitch of my clothing and I was in no mood to linger.

Easy ground continues north-east to the 1,935ft/590m cairn on Mitchell Hill, whence a descent to the head waters of the North Glendearg Burn and a continuation over Phawhope Hill and Hope Head brings you to the bridge over Ettrick Water at Ettrick House. But be warned, much new forestry has been planted in this area and we became hopelessly lost before finally reaching the bridge at Shorthope. A safe way in bad weather would be to head north from the 1,935ft/590m cairn to reach the bridge at Nether Phawhope.

Although we were tired, thoroughly chilled and annoyed at our incompetent navigation, our descent of the East Grain Burn had its rewards. The banks were carpeted with primroses and wood anemones, a buzzard flew overhead and a herd of deer was sheltering under the trees. It had been an unforgettable and eventful day and I had no doubt that the hills of Ettrick firmly deserved their place in *Wild Walks*.

Ascending Knockwhirn with Benloch Burn in the valley below.

Approaching Windy Standard from the south-east.

Windy Standard from Dugland.

[96]

CAIRNSMORE OF CARSPHAIRN

'There's Cairnsmore of Fleet,
And Cairnsmore of Dee,
And Cairnsmore of Carsphairn:
The biggest of the three.'

As soon as you turn off the A75 and leave behind the snarling container lorries bound for Stranraer, you enter another world. Smoothly contoured, rounded and folded hills rise from unspoilt valleys containing blue lochs, tumbling salmon rivers and villages of grey stone houses. On the low ground the fields are grazed by fat cattle and sheep, the farms are tidy and prosperous and the farmhouses are whitewashed and often sheltered by a windward belt of trees.

The open landscape is ideal for walking, the hills are high but gentle and difficulties are few. The bedrock is granite and attractive outcrops of the coarse, weathered rock occur high up on some of the hills. Quite steep escarpments of loose, vegetated rock are found on Cairnsmore, Beninner, Moorbrock and Windy Standard but these are easily avoided. As on the fells of Northumberland you are always conscious of the great vault of sky overhead, and on a windy day, with clouds racing in from the west, there cannot be a more exhilarating experience than a long walk over the roof of Galloway.

Visitors tend to favour Glen Trool and the picnic sites and forest walks organised by the Forestry Commission. Indeed, the FC is doing all it can to preserve its public image in a region where the blanket of conifers on the low ground is ever expanding, with tentacles reaching high into the exquisite upland valleys.

Outside the main group of hills, centred on Merrick and the Rhinns of Kells, the wildest hill area in Galloway is that of Cairnsmore of Carsphairn and its satellites. East of Loch Doon, Cairnsmore rises to 2,614ft/797m and magnificent rolling hills continue north, round the watershed of Water of Deugh and on for many miles. At present, Cairnsmore and its neighbours are still untouched by the planters; on the map they appear as an oasis in a green desert. Thus, exceptionally, the walk avoids all existing forestry, but this situation may not remain for very much longer. In 1985 I noticed ominous signs of a forestry extension south of Moorbrock Hill: ugly new bulldozed roads, brutal fencing and the scars of drainage furrows.

However, the high tops, ridges and plateaus of Cairnsmore continue to provide superlative walking country, where your eyes are drawn to far horizons rather than to the creeping forests of the lowlands.

Leave the car one mile north of Carsphairn at the bridge over Water of Deugh, marked Green Well of Scotland on the map. Easy slopes lead to the summit of the prominent conical hill, Craig of Knockgray. This hill is a wonderful viewpoint for the Cairnsmore group: you look right up to the source of the Benloch burn enclosed between the shoulders of Cairnsmore and Beninner, while to the south the long Cairnsgarroch—Corserine—Rhinns of Kells ridge rises beyond Carsphairn village, and its outline becomes increasingly more familiar as the day goes on. A more delightful backcloth to a walk cannot be imagined.

Map O.S. 1:50,000 Sheet 15.
Grading A tough walk over remote and trackless hills. In misty weather care should be taken to avoid crags on Beninner, Moorbrock Hill, Windy Standard and Cairnsmore.
Start / Finish Green Well of Scotland, near Carsphairn (557945).
Distance / Time 16 miles/8-9 hours.
Escape Routes Few. From Windy Standard descend N to reach the Afton reservoir access road. Emergency shelter could be found in the byre at Clennoch.
Telephone Carsphairn.
Transport Daily bus service (not Sun) New Galloway to Ayr passes through Carsphairn.
Accommodation Hotels at Carsphairn, Dalmellington and St. John's Town. B & B locally. Youth Hostel at Kendon.
Guidebooks S.M.T Guide 'The Southern Uplands'; 'Guide to Walks and Climbs in Dumfries and Galloway' by R. D. Walton (T. C. Farries).

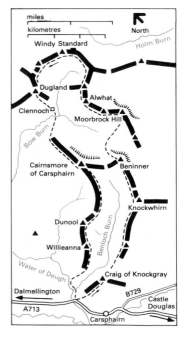

The smooth appearance of the hills is misleading. Galloway grass is of the long, thick and cutting variety and is legendary in its toughness. The going is hard; I reckon one Galloway mile is worth two elsewhere. Mercifully, above about 1,500ft, short heather and moss take over from the coarsest grass and this acts as a spur to climb up out of the valleys.

As we descended the north side of Craig of Knockgray we disturbed a fox which ran off into the rocks. But we were less enthused by the sight of a massive black bull grazing the flat moor below; there was no protective wall or fence nearby so we gave it an extremely wide berth which wasted much time and energy.

Our adventures were not over because on the east side of Quantans Hill, down by the burn, we came upon two men operating a small, mobile drill, collecting mineral samples from beneath the peat. They were not very forthcoming, but a local farmer told us later that they were sampling the rock for gold.

Under Knockwhirn a small block of ancient pines surrounds a derelict cottage, yet inexplicably neither is marked on the map. When this is passed a stone wall, and then a line of old iron fence-posts, leads up to the windswept plateau of Beninner, one of the best viewpoints on the walk. Early cloud had just lifted from the tops and we could see our way ahead over Moorbrock Hill and Alwhat to Windy Standard in the far north. Cairnsmore was only a stone's throw away across the bealach but it was scheduled for the return route later in the day. The east facing slopes of Beninner are horribly steep and loose and it is best to head west towards the Cairnsmore bealach before attempting to descend to the marshy watershed under Moorbrock.

A new forestry road runs high up onto Moorbrock, this makes for a simple ascent but it is an appalling eyesore. Easy walking in a fine situation then takes you over the grassy hill of Alwhat to the south shoulder of Windy Standard. Here a vast granite block called the Deil's Putting Stone sits on the hillside; a bowl-shaped hollow has been worn or carved in its top.

Apart from the OS pillar, the summit of Windy Standard is featureless and typical of many of the Galloway hills. Range upon range of hills, as smooth and rounded as if they were moulded from plasticine, roll away in every direction, but most of the valleys, and even the summits of the lesser hills, are cloaked in forestry.

The return route to Carsphairn swings west over Trostan Hill, turns south to Dugland Hill and then descends to the valley floor at Clennoch where there is a stone shed. This is a remote and beautiful spot, hidden deep in the hills and having no obvious vehicular access. At Clennoch two big burns, the Clennoch and the Bow, meet to form a sizeable river. We were just able to cross each burn separately but, in wet weather, they could present problems involving long detours.

The major task of the day now lies ahead: the 1,440ft haul up the north ridge of Cairnsmore, which looks particularly daunting as you descend from Dugland. Taken slowly, though, the ascent can be enjoyable and the views back towards Windy Standard are lovely, especially when the hills are patterned by shifting cloud shadows. One or two cairns have been built on the ridge but they seem to have little significance, for there is no vestige of a path.

The rough boulders which are strewn over the slopes of Cairnsmore become more numerous as the summit plateau is approached, and the top is marked by a large pile of stones, a windbreak and an OS pillar. We could see north across the Firth of Clyde to the pointed Arran hills and south to Criffel on the Solway and Cairnsmore of Fleet overlooking Wigtown Bay.

An easy descent of the broad south ridge of Cairnsmore took us past a tiny lochan under Black Shoulder, over Dunool and Willieanna and down to a Land Rover track running beside Water of Deugh. This is a broad and fast river which sparkles over its bed of boulders as it rushes into Kendoon Loch, finally emerging into the Solway Firth.

Throughout the descent from Cairnsmore the uplifting view west to Loch Doon and the Rhinns of Kells was always with us and at the end of the day, the sun dipped behind the ridge and the purple outline of the ancient hills was imprinted indelibly on our consciousness.

Cairnsmore from the south-west from near the Water of Deugh.

Ken Andrew

LINHOPE SPOUT AND HEDGEHOPE HILL

The Northumberland National Park committee must be congratulated on their sensible management of the Cheviot hills. Their policy is one of low profile; thus their information centres are unobtrusive or tucked away out of sight, and waymarking of paths has been kept to a minimum.

A few signs have been erected on the Border Ridge to prevent walkers straying from the Pennine Way, and the tourist path up the Cheviot is tastefully indicated, otherwise the hills remain wild and unscarred. Walkers, wandering at will, do not beat out paths.

Designated long distance footpaths have introduced thousands of walkers to upland Britain, but at considerable cost to the environment. Heavy boots have destroyed the basic structure of the peat in a wide area surrounding the summit of the Cheviot, and many walkers, struggling through the deep black bog of Cheviot's plateau, gaze longingly at the wild, rolling hills to the south: Hedgehope, Comb Fell, Bloodybush Edge and Cushat Law.

While access to the main Cheviot range is restricted from the south by extensive artillery ranges at Otterburn and Redesdale, lovely river valleys penetrate deep into the hills from the east: College valley from Kirknewton, the valley of the Harthope burn from Wooler and the Breamish valley running west from Ingram.

The Breamish is a considerable river, fed by tributary burns which rise in the hills south of the Cheviot. Although the Forestry Commission have planted wide areas of hillside on the south side of the Breamish, near Alwinton, the hills to the north are wild, lonely and rarely visited except by shepherds. In many parts of the country the Forestry Commission are selling land, but in the Cheviots they are keen to buy up hill farms for planting. The National Park is desperately trying to preserve the open landscape, and it has had some success in dissuading the Forestry Commission from buying farms in certain key areas.

The Breamish rises in typical Cheviot country; the hills are rounded and smooth and they roll away irresistibly into the distance. Mercifully, grouse shooting has now been abandoned and there are no regimented lines of shooting butts to break up the smooth contours. Walking is excellent over close cropped grass and heather, but bracken is rapidly encroaching on the lower slopes. Curlews, plovers and larks abound and, on my last visit, I saw wheatears and, high on the fells, two young badgers scampering over the heather back into their set.

A narrow motor road runs west from Ingram alongside the tumbling river Breamish. The valley sides are mostly steep and covered with broom and gorse yet, in places, the river bank is wide and grassy providing delectable picnic sites. At Hartside farm a locked gate prevents further progress by car, and this makes a convenient point from which to start the walk.

A good track leads to Linhope, a remote settlement consisting of a solid grey stone manor house (now an old people's home) set behind exotic trees and rhododendrons, a collection of estate cottages and a bridge over the Linhope burn. Follow the sign to Linhope Spout, a most attractive waterfall half-a-mile north of the bridge. The Linhope burn plunges, in a cascade of white water, over a forty foot rock step into a deep, black pool overhung by trees and moss covered rocks. The Spout, set amidst barren hills, yet enclosed in a leafy glade, is one of the most romantic waterfalls in England. The Linhope burn rises exceptionally quickly after rain, when the falls become ferocious.

Linhope Spout is the last real feature for many miles and in summer it is the only source of water on the entire expedition. Make sure you fill your water bottle.

Cross the new Land Rover track which was built to provide access for the shepherd from Linhope farm. It is an appalling eye-sore but, with only one shepherd now working instead of three, it was deemed necessary for supplying winter fodder to the sheep. Now climb the fell just west of Ritto Hill and follow the broad ridge round over High Cantle to Shielcleugh Edge. A path is marked on the map but little or no trace of it can be seen through the heather and moor grass.

High Cantle looks down the upper reaches of the Breamish valley to High and Low Bleakhope, two of the remotest farms in the country. Looking north across the shallow valley of the Linhope burn the huge globe of Hedgehope Hill, the principal objective of the day, dominates the view. In the foreground, two sharp rocky outcrops on Great Standrop draw the eye and relieve the almost unbroken sweep of moorland.

Outcrops of pink Cheviot granite appear again on Coldlaw Cairn and on Hedgehope itself. This is plutonic rock, once molten magma

Maps O.S. 1:50,000 Sheets 81 and 80.
Grading A rough walk over lonely and trackless fells.
Start / Finish Hartside (975162).
Distance / Time 12 miles/6 hours.
Escape Routes Comb Fell and Hedgehope can be descended easily N to the sheltered Harthope valley near Langleeford.
Telephone Ingram where there is also a Mountain Rescue Post.
Transport The Newcastle – Morpeth – Wooler bus to Powburn, 6 miles from Hartside.
Accommodation Hotels/Guest Houses and Youth Hostel at Wooler.
Guidebooks 'The Northumberland National Park' (H.M.S.O.); 'Green Tracks and Heather Tracks' by H. O. Wade and W. Balman (J. and P. Bealls); 'The Scottish Borders and Northumberland' by John Talbot White (Methuen); S.M.T. Guide 'The Southern Uplands'.

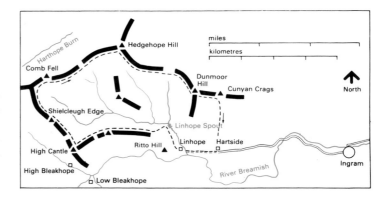

Linhope Spout.

that cooled beneath the surface of the earth and only became exposed after much erosion.

Comb Fell to the north is massive and featureless, but it is an excellent view-point for Scald Hill, the Cheviot and Auchope Cairn which dominate the head of the Harthope valley. Cloudberries grow in profusion on Comb Fell and in July I found the ground decorated by their white flowers. Less pleasant was the constant rumbling of the big guns on the ranges to the south. A steady crump of exploding shells echoed around Bloodybush Edge and Cushat Law; the hills themselves seemed to tremble.

At 2,343ft/714m, Hedgehope gives 331ft to the Cheviot, its loftier neighbour across the valley, but in many ways it is a finer summit. On each side the ground falls away quite steeply giving Hedgehope prominence, stature and individuality, while the shattered outcrop of rock at the very top has provided stone for a substantial cairn. On a clear day it affords wonderful views of the Northumberland coast, the Farne Islands and Holy Island.

Dunmoor Hill, two miles away down the broad south-east ridge of Hedgehope, is the next objective. A new forestry plantation stretches right up from Threestone Burn to the col between the two hills; the col is rather marshy and is covered with cotton grass.

Another mile leads to an area of rock outcrops called Cunyan Crags. These rough, rounded boulders make an ideal perch for a late lunch or tea, with views down the full length of the Breamish valley. A rich collection of Iron Age hill forts, earthworks and settlements indicate the popularity of this beautiful valley in pre-historic times.

Hartside farm is tucked away behind a screen of fir trees, just over a mile away across the bracken and heather.

Looking north-west from Great Standrop the rock outcrop south of Hedgehope Hill, over the ridge linking Comb Fell and Hedgehope Hill towards the Cheviot.

Ritto Hill (middle distance) and Hedgehope Hill from the slopes of Cushat Law above Low Bleakhope Farm.

Peel Fell from Deadwater Fell.

In the valley of the White Kielder Burn above Kielder Head.

KIELDER FOREST AND THE BORDER FELLS

The Scottish border cuts through some of Britain's wildest and most desolate country. Much of the thirty-two mile east–west crossing of the Cheviots from Wooler to Carter Bar, described in *The Big Walks*, follows the border, and the rolling fells continue untamed westwards to Kielder. I have chosen here a circular route from Carter Bar, crossing the highest fells to Kielder and returning via the forest, the valley of the White Kielder burn, Chattlehope Spout and Catcleugh reservoir.

Be prepared for an energy sapping, rough, tough walk of twenty-seven miles over England's remotest fells where, in emergency, help is far away. Allow at least twelve hours to complete the walk and in winter, when deep snow could be a major problem, it would be wise to arrange accommodation in Kielder village which is the half-way point.

Starting at Carter Bar, 1,370ft/417m, above sea-level, is a bonus and the climb up to Catcleugh Shin and Carter Fell is easily accomplished. The fells are trackless and the absence of boot prints in the peat indicate their unpopularity. Yet, they offer far ranging views of the Cheviots, Redesdale and north over the Wauchope Forest into Scotland and the broad valley of the Tweed.

On Carter Fell a group of cairns mark some old mine workings; lumps of poor quality coal still litter the surface. Beyond the mine, a small grey tarn is just visible and, at our approach, two mallard took off from the surface with much laboured flapping of wings and harsh quacking.

The boundary fence on Knox Knowe has rotted away and only the occasional low stump or marker stone emerges above the deep heather to aid navigation. Interestingly the boundary stones are inscribed N on the south side, referring to the Duke of Northumberland, and ꓷ (a back to front D) on the north side, referring to the Douglas estate; probably the work of an illiterate stone mason.

Whilst fording the Black Needle burn, which tumbles down an eroded cleugh, we noticed a spread of the delightful white flower, grass of parnassus. This flower grows on soils of high pH and thus we searched for, and found, thin seams of limestone in the cleugh. Disturbed by a falling rock, we looked up and saw a herd of feral goats slowly crossing the heather above the burn. About eight goats made up the herd, they had long shaggy coats, the nannies' mottled grey and the young billies' black. But the leader of the herd was a massive and magnificent billy with a beard trailing to his knees and long curved horns. We watched transfixed until they moved out of sight. The wild goat herd of the Cheviots is well known, and National Park wardens keep a watchful eye on it, but our sighting was probably of an independent border herd. The herds can never multiply to any great extent, for numbers are controlled by the severity of the climate and terrain.

Just before Peel Fell the impressive landmark known as the Kielder Stone is passed. This is a colossal chunk of gritstone, estimated to weigh 1,500 tons, which perches incongruously on the open fellside at a height of 1,490ft/454m. The whole of this border

Map O.S. 1:50,000 Sheet 80.
Grading A rough, tough walk over England's remotest fells. If fitness is suspect or bad weather approaches an overnight stop in Kielder village should be considered.
Start / Finish Carter Bar (698068).
Distance / Time 27 miles/12 hours.
Escape Route Kielder village is reached at the half-way point.
Telephones Kielder and Byrness.
Transport The Newcastle – Edinburgh and Newcastle – Glasgow bus services pass over Carter Bar.
Accommodation B & B at Kielder and Byrness. Youth Hostel at Byrness and Bellingham.
Guidebooks 'The Northumberland National Park' (H.M.S.O.); 'The Scottish Borders and Northumberland' by John Talbot White (Methuen); Information leaflets obtained from Information Office, Kielder Castle (Tel. 0660 50209).

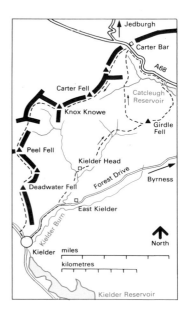

The view north-east of Kielder Stone to Kielder Head Moor.

region is steeped in bloody history and skulduggery and it is said that the Kielder Stone served as a *post office* in the days when messengers from one country dared not venture into enemy territory.

Peel Fell is the highest point on the walk at 1,975ft/602m and, on a clear day, you can see both the Solway Firth and the North Sea; one

of the few places in Britain from where a cross-country view is possible.

Deadwater Fell, two miles further on, is another compelling viewpoint, for Kielder reservoir stretches away to the south as a vast blue sheet, surrounded on all sides by forest.

The scale of the developments in the Kielder area is impressive if

monotonous green blanket.

Whereas it has taken over fifty years to plant out the open moorland of Kielder, it has taken the Northumbrian Water Authority only six years to totally transform the landscape. The Kielder dam, completed in 1982, has produced the largest man-made reservoir in the British Isles. From a landscape point of view I leave you to make your own judgement, but financially the project is questionable. At great expense the Water Authority can now supply large volumes of water to consumers on Tyneside, Wearside and Tees-side but, with the industrial recession, demand has flattened and the reservoir is a white elephant.

On a more cheerful note, you can obtain tea at the Forestry Commission Information Centre in Kielder Castle before turning for home. The 'scenic road', which runs through the forest linking Kielder with Byrness, is followed for two miles until it turns sharply right for East Kielder. Keep straight on at this point and make for Kielder Head. We found this stretch to be walking at its most pleasurable, with a stiff breeze at our backs and brilliant sunshine accentuating the various shades of green of the pastures and plantations, and sparkling on the Kielder burn as it hurried over its bouldery bed.

The valley of the White Kielder Burn is shallow and the purple moor grass was bending and rippling in the wind like a Kansas prairie. Further up the hillside the grass gave way to heather and boulders and it was dotted with rowan trees, heavy with brilliantly red berries.

At the valley head the burn is fed from numerous tributaries running down cleughs from the high fells. The cleughs are sheltered and support a luxuriant growth of heather, bilberry, bracken, ferns and cloudberry. In one of these cleughs, remnants of what is possibly the only natural pine wood left in England have been discovered.

Skirt White Crags to the south to reach the watershed near a massive flat-topped sandstone block on Girdle Fell. Below runs the Chattlehope burn which plunges over an escarpment in a 75ft waterfall, Chattlehope Spout. Sadly, on our last visit, following a dry summer, the spout was a mere trickle.

The Chattlehope valley is trackless and, choked with coarse grass and hummocky moraines, is tiresome to descend but, at Catcleugh reservoir, our labours were rewarded by the sight of roe deer amongst the trees near the shore. Although drawdown had left a muddy shoreline round the lake, the scar was diminished by coverage of pink flowering water bistort and banded marsh horsetail.

Two miles of road lead back to Carter Bar, but this could be avoided by a deviation on Kielder Head Moor to White Crags and a crossing of the fells above Bateinghope burn. By taking the alternative route you forfeit Chattlehope and Catcleugh. Either way this is a five-star walk with a unique Northumbrian flavour.

NOTE The Kielder Stone, Kielder Head, Peel Fell area is a Grade 1 Site of Special Scientific Interest. It is managed by the Nature Conservancy Council in collaboration with the Northumberland Wildlife Trust, and walkers are asked to be extremely circumspect and to avoid the area during the breeding season, March to July.

nothing else. Tree planting started in 1926 and the forest, now covering 80,000 acres, is the largest in the British Isles. Not all the land owned by the Forestry Commission has been planted, and they have co-operated with the Nature Conservancy Council and the Northumberland Wildlife Trust in the non-planting of certain elite areas. These areas of open moorland do much to alleviate the

FAIRFIELD AND THE DEEPDALE HORSESHOE

In the heart of Lakeland, not far removed from the most popular peak of Helvellyn, it is still possible to find peaceful dales and wild, lonely crags and coves.

From the fells further west Fairfield appears as a flat grassy hump, and walkers looking for an exciting day's expedition would not give it a further glance. However, to the east and north, Fairfield presents a steep face, broken by cliffs and rocky spurs while three delectable green valleys, Grisedale, Deepdale and Dovedale run down to Patterdale and Brothers Water.

The upper reaches of Deepdale, the middle of the three dales, run right up to the seamed rock-face of Fairfield. Deepdale is bounded by the ridges of St Sunday Crag and Hartsop Above How, and they are linked to the main massif of Fairfield by two prominent rocky bluffs: Cofa Pike and Hart Crag. This horseshoe provides a day's walk of startling contrasts, which encompasses the best that Lakeland can offer: lush green lower slopes, airy ridges, steep scrambles and bird's-eye views of hidden coves, deep gills and mossy crags with lakes and peaks stretching away to far horizons.

Park in Patterdale or Glenridding and follow the narrow metalled road which runs up a short way into Grisedale. After a quarter-of-a-mile cross the wall by the solid wooden stile and climb steadily through the birch trees towards Black Crag. This is a fine start to the walk, for in spring the ground is thick with primroses and, with every foot gained, more of Ullswater comes into sight in its exquisite setting of rolling fells, crags and woods.

A cairn marks the beginning of a lower path traversing round Birks, a grassy flat-topped hill, but it is preferable to gain height early to enjoy the panoramic view east of the High Street range, stretching from Yoke to Loadpot Hill.

As St Sunday Crag is approached the ridge steepens and becomes

Maps O.S. 1:50,000 Sheet 90; O.S. 1:63,360 Tourist Map 'The Lake District'; O.S. 1:25,000 Outdoor Leisure Map – 'The English Lake District N.E.'
Grading A fine mountain traverse in the heart of Lakeland. Some scrambling is involved on the approach to Fairfield which could be tricky in winter conditions. Careful route finding is necessary on the descent from Hart Crag.
Start / Finish Patterdale (390161).
Distance / Time 10 miles/5-6 hours.
Escape Routes Descents may be made from Deepdale Hause into either Grisedale or Deepdale.
Telephones Patterdale, Bridgend and Hartsop.
Transport Railway Stations at Penrith and Windermere. Bus Penrith – Patterdale. Mountain Goat bus service Glenridding – Windermere – Ambleside.
Accommodation Hotels/Guest Houses abound. Youth Hostels at Grasmere (2), Greenside and Patterdale.
Guidebooks 'Guide to the Eastern Fells' by A. Wainwright (The Westmorland Gazette); 'The Lakeland Peaks' by W. A. Poucher (Constable).

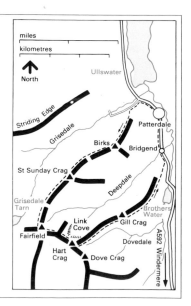

*Descending the East Ridge of Fairfield
on a route to Hart Crag.*

Stephen Greenwood

Deepdale Head and The Step with Link Cove and Scrubby Crag beyond.

silhouette on a grey day, grim and forbidding. It is not easy to believe that every year thousands of walkers safely negotiate its jagged crest on their way to Helvellyn's summit.

Looking up from Deepdale Hause, Cofa Pike, with its broken buttresses and pinnacles, appears to be a challenging obstacle but, in reality, it is a very easy scramble in all but the severest of winter conditions. Cofa Pike looks daunting because of its superb position; steep slopes on the west side lead down to Grisedale Tarn, set picturesquely between Seat Sandal and Dollywaggon Pike, while on the east side you can look into Sleet Cove with its dripping, precipitous walls, more popular with ravens than climbers because of the loose rock.

The summit plateau of Fairfield, 2,863ft/ 873m, is flat and rather confusing in mist because of the profusion of cairns, seemingly built at random. Easy descents from the summit abound, particularly to the south and west, but great care must be

rocky, particularly on the Grisedale side where a long line of crags gives some rock climbing. The routes are mostly easy and only two or three pitches in length, but the gullies can provide good winter climbs and Pinnacle Ridge gives a 600ft scramble; an enjoyable way to ascend St Sunday Crag from Grisedale.

Beyond St Sunday Crag the ridge narrows and descends 700ft to Deepdale Hause. As you descend the beautifully proportioned ridge you experience an exhilarating feeling of space: on either side, in Grisedale and Deepdale, the becks are mere threads and the grazing sheep spots of white on the green backcloth. North, beyond Grisedale, Striding Edge cuts across the top of Nethermost Cove looking, in

taken when descending to the east. The long line of cliffs is broken only at Hart Crag, where the ridge running to Hartsop Above How divides Deepdale from Dovedale. In mist many walkers have turned off east before reaching Hart Crag only to find their way barred by the sheer escarpment of Greenhow End.

On my most recent visit to Fairfield great banks of snow ringed the eastern combes, a gloomy sight in the twilight of the late winter's afternoon but, further west, light was streaming down through a break in the clouds, turning Windermere and Coniston Water to liquid silver.

The descent north-east from Hart Crag is rocky in places but less

Looking across Link Cove to Fairfield, with The Step on the right.

Richard Gibbens

steep than Cofa Pike. The ridge is broad and it is well worth while to deviate north to gaze into Link Cove and south to marvel at the bare rock buttresses of Dove Crag. Link Cove is secluded and intimate and it is one of the most secret corners of Lakeland. Set high above the main valley of Deepdale and hidden from below, it has the aura of the Lost Valley of Glen Coe. Dove Crag, on the other hand, presents a 300ft high rock face, clean and open, up which runs Hangover, one of Lakeland's classic Very Severe rock climbs. A cave is clearly visible in the lower part of the face, it runs several feet into the rock and makes an excellent bivouac site.

The rugged scenery of upper Dovedale and Deepdale is left behind as delightful walking over Hartsop Above How (Gill Crag on the map) leads gently back to Patterdale. Your last impression of this marvellous walk will be of the High Street ridge dominating the eastern skyline as you drop down through the woods to the road near Bridgend.

Climbers beginning the ascent to St Sunday Crag from Deepdale Hause, with Grisedale Tarn, Seat Sandal and the peaks of the central Lake District beyond.

Cofa Pike and St Sunday Crag from Fairfield.

The High Street range from below Hart Crag.

THE BACK O' SKIDDA'

Over the years I have paid many visits to Lakeland's northern fells, where I have enjoyed exciting days clambering up the narrow ridges of Blencathra and striding along the broad shoulders of mighty Skiddaw. From the wind scoured summits of these characteristic and much loved hills my eyes have been drawn south across Keswick and the Vale of St John to the old favourites: Grisedale Pike, Causey Pike, Great Gable and Helvellyn. In contrast, the fells Back o' Skidda': Great Calva, Knott, High Pike and Carrock Fell look rounded, grassy and rather ordinary.

However, appearances are deceptive and even though my first visit Back o' Skidda' took place on a most unprepossessing day in mid-winter, I was captivated by the loneliness of the area. Deep snow lay on the hills and Carrock Fell was enveloped in white mist, only compass work took us on to High Pike and Knott. The occasional glimpse south across the Caldew to Bowscale Tarn in its dark hollow, and a watery sun mocking us over the top of Skiddaw were our only rewards, and even these crumbs were soon snatched away by the fog. The peat hags of Miller Moss, which guard the north slopes of Knott, were festooned with icicles of such length that they would not have disgraced the Scottish Highlands.

At the end of the day Mosedale was empty and silent, save for a few Herdwicks nibbling the heather under the snow. I realised that here was a unique area of Lakeland, an area devoid of people, paths, enclosures and marker cairns, an area more in tune with the bare Northern Pennines than cosy Lakeland. I resolved to return in the spring.

A crossing of the fells, Back o' Skidda', from Mosedale to Bassenthwaite is an easy day's walk. There are no difficulties and escape routes abound, yet the fells are wild and remote; a haven of peace and solitude even on the busiest holiday weekend. A good bus service will return you from Bassenthwaite to Keswick and thence to the Mungrisdale junction on the Penrith road; three miles walk from Mosedale.

Carrock Fell rises steeply north of the cluster of stone-built cottages at Mosedale. A gabbro intrusion has produced crags on the east side and the lower slopes are strewn with rocks, quite unlike any other fell in the locality. A tangle of deep heather, gorse and juniper grows amongst the boulders and it is a fight to gain the higher ground where the going is much easier. The summit of Carrock Fell was the site of an ancient, possibly Iron Age, hill fort and the remains of the walls, which enclose an area of several acres, can be seen clearly.

Keeping to the high ground, the broad ridge is followed west over Miton Hill to High Pike, principal hill of the Caldbeck Fells at 2,159ft/ 658m. The summit lies on the north side, overlooking Caldbeck village, and it sprouts an extraordinary array of accessories: a stone bench, wind shelter, OS trig. point, ruined building and various cairns and stakes. The hill is easily climbed from the north and it has been used throughout the ages as a beacon, for it is clearly visible from Carlisle.

Continuing the walk south, the route crosses the swelling eminence of Great Lingy Hill keeping well above the shooting hut at the head of Grainsgill. Extensive mine workings scar the lower reaches of Grainsgill from where, earlier this century, the rare mineral wolfram was extracted.

The horrors of our winter crossing of Miller Moss were still in our minds as we scrambled across the black peat hags, and jumped the light green areas of ooze. But, in the sharp light of one of those rare, magical evenings of early summer, our spirits were high and we had no trouble in picking a dry route.

Some Swaledale ewes and their lambs were grazing the short turf beside the small pile of stones marking the summit of Knott, and we joined them to eat our sandwiches. Knott at 2,329ft/710m is the highest of the fells Back o' Skidda', and it provides wonderful views

The view south from Great Calva, through the valley of Glenderaterra Beck with Helvellyn in the distance.

Descending the western slopes of Great Sca Fell with the Uldale Fells on the right.

of the western seaboard. The sun was turning the Solway estuary to liquid gold and the hills of Galloway were silhouetted against a crimson sky; further south Snaefell on the Isle of Man looked a mere stone's throw away across the mirror calm Irish Sea.

Great Calva appears as a prominent knob at the end of a broad ridge and it is easily reached via a grassy col, 500ft below the summit of Knott. We found Great Calva to be the best viewpoint of all. The northern slopes of Skiddaw were in shade but the rolling fells of Knott, High Pike and Bowscale were smooth and green, manicured like a golf course and speckled white with sheep. A few fleecy clouds threw shadows across the fells producing patterns of dark and light. The coombs and folds were accentuated by the acute angle of the sun's rays and many carried white thread-like becks rushing head-long down to the dales.

The valley of Glenderaterra, dividing the massifs of Skiddaw and Blencathra, provides a narrow window to the hills beyond. Through it we could see Thirlmere and Helvellyn, its sharp eastern ridges highlighted by the sun.

Reluctantly we descended the gentle slopes to the south, meeting the bridle-path to Skiddaw House. Standing staunchly under the immense slumbering giant of Skiddaw, it is a long, grey building set in a protective belt of trees.

The path runs under Little Calva and then drops steeply towards Bassenthwaite. It skirts a strange craggy coomb scooped out of the northern shoulder of Skiddaw and known as Dead Crags. This is the sole precipitous feature on the north side of Skiddaw, where an unbroken sweep of grass, bilberry and heather falls relentlessly from the summit ridge.

Below Dead Crags, on the other side of the path, the Dash beck plunges down to the lower dale through a wooded ravine. The falls, called Whitewater Dash, are best seen from further down the dale or

from the whitewashed farm of Dash, commanding a magnificent position on the slopes of White Hause. Coleridge visited the falls and described them as, 'the finest water furies I ever beheld'.

The track meets the road at Peter House, where a signpost indicates a short-cut across the fields to Bassenthwaite. The sun was still catching the tops of the Uldale Fells, the hawthorn was in full bloom and the scent of may was heavy in the air as we strode into Bassenthwaite and a warm welcome at the Sun Inn. Six leisurely and unforgettable hours over the gentle and lonely fells Back o' Skidda'.

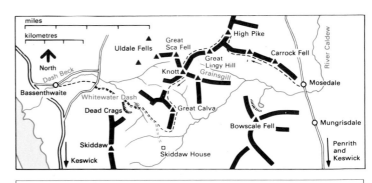

Maps O.S. 1:50,000 Sheet 90; O.S. 1:63,360 Tourist Map 'The Lake District'.
Grading An easy traverse of rounded and mainly heather-clad hills.
Start / Finish Mosedale (356322); Bassenthwaite (230323).
Distance / Time 12 miles/5-6 hours.
Escape Routes N from High Pike to Nether Row and Caldbeck. S from Great Lingy Hill to Grainsgill and the Caldew valley.
Telephones Mosedale, Bassenthwaite and Fell Side above Caldbeck.
Transport Railway Stations at Penrith, Carlisle and Workington. Bus services Keswick to Penrith and Keswick to Carlisle.
Accommodation A wide variety of accommodation in Keswick. Youth Hostels at Keswick, Cockermouth, Derwent Water, Thirlmere and Carrock Fell.
Guidebooks 'Foothills of the Fells' by Frank Goddard (Hale); 'Walking Through the Lake District' by Michael Dunn (David and Charles); 'The Northern Fells' by A. Wainwright (The Westmorland Gazette).

THE WAST WATER CIRCUIT

Wast Water lies amidst the grandest mountain scenery in Lakeland. Perhaps it is the great depth of the lake (at 250ft the deepest in England) and the unrelenting fans of scree falling straight into the dark water from the crags of Whin Rigg and Illgill Head that give it an aura of gloom and foreboding.

In only a few miles Wasdale runs from the pastoral coastal strip of West Cumbria right into the heart of the mountains. The stupendous rock peak of Great Gable fills the head of the dale, while the cliffs and rock buttresses of Yewbarrow, Middle Fell and Buckbarrow rise steeply on the west side. The rugged setting is more in tune with Snowdonia or North West Scotland than the predominantly gentle fells of the English Lake District.

Most walkers visiting Wasdale hasten on to Pillar, Kirk Fell, Gable and the Scafells and ignore the lesser hills overlooking the lake. Thus the Wast Water circuit can provide a high walk over rocky peaks, giving some fine situations, yet avoiding the crowds even on a holiday weekend.

From the stone bridge over the River Irt at Nether Wasdale take the footpath which is signed to Eskdale. The path crosses a field studded with mature oaks and Scots pines and then climbs steeply to Irton Fell. At the plantation turn left and head north-east to Whin Rigg.

The broad ridge is grassy and the walking easy, but it is worth a peep over the cliffs on the west side down to the lake and the great sweeps of scree for which Wast Water is famed. The cliffs continue to Illgill Head, the highest point of the ridge (1,998ft/609m), a distance of nearly two miles. A French student disappeared in Wasdale a few years ago, her body finally being found below the cliffs over a year later. During the search the police dragged the lake and discovered, by chance, the body of another woman. She was identified by her wedding ring and her husband was brought to trial and convicted of her murder. However, all was tranquil on my last visit; a buzzard was riding the thermals and avoiding the attentions of two crows with disdainful ease, while the mournful whistle of the Ratty, puffing along its fifteen inch gauge track to Ravenglass, floated up from Eskdale.

A gentle descent from Illgill Head, down the north-east ridge, leads to Brackenclose, a climbing hut owned by the FRCC, and then to the bridge over Lingmell Beck. Follow the road to the Wasdale Head Inn, centre of much of the early Lake District climbing and still regarded as a shrine.

Whilst the traverse of Whin Rigg and Illgill Head is only gently undulating, the return route across the western fells overlooking Wast Water is demanding. The imposing wedge of Yewbarrow is guarded by rocky spurs at the north and south ends, and by buttresses and gullies on its faces. Without doubt it is one of Lakeland's shapeliest peaks and its appearance when viewed from

Illgill Head is inspiring, but its actual traverse has to be paid for in sweat.

From Mosedale a narrow path zig-zags up the steep and stony hillside on the north side of Dore Head scree, once one of Lakeland's finest scree runs but now run-out down to bedrock, where pebbles as loose as ball bearings make the descent hazardous.

Once at Dore Head the benefits of the climb start to accrue. An exhilaratingly steep and rocky scramble up Stirrup Crag takes you to the narrow crest of Yewbarrow and the principal summit (2,058ft/627m) which commands one of Lakeland's finest views. From the dress circle of Yewbarrow you look straight into the amphitheatre bounded by the rock walls of Great Gable, Lingmell and the Scafells; this is classic Lakeland country where every rib, buttress and gully has its own history and traditions. On the other side of the ridge you can see up to the head of Nether Beck and Mosedale to the more rounded hills of Haycock, Red Pike, Pillar and Kirk Fell.

The south ridge of Yewbarrow falls away abruptly in the crags of Bell Rib overlooking Bowderdale farm, but it can be descended as far as the remarkable cleft of Great Door, a deep gully set between vertical rock walls which runs down towards the head of Wast Water. A traverse path leads down the north side of Bell Rib to the car-park at Overbeck bridge beside the lake.

The sight of the rough, bouldery and craggy slopes of Middle Fell rising steeply above Nether Beck may be too much for some walkers at the end of a long day; in which case Nether Wasdale is a pleasant three mile walk away, along the banks of Wast Water.

Purists will enjoy the east flanks of Middle Fell which are trackless and wild; as you pick your way through the crags and bracken, and over the deep carpet of bilberries you can imagine yourself to be in remote Wales or the wilds of Galloway. In the dale below, Nether

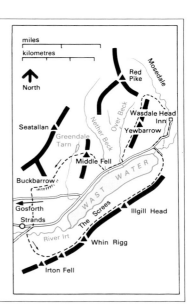

Maps O.S. 1:50,000 Sheet 89; O.S. 1:63,360 Tourist Map 'The Lake District'; O.S. 1:25,000 Outdoor Leisure Map – 'The English Lake District S.W.'
Grading A long hill traverse with plenty of steep, rough ground. Yewbarrow needs care under winter conditions.
Start / Finish Strands (125040).
Distance / Time 17 miles/10 hours.
Escape Routes The route may conveniently be cut short at Wasdale Head or Overbeck Bridge.
Telephones Wasdale Head and Nether Wasdale (Strands).
Transport No bus service to Nether Wasdale or Wasdale Head. Nearest services Gosforth (Whitehaven – Millom route) or Eskdale (Ravenglass Railway).
Accommodation Hotels at Strands and Wasdale Head. B & B locally. Youth Hostels at Wasdale Hall and Eskdale.
Guidebooks 'Foothills of the Fells' by Frank Goddard (Hale); 'The Lakeland Peaks' by W. A. Poucher (Constable); 'Guide to the Southern Fells and Guide to the Western Fells' by A. Wainwright (The Westmorland Gazette).

Left: Approaching Great Door on the south ridge of Yewbarrow above Bell Rib and Wast Water.

On Yewbarrow – the view down Great Door to Wast Water.

Wast Water from the lower slopes of Whin Rigg, with Yewbarrow, Kirk Fell and Great Gable in the background.

Illgill Head, Whin Rigg and the Wast Water Screes from High Fell below Red Pike.

The South Ridge of Yewbarrow with Great Gable and Wast Water on the right.

Beck runs through a belt of trees (oak, alder, rowan, hazel and birch) in a series of delightful falls and deep, clear pools.

Once again the superb view up Wasdale is yours on reaching the summit plateau of Middle Fell and, with the major efforts of the day now accomplished, you can afford to take a leisurely tea-break beside the cairn.

Grassy slopes now descend to the out-flow of lonely Greendale Tarn and a simple traverse leads to the line of low cairns on Buckbarrow, more a rocky bluff on the end of the south ridge of Seatallan than a peak in its own right. The crags on Buckbarrow extend for at least half-a-mile and, although broken, they provide a number of worth-while rock climbs.

From the west end of the crags a gully and then grass slopes lead to the Wasdale road near Gill farm. A footpath passes Tosh Tarn, one of Lakeland's most elusive tarns, and then runs through the fields back to Nether Wasdale.

HARTER FELL AND BLACK COMBE

by ROGER PUTNAM

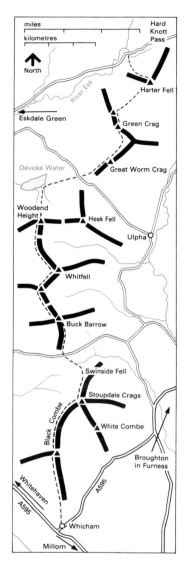

The view north from Buck Barrow to Whitfell, wi

Harter Fell seen from Ulpha Fell to the north.

There are very few places in the well trodden fells of Lakeland where one can walk all day away from the footpaths which spread like tentacles across the landscape. Even twenty years ago path erosion was minimal, cairns infrequent, and scree slopes relatively disturbed. Ease of access to the Lake District National Park is rapidly destroying it, despite the best efforts of the authorities to repair the damage of the multitude of visitor feet.

This presents a dilemma for every guide book writer – how to describe a favourite area without destroying it by doing so. The answer, surely, is to indicate only the possibilities for the walker rather than set out in detail the pathways to the delights of the fells. I propose, therefore, to hint at possibilities and alternatives and to avoid recommending a specific route between the ancient rocks of Black Combe and the shapely cone of Harter Fell, or vice versa.

Black Combe shoulders its massive bulk into the coastal plain, forcing road and railway alike onto a windy coastal shelf at Silecroft. The fell broods over the Millom peninsula, an oppressive presence, its great eastern combe biting into the smooth contours of the Skiddaw slates.

Harter Fell is in total contrast; its shapely summit, crowned by tors of hard volcanic rock, is a fitting climax for a fell so well endowed with outcrops, gullies and secret buttresses; it is always a rewarding walk. Try climbing to the summit direct from the footbridge over Hardknott Ghyll at the foot of Hard Knott Pass, or more adventurously scale one of the ghylls which descend the heathery northern slopes towards the Hardknott road.

The summit, when it eventually appears, is a splendid viewpoint. Far below the Roman fort is perched on its spur overlooking the Esk. Behind are the gaunt fells of upper Eskdale, the finest mountain vista in Cumbria.

You will now head south-west for Green Crag across peat hags which would not disgrace the Pennines, full of ancient remnants of the forest which once flourished here. The grey tors of Green Crag and Crook Crag have mountain stature, despite their lowly elevation. They dominate the heather-clad slopes of Ulpha Fell and much of the view from mid-Eskdale. Below these summits lies the remote and beautiful Low Birker Pool, truly a teardrop tarn, and nearby the shattered rocks of Fox Bield, often a safe haven for the hard pressed quarry of the Eskdale Pack.

From Green Crag, head across undulating moors to the Birker Moor Road at Brown Rigg, passing the extensive remains of pre-historic settlements on the slopes of Great Worm Crag. At this point you have numerous choices. A pint of real ale in Eskdale is only a successful hitch-hike away, but resisting that temptation you can strike out for Hesk Fell, or more interestingly head for Devoke Water via Woodend farm. Woodend was once a Quaker settlement – in a suitably remote and austere location. Devoke Water is a delightful place of reflection and colour, best seen against the setting sun. It is hard to imagine it surrounded by woodland as it

...ter Fell the shadowy cone on the right and the snow-covered Scafell range beyond.

Green Crag from Great Worm Crag, with Illgill Head and the snow-flecked Pillar range beyond.

must have been 3,000 years ago before the first forest clearances.

From Devoke Water, strike out for Woodend Height and its neighbouring tor, Yoadcastle, a wet and time-consuming trudge. From this fine summit head south and steel yourself for miles of trackless going over difficult tussock-grass and bogs. This can be a wet walk indeed and you will no doubt be tempted to skirt Whitfell to the west, particularly if you have visited Holehouse Tarn, at 1,500ft the highest tarn on the route and certainly the least known. Again the traces of ancient settlements abound, a standing stone on the northern spur of Whitfell is eighteen feet in height, and bronze-age hut circles cover the western slopes of these fells.

Soon you will approach the last of the castellated tor-like summits on the walk, Buck Barrow and Kinmont Buck Barrow. Not far from here, the last of the Lake District golden eagles was shot by a

> **Maps** O.S. 1:50,000 Sheets 89 and 96; O.S. 1:63,360 Tourist Map 'The Lake District'; O.S. 1:25,000 Outdoor Leisure Map – 'The English Lake District S.W.'
> **Grading** A rough, tough walk over mainly trackless Fells.
> **Start / Finish** Hard Knott Pass (203009); Whicham (132825).
> **Distance / Time** 20 miles by the longest recommended route/9 hours.
> **Escape Routes** Minor roads cross the line of the walk at Brown Rigg and one mile S of Buck Barrow.
> **Telephones** Whicham, Bootle, Ulpha and Foot of Hard Knott Pass.
> **Transport** Railway Stations at Silecroft, near Whicham, and Ravenglass on Barrow to Carlisle line. Narrow gauge railway Ravenglass to Eskdale.
> **Accommodation** Hotels/Guest Houses abound in Eskdale, Millom and the Duddon valley. Youth Hostels at Boot in Eskdale and Black Hall east of Hard Knott Pass.
> **Guidebooks** 'The Lakeland Peaks' by W. A. Poucher (Constable); 'Guide to the Southern Fells' and 'Guide to the Outlying Fells of Lakeland' by A. Wainwright (The Westmorland Gazette).

delighted farmer in the early nineteenth century. It took one hundred and fifty years for this splendid bird of prey to return to the Lake District to nest. Less than a mile beyond, the Corney Fell road is reached, a surprisingly busy commuter route in early morning and evening. There is still some tough walking ahead, and only the most energetic will make the two-mile detour to see the finest Neolithic circle in Cumbria at Swinside. These grey stones on inbye land near the farm have an eerie and mysterious quality. Who built them, and why?

Leaving such speculation for your recuperative bath, head south-west from Swinside Fell for a long two miles to Black Combe. The sea view bursts upon you, signalling the end, for there are no more heights to conquer. Descent to the Whicham village is easy on a well-made track; a mountain bike would be the best means of travel on this final stage of your walk, which I hope has kept you free of mountain paths for nine-tenths of your journey.

Of course, you may prefer to reverse the route, with promise of equal satisfaction.

Looking east to the Duddon Estuary from Black Combe.

THE SWALEDALE WATERSHED

In early summer Swaledale is peerless. Take the road west from the historic town of Richmond and you will discover a corner of England, little changed over the centuries. The road up the dale winds between hedges of blackthorn, hazel and oak, the bridges are hump-backed, every house is stone built and many have narrow mullioned windows and stone-slabbed roofs.

The hay meadows are bright with flowers (spraying is rare): clover, buttercup, cranesbill, vetch, bedstraw and birdsfoot trefoil. Higher up the valley side, above the lush gills, heather and rough moorland take over and in several places remnants of the lead mining industry are visible. The ancient trackways and spoil heaps are now overgrown, the smelt mills and chimneys tumbled down and lichen covered.

The head of Swaledale is surrounded by high fells, seamed by gullies and gills which carry down the water in falls and cascades and through deep gorges.

A circular walk over the high tops of the Swaledale watershed involves thirty miles of tough going and, although the Pennine Way and the Coast to Coast Walk cross the watershed, the fells are mostly quite barren and trackless.

Setting off from the hamlet of Thwaite, between Muker and Keld, I took the Pennine Way path to Great Shunner Fell. It was one of those perfect June mornings when the sounds, sights and smells of the countryside elevate your spirits and bear you on effortlessly. Spring had been late and the ash trees were still in bud, but the bluebells were startling, bracken tips were pushing up through the turf

and the air was heady with the aroma of sun-warmed meadows. Throughout the day larks, curlews, dunlin and plovers kept up their calls. Life was emerging with vigour; even the puddles were black with threshing tadpoles.

Great Shunner Fell, 2,340ft/716m, is the highest point of the day, but it is rather a featureless lump and I was depressed by the cairn

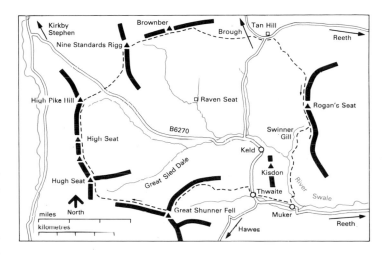

stuffed with coke cans and sweet papers. Thankfully I turned west off the Pennine Way and made my way across rough grass, heather and peat hags to Hugh Seat. The skyline was one continuous sweep of

Approaching Nine Standards Rigg.

Stephen Greenwood

River Swale near Keld.

The view west to Great Shunner Fell from Thwaite.

At the summit of Rogan's Seat.

moorland, broken only by the sun's rays glancing off Birkdale Tarn west of Keld.

The next four miles along the broad ridge to High Pike Hill is walking for the virtuoso. Heat haze had settled in the valleys, but a cooling breeze on the tops was welcome and I delighted in the familiar surroundings that are typical of upland country anywhere in Britain. Exposed slabs of gritstone emerged at intervals from the heather, and beautifully constructed stone cairns, of doubtful origin and purpose, sprouted from unlikely ridges and hillocks.

To the west the ground fell away steeply, even precipitously in places, to Mallerstang through which runs the famous Settle to Carlisle railway. Beyond Mallerstang the view was dominated by the whaleback ridge of Wild Boar Fell, but, to the northwest, the fertile, chequered Vale of Eden temporarily alleviated the upland scene, before the mighty Great Dun Fell – Cross Fell massif made me realise my position in the heart of the Northern Pennines.

Descending steeply from High Pike Hill I crossed the B6270 road at the head of Birkdale. A stretch of limestone pavement above Nateby appeared invitingly white in the sunshine, but my route lay across a marshy area of coarse reeds and black oily water before climbing to a prominent cairn on the horizon.

The aptly named Rollinson Haggs guard the spectacular ridge known as Nine Standards Rigg on which are built nine massive stone cairns, between twelve and fifteen feet high. I walked round the pillars, feeling the rough texture of the rock and marvelling at their construction.

The peat was baked dry and my throat was parched, the mouthful of brackish water which I had scooped up from Rollinson Haggs had left me retching. But only five miles away, across Brownber Fell, lay the Tan Hill inn and liquid refreshment.

Walking across remote and trackless fells is one of my favourite pastimes, and I have covered many hundreds of miles from the Cheviots to Bleaklow and from Cross Fell to Lilla Howe, but nowhere has compared with Brownber Fell for tough, featureless and energy sapping moorland. The heather is as coarse and thick as barbed wire, the peat hags are as deep as elephant traps and the black bogs suck hungrily at your boots.

I failed to take a compass bearing from Nine Standards Rigg and, with head down and teeth clenched, I strayed too far south. Only when I reached the tiny tarn on

Maps O.S. 1:50,000 Sheets 91 and 98; O.S. 1:25,000 Outdoor Leisure Map – 'The Yorkshire Dales Northern and Central Areas'.
Grading A long and arduous walk over high, open fells. Much of the way is trackless, crossing coarse grass, deep heather and peat hags.
Start / Finish Thwaite (892982).
Distance / Time 30 miles/12-13 hours.
Escape Routes Roads are crossed at Birkdale, Tan Hill and Muker.
Telephones Thwaite, Keld, Lower Birkdale, Tan Hill and Muker.
Transport Railway Station at Darlington. Daily bus service (United) to Richmond, Reeth, Muker and Gunnerside, continuing to Keld on Tues and Sat.
Accommodation Hotels/Guest Houses at Reeth and Richmond. Inns and B & B at Muker and Gunnerside. Youth Hostels at Grinton and Keld.
Guidebooks 'The Yorkshire Dales' by Gladys Sellers (Cicerone Press); 'Swaledale' by L. Hinson and T. Sykes (Dalesman); 'Walks in Swaledale' by Geoffrey White (Dalesman).

The Tan Hill Inn.

Slatepit Moss, with its bevy of screaming black headed gulls, did I realise my mistake. As I worked my way back north through hideous and relentless tussocks of coarse grass, I cursed my carelessness. It was tea time before I located Great Wygill which led me to the road just north of Tan Hill.

The Tan Hill inn stands gaunt and grey 1,732ft above sea level, the highest hostelry in England. Whatever the weather it is warm and friendly and it has long been a favourite with sheep farmers and Pennine Way walkers. At 6 p.m. I emerged from the dark bar and blinked in the strong light, searching the horizon for Rogan's Seat, my final objective.

Just east of Tan Hill, nestling in a hollow and emitting a low hum, is a radio beacon. An ancient trackway, just discernible through the grass, bypasses the beacon and leads to an old mine shaft and some spoil heaps, but from there onwards only rolling moorland rises to the south, culminating in Rogan's Seat, 2,203ft/671m.

I made my way south-east to Water Crag, a band of grey rocks which emerge from the heather and bilberry as a most attractive feature. But high on the fells, beyond the crags, I came unexpectedly to a new and brutish bulldozed road. Heavy machinery has torn into the peat, and tons of yellow quarry bottoms have been rolled in leaving an ugly scar.

Prominent to the south-east was Gunnerside Gill, an important lead mining centre, and I could pick out the spoil heaps, hushes and derelict mills. Heading south I made for the path leading down to Swinner Gill, a lovely deep, green valley decked with flowers and fringed with crags.

Evening was well advanced as I ambled through the fields beside the river Swale into Muker and, after the exertions of the day, I could unwind and reflect on the pleasures of a magnificent twelve-hour walk over the roof of England.

From the narrow path that runs through hay meadows beside the Muker beck I caught the flash of a dipper; then I was at Thwaite and the car with the Black Bull in Reeth beckoning only twelve miles away.

Looking east towards Rogan's Seat from the largest of the Nine Standards.

PEN HILL AND BUCKDEN PIKE

Pen Hill stands proudly at the gateway to Wensleydale. It is the most prominent of the eastern fells of the Yorkshire Pennines and its conspicuous flat top and sharp escarpment make it easily identifiable from the Vale of Mowbray and the North York Moors. For centuries Pen Hill has been used as a beacon in times of national peril or rejoicing.

Pen Hill looks particularly fine when viewed from Leyburn on the north side of Wensleydale, but few visitors stop to take a blowy walk along its crest and enjoy a bird's-eye view down the full length of the dale to Great Shunner Fell and the distant Howgills. They may glance at the fringe of gritstone crags below the summit, but then they hasten to the popular tourist attractions of Aysgarth Falls, Castle Bolton and the cobbled market town of Hawes.

The hill walker should not look at Pen Hill in isolation, for it marks the end of a long and broad ridge of high fells running north all the way from Buckden Pike above Wharfedale. This ridge is wild, lonely and trackless and it makes a vastly superior ascent of Buckden Pike than the trade-route from Starbotton. A return can be made north-west across Naughtberry Fell and Wasset Fell to the delightful dales village of West Burton. This horseshoe walk encloses sleepy, rural, undiscovered Waldendale. Where else in the Yorkshire Dales can you walk eighteen peaceful miles over high fells without crossing a single road? This is a walk for the connoisseur of the old Yorkshire Dales, before the coming of the trail riders, the fell runners and the charabancs. It is quite perfect.

The Wensleydale Heifer, a seventeenth century inn at West Witton makes an ideal base for the walk. Easy access onto the east ridge of Penhill Beacon is gained just beyond Penhill farm, a pleasant walk up a winding lane from West Witton. Alternatively, a car can be taken up the road and parked on the wide verge beyond the farm.

A narrow path runs along the gritstone edge, passing the OS pillar and various cairns marking the beacon. But the highest point of the hill, Height of Hazely, lies one mile south-west, and you must find your own way there through the heather and coarse grass. This stretch of typical Pennine moorland, wet, tussocky and trackless, ends at a collection of ancient pit shafts and boulder heaps, beyond which the going becomes much easier.

The way ahead is now revealed over Harland Hill and Brown Haw to the distant blue outline of Buckden Pike. Far below, on either side, the farms, patterned fields and woods of Waldendale and Coverdale can be seen.

Over many centuries the landscape of the dales has been gradually tamed by man, and the use of local materials has preserved their charm, but the high fells have remained wild. A few walls, some drainage and intermittent heather burning has helped the grazing and that is the extent of upland improvement in this corner of the dales. Thank goodness the farmers here have not attempted to extend their grasslands by the application of massive doses of lime, nitrogen and phosphorus.

Old fence posts and some boundary stones make a useful guide as you walk south, but Great Whernside, at the head of Coverdale, and the seamed face of Buckden Pike are the best indications of progress. This is magnificent Pennine country where a breeze blows constantly, ruffling the wool of the Swaledales and bearing away the curlew's cry. On Brown Haw stretches of fence have been constructed from rusty steel rails; a job-lot perhaps, purchased from a bankrupt mining company in the nineteenth century and dragged up onto the fell by ponies.

The high ground can be followed over North Moor and Windle

The summit plateau of Buckden Pike – looking south-east to Little Whernside.

Ernest Shepherd

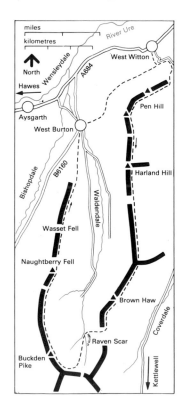

A view down Waldendale from Buckden Pike to Pen Hill (left) and Brown Haw (right).

Side to meet the north–south ridge of Buckden Pike near the memorial cross. However, it is much more interesting to descend to the upper reaches of Waldendale near Raven Scar. This hidden valley, deeply set midst rough peat moorland, is a gem; one of the secret treasures of the dales. It was here that the last pine marten was seen in Yorkshire. A beck tumbles down its rocky course in waterfalls and cascades; cutting into the limestone it has carved out a steep-sided ravine where rowans, holly and ferns grow. Here are deep, mysterious pools and grassy platforms which make delectable picnic sites.

Easy slopes lead straight up to the summit of Buckden Pike where the tourist path, pounded to a sticky black bog, comes as something of a shock. In spite of the bog, Buckden Pike is one of the finest viewpoints in the Pennines and, for the first time on this walk, a complete panorama of Pennine fells is enjoyed with Penyghent and Ingleborough prominent to the west.

A narrow path, just discernible through the heather, leads down the broad north ridge over Naughtberry Hill. We are now back on open, featureless moors relieved only by a line of shooting butts, a tumbledown wall and some spoil heaps. Lead was mined on the north side of Naughtberry Hill in the eighteenth century, ore being carried by packhorses to a smelter at Cote in Waldendale.

Wasset Fell sprouts several round cairns, a ruin and a wooden hut. It also marks the end of the rough ground, because limestone outcrops break through the surface encouraging the growth of springy turf.

A good path follows the west edge of the Forelands Rigg plantation, where buzzards nest in the sweet smelling spruce trees. The picture postcard village of West Burton, set at the junction of Waldendale and Bishopdale, lies only a mile away across the fields.

The village has a wide green surrounded by stone houses with slate or flagged roofs. Ancient wooden stocks and a stone obelisk, dated 1820, stand on the green, while facilities include a post office, store and pub, the Fox and Hounds.

At the end of the village a packhorse bridge crosses the beck near the Cauldron Falls, whence a path leads through a wood to meet Morpeth lane. This is one of the famous 'green lanes' of the dales and it contours Pen Hill at a height of about 1,000ft, meeting the Melmerby road less than half-a-mile from West Witton. A more delightful completion of the walk cannot be imagined; the lane passes under overhanging ash trees and skirts limestone crags before opening out into a broad, level ride enclosed by dry-stone walls. It was constructed as a drove road, part of a network along which cattle would be driven from Bishopdale to York market in only three days. Now Morpeth lane provides the easiest of footpaths, a welcome boon to tired legs and the ideal finish to this enchanting dales walk.

Maps O.S. 1:50,000 Sheets 98 and 99; O.S. 1:25,000 Outdoor Leisure Map – 'The Yorkshire Dales Northern and Central Areas'.
Grading A rough walk over high Pennine moorland.
Start / Finish West Witton (058884).
Distance / Time 22 miles/8-9 hours.
Escape Routes Numerous easy descents into Coverdale, Waldendale or Bishopdale. An overnight stop could be made at Buckden or Kettlewell.
Telephones West Witton, Hill Top Waldendale, Buckden and West Burton.
Transport Railway Station at Darlington. Daily bus service (United) Richmond – Leyburn – Hawes, to West Witton with connections from Darlington, Ripon and Northallerton.
Accommodation Inns/B & B at West Witton, Aysgarth and West Burton. Youth Hostels at Aysgarth Falls, Hawes, Ellingstring and Kettlewell.
Guidebooks 'The Yorkshire Dales' by Gladys Sellers (Cicerone Press); 'The Yorkshire Dales' by M. Hartley and J. Ingilby (Dent); 'Walking in the Yorkshire Dales' by the Ramblers Association (Dalesman).

THE NORTH YORK MOORS FROM NORTH TO SOUTH

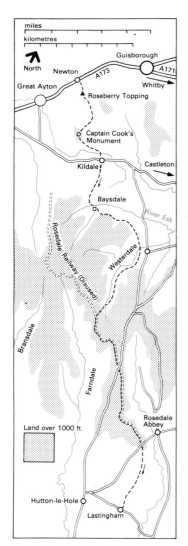

The North York Moors is one of the largest of our National Parks and one of the least known. Its 553 square miles are bounded on the west side by the Hambleton Hills and a limestone escarpment falling 600ft to the Vale of Mowbray, while on the east the North Sea pounds even higher cliffs and headlands, which descend in places to tiny fishing villages and smugglers' coves.

To the north and south the moors are intersected by sheltered wooded valleys, where settlements of Mesolithic and Bronze Age man, the Romans and the Vikings have been discovered. In the twelfth century Cistercian and Carthusian monks built glorious abbeys in choice sites on the fringes of the moors.

Today the moors and dales are largely unspoilt; notable exceptions being the Fylingdales Early Warning Station, the Bilsdale TV mast and some deep erosion following the disastrous fire of 1976 which burned for six months and destroyed huge tracts of peat.

Scenically, the famous Lyke Wake Walk which keeps solely to the high ground is disappointing. A more rewarding walk is a north-south crossing from Roseberry Topping to Lastingham, which combines the delights of open moorland, wild, upland valleys, sleepy pastoral dales and charming stone-built villages. It should not be seen as a challenge walk, to be completed head down and teeth gritted, but as an excursion through some of Yorkshire's most richly varied hill country.

Over the years erosion has eaten away the north edge of the moors, but a cap of hard rock has protected the isolated hill of Roseberry Topping, a feature much loved by the population of Tees-side and recently acquired by the National Trust. Old prints show the Topping as a perfect cone, but iron ore and jet mining, followed by rock falls, have now produced a cliff on the north side. Geologists reckon the Topping to be the most rapidly eroding hill in Britain.

Early one perfect morning in mid-May we left Newton-under-Roseberry bound for Lastingham. Clear skies had produced a sharp frost, turning to iron the muddy path through the woods and nipping the bluebells and ramsons. Seen from our perch on Roseberry Topping the tower blocks, cranes and cooling towers of industrial Tees-side appeared in sharp focus, already seeming part of another

Heading south up Westerdale, towards Esklets

The summit of Roseberry Topping.

Maps O.S. 1:50,000 Sheets 93, 94 and 100; O.S. 1:63,360 Tourist Map 'The North York Moors'; O.S. 1:25,000 Outdoor Leisure Map – 'The North York Moors, West'.
Grading A long but easy walk through upland dales and across rolling, heather-clad moors.
Start / Finish Newton (570129); Lastingham (730904).
Distance / Time 25 miles/9-10 hours.
Escape Routes The walk may be cut short at Westerdale and sanctuary sought at Castleton (2 miles) or at the Lion Inn on Blakey Bank or at Rosedale Abbey.
Telephones Great Ayton, Kildale, Gribdale, Westerdale, The Lion Inn, Blakey, Rosedale Abbey and Lastingham.
Transport Railway Station at Great Ayton on Middlesbrough to Whitby line. Frequent bus service Great Ayton to Middlesbrough. No bus service to Lastingham.
Accommodation Hotels/Inns at Great Ayton, Lastingham and Hutton-le-Hole. B & B locally. Youth Hostels at Westerdale, Helmsley and Lockton.
Guidebooks 'The North York Moors' by Geoffrey White (F. Warne); 'Eskdale Way' by Louis S. Dale (Dalesman); 'North York Moors National Park Guide' (H.M.S.O.); 'Walking on the North York Moors' by the R.A. (Dalesman); 'Rosedale Mines and Railway' by R. Hayes and J. Rutter (Scarborough Archaeological Society).

Richard Gilbert

...est of the North York Moors.

Andy Hosking

world. We followed the Cleveland Way round to Captain Cook's Monument on Easby Moor and then descended to Kildale. The sun was rising slowly into a cloudless, pale blue sky, yet inversion had created a thin layer of freezing mist which submerged the village, decorating the bracken, gorse and telephone wires with frost feathers.

From Kildale the Cleveland Way continues over Ingleby Moor but, at the second gate on Warren Moor, we took the narrow path down into Baysdale. The imposing grey farmhouse, nestling in a hollow beside the beck, is known as the 'abbey' and was built on the site of a twelfth century Cistercian nunnery. There is no easy access to Baysdale by road and it is rarely visited by day trippers. Heather moors descend almost to the valley bottom where a beck runs swiftly through woods of oak and sycamore.

Half-a-mile down the dale a path climbs up the hillside, passing Low House and a patch of forestry before contouring round into Westerdale. This is an ancient route known as Skinner Howe Cross Road, and a beautifully constructed pack-horse bridge takes it across Great Hograh beck just above a ravine overhung with rowan and oak. A shepherd was checking the progress of the lambing and I remarked on the lack of grouse in the heather. 'Ay, tha's reet, tha's as

Roseberry Topping from the north.

it shood be,' he said, 'when tha sees plenny, tha's nowt mooch thar, an' when tha sees nowt, tha's grouse a plenny.' I walked on baffled at the apparent contradiction in the countryman's lore.

Round the corner, beyond the bridge, lies Westerdale, loveliest of upland valleys and bedecked in spring with primroses, wood anemones, violets, cowslips, bugle and bluebells. A Land Rover track leads to New House farm and from there a marked footpath crosses lush meadows to the ford under High House.

Beside the beck runs an ancient path, flagged in places, leading to the ruins of Esklets, the site of a monastic grange once owned by the monks of Rievaulx. An adder lay curled up on a bed of dry bracken beside the path; at my approach it glided away to the safety of a dry-stone wall where it watched me, head moving from side to side and forked tongue darting in and out.

The early monks built their settlements in the most secluded corners of the moors and Esklets must be one of the wildest. The ruins stand near the confluence of springs and streams which drain the upper reaches of Westerdale, merging into a torrent which establishes the infant river Esk which runs into the sea at Whitby, only twenty miles away.

A wide track leads south from Esklets, climbing steeply to meet the old Rosedale Railway above Farndale. The next seven miles is flat, fast walking along the course of the old railway which is still in excellent repair, although the last train passed in 1928. The track clings to the hillside high above Farndale before crossing the Hutton-le-Hole to Castleton road at Blakey Ridge; it then winds along the west side of Rosedale to the terminus at Bank Top. Here, a row of

cottages and some old kilns remain from the era of ironstone mining which can be traced back to medieval times, but blossomed in the last century.

The railway was built in 1861 to carry the ore across the moors to Tees-side and it is not hard to imagine the scene one hundred years ago. The population of Rosedale was then nearly three thousand, for not only was the ore mined but it was roasted on site before being loaded into the wagons. Night working of the railway was necessary to shift sufficient ore, while incoming trains brought coal for the kilns. During the day the brake-van would carry school children to Farndale, and railwaymen's wives to Stokesley and Middlesbrough.

The village of Rosedale Abbey, built on the site of another Cistercian nunnery, can be seen in the valley; it is worth a slight diversion to explore, if only to visit the Milburn Arms. A path runs down to the village from the railway track, passing through the hamlet of Thorgill.

Back at Bank Top head south across the heather to Ana Cross, one of the most prominent of the stone crosses on the high moors. The origin of these crosses is obscure, but they may have been erected by the abbeys as boundary markers or guides for travellers.

A good path now crosses Spaunton Moor to Lastingham, a lovely old Yorkshire village where St Cedd founded a monastery in 654. Bede described Lastingham as being set among 'steep and solitary hills, where you would rather look for the hiding places of robbers and the lairs of wild animals than the abodes of men'. Nowadays it is more civilised with a pub, hotel, shop and an eleventh century church boasting one of the finest crypts in England.

THE FOREST OF BOWLAND:
WOLF FELL AND FIENDSDALE

Smoke was streaming from the chimneys of the great cement factory at Clitheroe, windows in the office blocks and high-rise flats of Preston were catching the morning sun and, to the north, the Heysham nuclear power station dwarfed even the wide blue estuary of the Lune. Yet I surveyed the distant industrial landscape with complete detachment for I was walking the fells of the Forest of Bowland, the westernmost extension of the Pennines, but a distinct area of wild uplands with its own history, traditions and character.

On this sparkling summer's morning a strong north-west wind was rippling the heather and moor grass and driving white fleecy clouds across a broad expanse of sky. As I approached the summit of Fair Snape Fell a flock of several hundred twite, who were resting in the heather and bilberry plants, rose into the air, wheeled as one and with a flash of white moved down the steep flanks of Wolf Fell.

The three hundred square mile area of the Forest of Bowland is designated by the Countryside Commission as an Area of Outstanding Natural Beauty, but it is still relatively undiscovered. Over the years it has gained a sad reputation as a no-go area and even now only certain parts have free access. Lancashire County Council has won access agreements from private landowners for Clougha Fell in the north and Fair Snape Fell, Wolf Fell and Saddle Fell in the south; in addition certain rights-of-way have been negotiated. Although existing access is limited there is scope for several long moorland expeditions across Bowland, but the penalty exacted is harsh: yellow marker posts, brutal fences, official notices and the channelling of walkers along fixed routes.

It seems that the restrictions are more a result of tradition than necessity. A hill farmer I spoke to had no objection to walkers on the fells provided they left their dogs behind. He pointed out that walkers' feet were unlikely to have a significant effect on grouse when the fells were extensively grazed by sheep anyway. The Water

Board maintain a total exclusion zone, which includes the shapely Totridge Fell above Hareden. The reason given is pathetic, namely that Totridge Fell is in a catchment area and walkers could pollute the water supply.

Access restrictions are a constant irritation to walkers in Bowland but several wonderfully wild and diverse walks can be enjoyed. Not only does Bowland offer bleak and rugged fells, but it is surrounded by picturesque old villages, hay meadows, woods, deep valleys and bubbling streams. Iron Age man, the Romans, Angles and Norse all settled in Bowland and it became a Royal Forest under the Normans.

My recommended walk starts from Chipping, a delightful village set under the southern slopes of the fells. Chipping has stone houses dating from the seventeenth century, three pubs and, appropriately, a thriving chair factory.

Take the lane which runs beside the factory, from which emanates the delicious smell of freshly sawn wood. Above the factory the beck runs into an old mill-pond which powered the saws in the last century, but now all is serene and ducks glide among the water lilies. Opposite the mill-pond a footpath signed to Burnslack follows the bank of a small beck, passes through a wood of foxgloves, and then breaks out onto the open fellside at Saddle Side farm.

A good track continues north up Saddle Fell for half-a-mile, but then becomes indistinct and you are left to pick your own way across the rough grass and heather. A fence with stout LCC stiles and persuasive access notices awaits you on Saddle Fell, while an area of badly eroded peat hags make for hard going westward towards Fair Snape Fell. But the plateau opens out distant views north, beyond the Trough of Bowland and Ward's Stone, to Whernside, Ingleborough and Penyghent.

Swing round the head of Wolf Fell and make for the old wall which runs south along Blindhurst Fell towards Parlick. Parlick is a symmetrical cone which rises at the end of an arm thrown out to the south by Fair Snape Fell, and the one mile detour to its summit is well worth the effort. It is a magnificent walk along the broad ridge with lonely coombs on either side. To the west some rocks and boulder fields give stature to Fair Snape Fell, while on Wolf Fell, to the east, heather gradually gives way to bracken and grass and the hillside is heavily grazed. Parlick is the principal landmark on the south side of Bowland and its summit gives a bird's-eye view over the chequered fields, hill farms and villages of the Ribble valley. On my last visit, after a night of rain, the air was so clear that I could see Blackpool Tower away to the west and the mast on Winter Hill, south beyond Blackburn.

Returning to Fair Snape Fell, a huge stone-built cairn marks point 1,674ft/510m, yet the true summit at 1,707ft/520m, a quarter-of-a-mile away to the north, warrants only an insignificant pile of stones. The fence is now followed north for a mile across cheerless, boggy and hag-ridden fells until a low line of marker cairns indicates the path down the deep valley of Fiendsdale.

Fiendsdale is an astonishing feature; without warning the fell falls

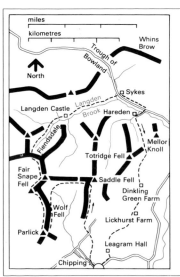

miles
kilometres
North

Whins Brow
Trough of Bowland
Sykes
Langden Castle
Langden Brook
Hareden
Fiendsdale
Mellor Knoll
Totridge Fell
Fair Snape Fell
Saddle Fell
Dinkling Green Farm
Wolf Fell
Lickhurst Farm
Parlick
Leagram Hall
Chipping

Map O.S. 1:50,000 Sheet 102.
Grading A magnificent walk over wild upland country. In bad weather route finding on the bleak and exposed moors above Fiendsdale could be difficult.
Start / Finish Chipping (623433).
Distance / Time 19 miles/7-8 hours.
Escape Routes The walk may be cut short at the Trough of Bowland.
Telephones Chipping, Dunsop Bridge and lane end near Lickhurst Farm.
Transport Regular daily bus service (including Sun) from Preston to Chipping via Longridge.
Accommodation Brick House Hotel, Chipping. Hotels/Guest Houses at Longridge and Clitheroe. Youth Hostel at Slaidburn.
Guidebooks 'Wandering in Bowland' by A. A. Lord (Westmorland Gazette); 'Walks in the Forest of Bowland' (Frederick Warne); 'Walking in Bowland and Pendle' by Cyril Spilby (Dalesman).

The Notice Board below Saddle Fell.

Parlick from Fair Snape Fell.

away abruptly into an almost bottomless ravine-like valley with steep, and in places precipitous, sides.

A narrow path clings dizzily to the rim of the valley and a tiny beck rushes below like quicksilver. By the time Langden valley is reached tributaries have swelled the beck to respectable size. To reach the main path, which runs along the north side of the Langden valley, the Langden Brook must be forded. Great care must be taken in wet

weather, when the crossing is likely to be difficult or impossible without the use of a safety rope.

A building, marked on the map as Langden Castle, turns out to be only a cow byre, after which the path allows fast walking to the Trough of Bowland road at Sykes.

We are now in the heart of Bowland, with crystal clear streams and inviting valleys running deep into green, steep-sided fells. On a

The view down Fiendsdale from Fiendsdale Head.

Totridge Fell and Fair Snape from Whin's Brow above the Trough of Bowland.

summer's day the scene is tranquil beyond measure and a welcome contrast to the wind-swept moors.

With access being denied to Totridge Fell, the col between Totridge and Mellor Knoll provides a pleasant low-level return route to Chipping. Walk down the road to Hareden and cross the river by the new bridge. The path starts opposite a beautiful stone farmhouse with mullion windows, but, although the path is signed, it is so infrequently used that no trace exists underfoot.

The right-of-way passes through Whitmore plantation, the farms at Dinkling Green and Lickhurst, and finally the landscaped estate of Leagram Hall before entering Chipping.

This easy walking through woods and meadows beneath the Bowland escarpment provides a gradual return to civilisation. Refreshments are usually available at Lickhurst farm, or you can wait for a cream tea at Chipping.

Looking south-west to the upper reaches of the Langden valley.

Langden Castle.

THROUGH THE WHITE PEAK
BY EIGHT PICTURESQUE DALES

Go to Lathkill Dale in May. The purest water in England cascades over the weirs into deep, clear pools bordered by brilliant beds of kingcups and butterbur. The leaves on the hawthorn and elm are that delicate, transient green, which appears only fleetingly in springtime, and the ash buds are just beginning to burst. Limestone crags and bluffs overlook the steep valley sides which are yellow with a profusion of cowslips, while in the woods bluebells, violets, forget-me-nots, red campions, ramsons and dog's mercury add to the blaze of colour. It is heartening to think that this beautiful natural scene, which is a Nature Reserve, is only a handful of miles from some of our largest conurbations.

Lathkill Dale is popular with walkers, but it can be linked to a string of other dales to give a much longer and more varied walk through some of the Peak District's loveliest scenery. A route from Alport to Peak Forest or Brierlow Grange includes delectable limestone dales with rushing rivers, shady woodlands, dry valleys, high open pastures, picturesque stone villages and a sprinkling of mills, viaducts, lead mines, water wheels and other relics of the industrial revolution. It is most convenient to leave a car at the finish, at either Peak Forest or Brierlow Grange, but if this is not possible a good bus service runs from Peak Forest to Buxton which connects with Bakewell, thence Alport.

The lower reaches of Lathkill Dale are broad, and the path from Alport meanders through water meadows in the most tranquil of settings. After a mile it crosses a packhorse bridge and winds through trees on the north bank, while the river rushes past in a series of weirs and trout can often be seen leaping from the pools.

As the dale climbs up to higher ground the woods thin out to be replaced by outcrops of white limestone, and the river's flow rapidly diminishes. Eventually the river emerges from the mouth of a gaping cavern under the cliffs and a dry valley leads to the village of Monyash, once a market town and centre of the lead mining industry which flourished from the Roman occupation through to the nineteenth century.

Our visit to Monyash coincided with the festival of 'well dressing'. Boards of wet clay had been set up beside the two natural wells in the village and, using only petals, leaves, rowan berries, bark, lichen and moss, the primary school had constructed colourful mosaics: a sea-scape and a scene from the Battle of Hastings as recorded on the Bayeux Tapestry.

The high pastures behind Monyash rise to over 1,000ft and, although they are now enclosed with drystone walls and are grazed by sheep, land reclamation did not take place until the late eighteenth century and odd patches of heather and bilberry remain. Ancient bell pits and spoil heaps from lead mining days abound, in spring they are covered in yellow pansies.

Deep Dale is a dry valley with woods on the north side and open slopes of limestone scree, scrub and rough grass on the south;

cowslips and early purple orchids grow here in abundance. But, as the dale descends towards the Wye, it suddenly narrows and you must pick your way through a dank, dark, gully, scrambling over moss-covered boulders while overhanging cliffs trail creepers and ferns. The atmosphere is heavy and Victorian and it is a relief to emerge into Monsal Dale.

Part of the charm of Lathkill Dale and Deep Dale lies in the modest scale of their natural features. Monsal Dale and Miller's Dale, however, are altogether grander. The river Wye is deep and fast flowing, the wooded valley sides rise steeply to over 1,000ft and towering cliffs of white limestone thrust upwards through the trees.

At Monsal Head a viaduct strides boldly across the dale. For a period of over a hundred years, ending in 1968, the viaduct carried the Midland Railway; now the old track forms part of the Monsal Trail which runs right through Miller's Dale and Chee Dale. It makes for easy walking, leaving you free to concentrate your attention on the winding river, the woods, flowers and butterflies. On the north side, in particular, the slopes are patched with boulder screes where

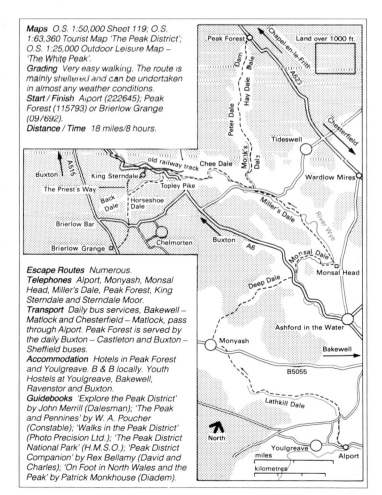

Maps O.S. 1:50,000 Sheet 119; O.S. 1:63,360 Tourist Map 'The Peak District'; O.S. 1:25,000 Outdoor Leisure Map – 'The White Peak'.
Grading Very easy walking. The route is mainly sheltered and can be undertaken in almost any weather conditions.
Start / Finish Alport (222645); Peak Forest (115793) or Brierlow Grange (09/692).
Distance / Time 18 miles/8 hours.

Escape Routes Numerous.
Telephones Alport, Monyash, Monsal Head, Miller's Dale, Peak Forest, King Sterndale and Sterndale Moor.
Transport Daily bus services, Bakewell – Matlock and Chesterfield – Matlock, pass through Alport. Peak Forest is served by the daily Buxton – Castleton and Buxton – Sheffield buses.
Accommodation Hotels in Peak Forest and Youlgreave. B & B locally. Youth Hostels at Youlgreave, Bakewell, Ravenstor and Buxton.
Guidebooks 'Explore the Peak District' by John Merrill (Dalesman); 'The Peak and Pennines' by W. A. Poucher (Constable); 'Walks in the Peak District' (Photo Precision Ltd.); 'The Peak District National Park' (H.M.S.O.); 'Peak District Companion' by Rex Bellamy (David and Charles); 'On Foot in North Wales and the Peak' by Patrick Monkhouse (Diadem).

Left: An easterly view down the upper section of Lathkill Dale from near Monyash.

Stuart Bramwell

The idyllic riverscape in Lower Lathkill Dale with Over Haddon just visible on the hill in the distance.

The narrow section at the head of Lathkill Dale.

The old railway viaduct at Monsal Head.

Jerry Rawson

Phil Ideson

The river and lake at the east end of Miller's Dale below Cressbrook, seen from the old railway track that runs through the dale. The mudflats appeared in 1987 following a deterioration of the dam at Cressbrook Mill.

The Cressbrook Mill lake in Miller's Dale at its traditional level.

One of the railway viaducts in Chee Dale.

The narrow section of Miller's Dale where steep limestone crags flank the River Wye.

The narrows of Chee Dale near Chee Tor. Here stepping stones allow progress at river-level below steep limestone cliffs.

differential colonisation has occurred: ash growing on the screes and hawthorne on the grassland.

Cressbrook Mill, at the junction of Cressbrook Dale and Miller's Dale, is another impressive monument to the industrial revolution. Originally built in grey stone by Arkwright in 1815 it was powered by water, and the mill owner was notorious for his exploitation of child labour. A weir just upstream from the mill holds back a large mill-pond, and the path runs along the water's edge under an overhanging wall of clean limestone which is a popular venue with rock climbers.

At Miller's Dale village you leave the valley of the Wye and take a narrow path which runs beside the church, heading north into Monk's Dale, another National Nature Reserve. Solitude is now regained as you follow the bubbling stream, first through beds of kingcups and then through gloomy woods before emerging into the light amongst undulating green pastures and limestone outcrops.

Now follows a succession of minor dales: Peter Dale, Hay Dale and Dam Dale. These dales become progressively more open and each has its own particular feature. Peter Dale is bounded by a low line of limestone crags, in Hay Dale you walk down a proud avenue of elms and Dam Dale, true to its name, has an earth embankment across its upper reaches which once held back a sizeable reservoir. Now the dam is breached, cows graze the meadow which once lay under water, and the stream tinkles merrily through watercress beds.

The Devonshire Arms at Peak Forest can now be seen across the fields and this makes a fitting end to the walk. North of Peak Forest is the vast Eldon Hill quarry which has destroyed huge tracts of choice Peak District country.

Remarkably this long Peak crossing has been free from major eyesores, and it is best to return home with memories of eight diverse and beautiful dales rather than a hideous man-made scar on the landscape.

Heading north up Monk's Dale.

Peter Dale at a point where small crags crowd in to create a gorge.

The Alternative Finish by Chee Dale and Deep Dale

Walkers, who are reluctant to leave the deeply cut valley of the Wye at Miller's Dale, can follow an alternative route through Chee Dale and (another) Deep Dale to finish at Brierlow Grange, three miles south of Buxton on the A515.

Chee Dale gives a three mile walk through grand scenery where river, woods and prodigious rock architecture are intricately combined. High above the River Wye limestone buttresses can often be seen thrusting out over the trees, while in other places sheer or overhanging walls of rock turn the dale into a gorge. The path follows the river as it twists and turns, rushing over boulders and down weirs or moving sluggishly through woods of ash and sycamore. Your constant companion is the old railway which takes a tortuous course: clinging precariously to the valley sides, criss-crossing the river by a succession of viaducts, or tunnelling through projecting buttresses.

In two places the cliffs rise from the water's edge and progress forward is by stepping stones. It only needs a rainy day for the stepping stones to be submerged and in times of flood the railway track provides the only feasible passage.

East of Topley Pike the A6 trunk road must be crossed and a way found through mounds of quarry spoils which effectively block the entrance to Deep Dale.

Deep Dale is a haven of peace and beauty, and it is surprisingly similar to its namesake traversed earlier in the day. Scrub hawthorn and ash grow on the limestone screes and the valley edges are fringed with crags. The cliffs encroach at the head of the dale, narrowing it to a neck, beyond which it opens out to the shallow and grassy Horseshoe Dale.

The final stretch follows the Priest's Way, an ancient green track linking the Monastic Granges at King Sterndale and Brierlow.

THE MANIFOLD VALLEY

by PHIL COOPER

Maps O.S. 1:50,000 Sheet 119; O.S. 1:63,360 Tourist Map 'The Peak District'; O.S. 1:25,000 Outdoor Leisure Map – 'The White Peak'.
Grading Easy walking through rural dales and hills.
Start / Finish at Ilam Hall (133506).
Distance / Time 18 miles/7-8 hours.
Escape Routes The walk is nowhere more than two miles from a village, any of which may be reached easily from the dale.
Telephones Ilam, Grindon, Wetton, Butterton, Warslow and Hulme End.
Transport Derby – Buxton service (Trent) to Ilam or Hulme End. Warrington's of Ilam (No. 442) runs Ashbourne – Hartington – Hulme End – Warslow – Buxton.
Accommodation Hotels at Ilam, Hartington and Hulme End. B & B locally. Youth Hostels at Ilam Hall, Hartington and Buxton.
Guidebooks 'Explore the Peak District' by John Merrill (Dalesman); 'Dovedale and the Manifold Valley' by B. Spencer and L. Porter (Moorland); 'The Leek and Manifold Valley Light Railway' by Keith Turner (David and Charles); 'Walking in Derbyshire' by J. Haworth (Derbyshire Countryside Ltd.); 'On Foot in North Wales and the Peak' by Patrick Monkhouse (Diadem).

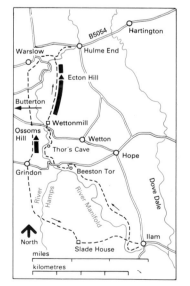

Some years ago, I was youth hostelling in central France. On booking in, the warden spotted my Derbyshire address and immediately questioned, 'Dovedale, oui?'. Such is the international fame and fortune of that dale, but even if my warden friend had been to the Manifold during his Peak District visit, it is doubtful if he would have remembered it quite so clearly. Whereas in Dovedale the finest walk is alongside the river, to make the most of the Manifold, it is better to explore the attractive paths on the hills and slopes which overlook the dale, avoiding the tarmac path along the former railway track in the dale, except in areas of particular interest. From the hills, there are spacious views across the limestone plateau of this corner of the White Peak and to the gritstone moors a few miles west; these moors form England's east–west watershed in this area. The uplands have been cultivated and grazed for centuries, yet often you will have only a few sheep or cattle for company. On the eighteen-mile route described, I met only two other parties of walkers, except in the dale itself, on a fine August day.

The walk is conveniently started at Ilam, where the National Trust will let you leave your car in the pleasant grounds of Ilam Hall, centre of Ilam Estate Country Park, for a small fee. There is a short walk from here towards Thorpe through meadows to the meeting of the Manifold and the Dove. The walk up the dale starts by following the bend past Hinkley Wood and the Ilam Estate. After a short distance, you can see a well with substantial volumes of water either augmenting the river's flow in a wet season, or turning a dry river bed into a proper river should the season be dry. For the Manifold knows the usual disappearing tricks of rivers in limestone country, and often disappears completely south of Hulme End, to reappear at this well. In the wet August of 1985 the river was full for its whole course, but in many summers the bed is bone dry. The Cross Stone, or Battle Stone, is associated with the struggle between the Saxons and the Danes. Its carving is thought to date from the mid-eleventh century.

'All persons using this road must pay 1np at the lodge', dictates a sign on the path approaching River Lodge. Be sure to take your cheque book; they do not accept credit cards. There is no right-of-way up the dale between Rushley Bridge and Beeston Tor farm. I must confess to walking down the river's stony bed during a dry spring, but there are superb bird's-eye-views of the dale and its many-folds from a path running along the rim of the eastern valley slopes. Walk up the farm track to Castern Hall from where the path at first contours the slopes, then climbs gently towards an area of disused mine shafts near the Weag's Bridge – Alstonefield Road. Beeston Tor comes into view along this path and there are good views of Hamps Dale, Oldpark Hill and Soles Hill, while Grindon church spire is a prominent landmark across the dale. To view the

Right: The view north up the Manifold Valley from the top of Thor's Cave. Ecton Hill and Whitton Hill are the principal heights.

Beeston Tor from the camping field east of Weag's Bridge.

On the southern spur of Ecton Hill looking south down the valley to Thor's Cave.

limestone crag of Beeston Tor at close quarters, take the track which leaves the Weag's Bridge road at a cattle grid and descends to the foot of the Tor; National Trust property again. A large hoard of Saxon coins and jewellery was found in the Beeston Tor cave in 1924. The stepping stones below the Tor were impassable in August 1985 on account of the monsoon, but normally you may cross the river dry-shod. Anyway, a rough path leads along the left bank towards Weag's Bridge, thus permitting progress up the dale.

Thor's Cave is another outstanding natural feature of the Manifold, and to reach it, the tarmac path is now followed up the route of the old railway line. From Weag's Bridge to near Wettonmill, the dale is free of cars. Below Thor's Cave and its limestone tower, a river bridge leads to a stepped path to the cave's mouth. From this viewpoint, there are fine views of the country ahead including Wetton and Ecton Hills. Thor's Cave was inhabited in early times, and today a flippant half-hour may be spent in scrambling into and between its different chambers, most of which have adequate day-light to permit their exploration.

At Wettonmill, the dale is again deserted in favour of the hills, and a path leads through Dale Farm up a dry valley which has descended from the south side of Ecton Hill. Past the Top of Ecton, the path leads close by the summit of Ecton Hill which commands a full 360-degree view, and is one of the highest hills in the area. There are views across the acres of wild upland, the Morridge being prominent beyond Warslow, and up-valley all the way to Oliver Hill and Axe Edge, close by the sources of the Manifold and Dove. In the eighteenth century, Ecton Hill had the richest copper mines in Europe and the profits paid for the construction of The Crescent in Buxton. After descending Ecton Hill's north side via Ecton back to the Manifold, a walk along the railway route into Hulme End is in order for refreshments and accommodation if required. Upstream from Hulme End, Manifold Dale becomes a broad slate valley, very rural and with a substantial cattle population. But the return route to Ilam, on the western side of the dale, permits further views of the lime-stone country and the traverse of several side valleys, which you will have noticed from the upland sections of the walk from Ilam.

Proceed to Warslow, from where a route leads due south all the way to Lee House in the Hamps Valley. The track is so remarkably straight that one suspects its origins to be Roman; it certainly crosses the side valleys in a straight-up, straight-down fashion uncharacter-istic of the later medieval ways and packhorse routes. The straight track leaves Warslow by the 'no through road' which runs south from the village, and passes down what appears to be a private driveway, but there is a small 'public footpath' sign to encourage you. The path crosses Warslow Brook and Hoo Brook before ascend-ing to Grindon. You could divert to ascend the National Trust area of Ossoms Hill, which gives a good view along the dale and across to Thor's Cave. Becoming a track, the way south slowly descends into the normally dry Hamps Valley. A bridge at Lee House points the way ahead, steeply up the valley side, across the Calton-Throwley road, then to Slade House. From there it is only a mile or so to Rushley farm and the path returning directly to Ilam Hall, crossing the Manifold by a footbridge on the way.

Manifold Dale north from Hulme End is less spectacular but nonetheless worth the walk, using the network of footpaths avail-able, all the way to Flash village below Oliver Hill. You might even like to continue by walking across the watershed to Three Shire Heads and the Dane Valley, but there is another story.

Two views of Thor's Cave.

THE ROACHES AND AXE EDGE

by JOHN BEATTY

I am glad of Snowdon, Ben Nevis and the Roaches because I am left with the Carneddau, Knoydart and Goldsitch Moss. White spirits walk in cluttered company, black spirits walk alone and wild.

The October rain lashed the village of Upper Hulme. I sat in the soporific warmth of the car. Rivers of water guttered along the wipers. Next, the opening of the door, an extempory moment. We were bound for Buxton on an eighty mile horseshoe of the Peak. Victory, we stepped out into the sloppy farm track leading up behind Hen Cloud. Redwings and fieldfares gusted up and out of the thorns and ran with the wind with us into the flooded farm fields. We could see Hen Cloud through the driving rain and mist, ahead in the wind. It always takes me a few miles to collect my senses, the freshness and abandonment of winter rain, the wet scent of bilberry and gritstone, drawing me, heedless, to the black edges flanking the supreme and tragic landscape of Goldsitch to the east.

A snipe bolted from a clump of rushes, then, wading in deep wet heather, up to the back of Hen Cloud, I was eager to be on drier ground.

Find your own way to the Cloud. Scramble, the rock will enfold you, and stand on the monolithic summit. Hen Cloud has great power, Orthanc. In summer it is sweet bilberries and brilliant clean rock fun. In winter, green, impenetrable and sinister. I wait awhile, scouring the marshes on Goldsitch for the heron, but he has gone.

Ahead lies the Roaches, a two-mile skyline of perfect gritstone. The rock is huge, castellated and windbitten, today shrouded in a grey cloak, the silent, primeval woodland to the west remains secret, abroad with spirits. Down there, a recluse, strange animals and at weekends up to a hundred cars. People flock to walk amongst these rocks. Great power indeed.

It is still winterblue up on our Skyline, the Doxy Pool is quite frozen. Only a shallow, peaty mire, but legendary. ... The singing woman, a recluse in the rocks, riders, Queen Anne, and the icy east wind. We wander in a dream, rising to the trig. Henry Moore must have walked this way because I have seen that boulder outside Euston, but it was silver!

Gloved and bouldering quite happily in the cold sunshine, I jumped off a rock down to my flask. From this high place I can lie in dry heather and scan a spectacular panorama. A pyramid to the north-west: Shutlingsloe. I might walk back that way tomorrow, she looks a sweet summery hill. Or I might be feeling black and stalk back over the tors east of Goldsitch with my hands plunged into pockets, and my collar up against the gale. There are mad geese over there, in Caithness, once talk of a yak too.

It is summer at Roach End, a simple little col spoiled by cars, but a plunge down through the bracken will bring you to a magical woodland, toadstools and a curious cleft, Lud's Church. Find it if you can. Steps lead down from the birchwood fringe into a hidden slot, just like Rupert Bear. Within its 70ft walls Christians hid centuries ago and held ceremony. Sir Garwain met the Green Knight and battled. You will find your voice drop to a whisper. Strange power indeed. Lud's Church today is a silent fern sanctuary.

Rain squalls and rushing autumn light, I am running now with friends along the River Dane upstream from Lud's Church, through Gradbach Youth Hostel and on to Gradbach bridge. We all stop on the bridge to read the plaque in the wall; a rainbow soars into the heavens. We run towards a blackening sky; Axe Edge.

Take field paths, straw stubble, manure and a couple of lost boy-scouts, head for Wicken Walls, up past the black and white wooden chalet. Rise up, there are curlews up here.

After a mile up the meadows, a sandy walled track will lead you down into the Dane headwaters, to the pack-horse bridge of Three Shire Heads. I look down from the track; I am five years old and swimming in the waterfalls and green pools below the bridge, a picnic on the bank and ring-ouzels upstream. I take a drink from my favourite spring on the track, rush down the bank and plunge into a pool. Still swimming, still living, still learning.

The only time on Axe Edge is winter. There are sheets of ice flowing on the cobbled lane that leads from Three Shires to Orchard Farm. The snow no longer blows off us, but sticks wet and heavy on our woollens. Caught without anoraks we don bin-liners found in a barn. Heads down against the northerly, Axe Edge is so bitter and beautiful. We once found a dead sheep by the wall here, legs up in the stiff wind, the tongue and the grimace haunting in the grey light. She'd gone the next day, probably borne to where herons go. Axe Edge is so lonely. The tussocks might snap your ankles if you lose the path. Side-step west off the gravel track beyond Orchard Farm,

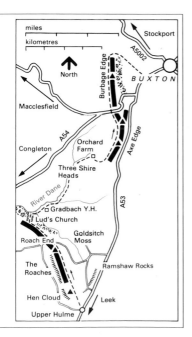

Maps O.S. 1:50,000 Sheets 118 and 119; O.S. 1:63,360 Tourist Map 'The Peak District'; O.S. 1:25,000 Outdoor Leisure Map – 'The White Peak'.
Grading A fine day's walk along rocky escarpments, moorland edges and through a beautiful river valley.
Start / Finish Upper Hulme (013609); Buxton (059734).
Distance / Time 14 miles/6 hours.
Escape Routes Numerous. The route is never far from a minor road or a village.
Telephones Upper Hulme, Flash, Canholes, Burbage and Buxton.
Transport Railway and Bus Stations at Buxton. Buxton to Leek and Hanley to Sheffield bus services link Upper Hulme with Buxton.
Accommodation Buxton is the best centre, but Inns and B & B abound in the surrounding villages. Youth Hostels at Buxton, Gradbach and Meerbrook.
Guidebooks 'High Peak Walks' by M. Richards (Cicerone); 'Walks in the White Peak' by John Merrill (Dalesman); 'South Pennine Country' by Roger Redfern (Hale); 'Walks in the Derbyshire Dales' by J. Haworth (Derbyshire Countryside Ltd.); 'On Foot in North Wales and the Peak' by Patrick Monkhouse (Diadem).

The Roaches/Hen Cloud escarpment seen from the north-west. Hen Cloud is the pointed hill on the right.

Looking north towards Shuttlingsloe from Roach End.

On the Roaches escarpment: looking south to Hen Cloud and north (inset) from the summit rocks.

The two arms of the infant River Dane at Three Shire Heads.

Lud's Church – the mysterious gritstone gorge in the northern slopes of Back Forest.

make for the crown of walls and a stile.

We are high now on the moors, the open moors, and at last the sky. I was up here once when the freezing cloud sank away all round me leaving only islands of land on which to walk. Gateways, pools, enclosures infused in deep pink mist. I sit on the stile and warm my palms on the flask cup. The sunrise is blazing through the mist. I drink the silence and laugh in love.

Further on the clouds roll off the Cat and Fiddle summit. Morning traffic on the distant high road is dazzled briefly before descending to dank towns.

I sit on that stile at all times of the year, but today it is a heavy July afternoon, I have been out all day with the skylarks. I want to stay high in the warm evening air.

Cross the road to Axe Edge cutting and descend a little to the Cat and Fiddle road and a collapsing gate that tests your age. We are on home ground, an ancient grassy trackway keeps you on the skyline to a gritstone fingerpost and the Roman track to Burbage and the Goyt. The night has fallen, it would be so easy to drop to the east into Buxton, but the curlews have not settled yet. I want to hear them.

There are foxes up here beneath the stars. The path skulks along the skyline wall to the trig. point. A primitive wood, bent by the east wind, hisses in the gloom. Dropping a hundred feet across a grassy col, I glimpse the cold blue lights of Buxton. Sister moon lifted from the dim horizon, and rose triumphantly into the night sea to illuminate my descent round the north end of the wood. Down, down by the shadowy birches and into the lane leading to the velvet, dewy golf course.

Maybe I will awake tomorrow and walk back to Upper Hulme. I may race with friends up to the windy summit of Shutlingsloe, collect bilberries on Gib Tor, or simply lie in a sunny hollow on the Roaches Skyline hidden from the path.

In this small landscape are etched all the places you have ever been. It is as enchanting and wild now as it was all those years ago when you first saw the redwings sweeping down in the winter wind.

The head of the Dane above Three Shire Heads looking past Reeve Edge Quarry to Axe Edge Moor.

A cloud inversion isolates the hills of upper Dovedale south-east of Axe Edge.

CAER CARADOC AND BROWN CLEE HILL

Shropshire is well wooded and pastoral, its deep, winding lanes and pretty villages stamping it as a very English county, yet it has a sprinkling of individual hills, as high and untamed as if they had spilled over from across the Welsh border. The tower blocks and smoke-haze of the industrial West Midlands can be seen clearly from the hill summits, but the urban sprawl stops short of the river Severn, allowing the hills to rise from unspoilt countryside.

The Wrekin, The Lawley, Caer Caradoc and Hope Bowdler are hog-backed hills with characteristic and well-loved shapes. These hills run north-south, parallel to the Church Stretton fault, and they bear a striking resemblance to the Malvern hills further south. Both ranges were formed by upthrust of Pre-Cambrian Uriconian lavas, some of the oldest rocks in England and Wales. Unlike the Malverns though, the Shropshire hills are wild, unspoilt by man and rarely visited.

There is some outcropping, particularly on Caer Caradoc, but the hills are mostly covered with grass, bracken, heather and bilberry, giving rich colouring at all seasons. Sheep are free to roam and graze at will, walking is easy over the close-cropped grass and access is

unrestricted. For the walker who does not demand rough boulders and scree the Shropshire hills are idyllic.

Apart from the Long Mynd, described in *Classic Walks*, there is no great massif in Shropshire; neither is there a linked network of smaller hills to provide a tough day's walk. For this reason I have chosen two half-day expeditions, both of high quality and both conveniently centred on picturesque villages where accommodation can be found.

Tucked away on the east side of the Church Stretton hills lies the peaceful village of Cardington. Here, the Royal Oak makes a convenient and hospitable base for the circuit of The Lawley, Caer Caradoc and Willstone Hill, a walk which can be accomplished comfortably between lunch and dinner.

Take the narrow lane which is bordered by a stream and runs between high hedges to Chatwall. From the top of the bank a footpath cuts across a field and leads up to the woods on Hoar Edge.

Caer Caradoc seen from the north, from the fields near Hollyhurst.

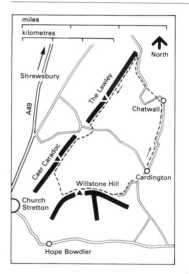

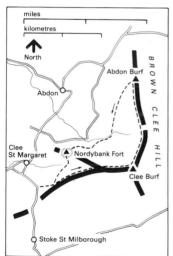

Map O.S. 1:50,000 Sheet 137.
Grading Two easy walks over open rolling hills.
Start / Finish Caradoc – Cardington (505952). Brown Clee – Clee St. Margaret (565844).
Distance / Time Caer Caradoc, 10 miles/4-5 hours; Brown Clee Hill, 8 miles/3-4 hours.
Escape Routes Numerous. The hills may be descended almost anywhere.
Telephones Cardington, Church Stretton, Clee St. Margaret and Stoke St. Milborough.
Transport Railway Stations at Church Stretton and Ludlow. A bus service (Boulton's) links Cardington to Church Stretton, Ludlow and Shrewsbury. Ludlow – Clee St. Margaret bus service run by G. Whittle, Ludlow 2491.
Accommodation Hotels at Church Stretton and Ludlow. Inns at Cardington. B & B at Cardington and Clee St. Margaret. Youth Hostels at Wheathill, Wilderhope Manor and Ludlow.
Guidebooks 'Welsh Border Country' by Maxwell Fraser (Batsford); 'Church Stretton and South Shropshire Rambles' by Robert Smart (available locally); 'Shropshire Hill Country' by Vincent Waite (Dent); Information leaflets can be obtained from the Information Centre, Church Road, Church Stretton, Salop; 'The Shropshire Landscape' by Trevor Rowley (Hodder and Stoughton).

Now the long undulating crest of The Lawley bursts into view, its smooth ridge rising in steps to a height of 1,236ft/377m. an irresistable sight to the walker.

A short way past Blackhurst farm, access to the north end of The Lawley is provided by a wicket gate. A broad grassy ride cuts through thick bracken and brambles on the lower slopes and the mile-long ascent up the springy turf is a joy. The huge bulk of the Long Mynd effectively cuts off the view westwards but, glancing back to the north, the Wrekin rises prominently to 1,334ft/407m commanding the north Shropshire plain. It was an important link in the chain of beacons warning of the approach of the Spanish Armada in 1588.

From the summit of The Lawley the route of the rest of the walk over Caer Caradoc and Willstone Hill can be traced. Caer Caradoc dominates the Church Stretton hills; from this direction it thrusts up steeply and with its bold outline and fringe of summit rocks it resembles a giant wart. Its superior height, 1,505ft/459m and abrupt shape made it a natural stronghold, and the earthworks of a prehistoric camp are clearly visible on the upper slopes. This camp is thought to have been used by Caractacus, who fought the Romans in 50AD. Caradog is the Celtic name for Caractacus.

Several paths wind through the tangle of scrub thorn, gorse and bracken on the lower slopes of Caer Caradoc to merge on the open ridge near a pond. The paths, though distinct, are not eroded and Caer Caradoc seems to have avoided problems of scarring suffered by many less attractive hills.

Weathered outcrops of rock provide delightful features on the summit of Caer Caradoc; useful as windbreaks, seats or tables for a picnic lunch. But the most impressive outcrop is called the Battlestones and can be seen across the Wilderness valley, high on Willstone Hill.

Caer Caradoc is easily descended on the east side to a farm track running through a dry valley with Willstone Hill rising beyond. It is worthwhile making a short detour from the summit of Willstone Hill, to inspect the spectacular perched block on the Battlestones, before walking down the broad ridge to Cardington Moor Farm. The tower of Cardington's Norman church can be seen through the trees, and half-a-mile of country lane leads back to the Royal Oak.

While the Long Mynd and the Wrekin dominate the western and northern horizons as seen from Caer Caradoc, the view east is equally entrancing. Running broadly north-south is Wenlock Edge, a sixteen-mile long escarpment of Silurian limestone. Immortalised by Housman in *A Shropshire Lad*, the woods of Wenlock Edge have recently been acquired by the National Trust. In spring Wenlock Edge is exquisite with the woods carpeted by snowdrops, primroses, wild daffodils and great swathes of bluebells. But the Edge is crisscrossed by roads, the paths are overhung by foliage and, after an exploratory walk, I did not consider it appropriate for inclusion in *Wild Walks*.

However, east of Wenlock Edge, Brown Clee Hill rises to the considerable height of 1,790ft/540m, a superb open hill of heather and boulders, the home of curlews and buzzards. Apart from a radio station the hill is wild and unspoilt yet, amazingly,

Outcrops on the southern slopes of Caer Caradoc with Church Stretton in the valley beyond.

The summit of Brown Clee Hill.

less than twenty-five miles from the centre of Wolverhampton.

The village of Clee St Margaret is an ideal base for the walk but be warned that, if approaching from Ludlow, the Clee Brook must be forded as it flows through the village street. A hazard in wet weather.

Half-a-mile along the Stoke St Milborough road, at a lay-by, another of Shropshire's broad green paths leads to Clee Burf, one of three prehistoric forts on Brown Clee Hill. The path follows a line of beech trees and, near the top of the hill, it passes a disused quarry and some bell pits. The rocks of Brown Clee Hill are more recent than those of the Church Stretton hills and Wenlock Edge, they are Old Red Sandstone capped with lava which has prevented erosion of coal measures. Brown Clee has a long industrial history: coal, iron, limestone, basalt and copper have all been mined.

Follow an old wall on the edge of another magnificent stand of old beeches, cross an area of coarse grass and reeds and plough straight through the deep heather to the radio mast. Set low down in the heather is a stone memorial to twenty-three Allied and German airmen who died in various accidents on Brown Clee Hill during the last war.

On my visit, in mid-March, a bitter wind scoured the summit of the hill, the highest in Shropshire and the site of the second hill fort, Abdon Burf. A shallow pond near the OS pillar was frozen. With eyes streaming I gazed far into Wales; west to Cader Idris and south to the Radnor Forest. Some of the distant hills were illuminated by shafts of sunlight while others were masked by white squalls of hail. It was a bracing day, ideal for walking.

A path leads down to the valley below Five Springs, and here it was sheltered and warm in the early spring sunshine. Oak, holly, alder and hazel grew beside the stream and I drank from a spring emerging from under a rock, before continuing down the valley.

A jumble of vast concrete blocks beside the track marks the terminal of an old mineral railway and, at this point, a path crosses a stile and leads to Nordybank Hill Fort. Extensive ditches and ramparts remain, the site is totally uncommercialised and you are free to explore this fascinating earthwork at will. Evidence has been found showing the fort to have been in occupation from Neolithic to Romano-British times. A wide traverse path leads easily back to the lay-by above Clee St Margaret.

THE MOORS AND TORS OF EASTERN DARTMOOR

The wildest walk on Dartmoor is probably the twenty-five mile north to south crossing described in *The Big Walks*, followed closely by *Classic Walks'* expedition to Cranmere Pool. These are superb walks with definite objectives and they capture the unique atmosphere of the moors, the atmosphere which makes them the most inscrutable and mystical area of England.

There are high, wild moors too on the north and west sides of Dartmoor, but they are in the clutches of the military who impose infuriating restrictions on access. I feel there is little pleasure to be gained from struggling along a contrived route across desolate and boggy hills just for the sake of wildness, when Dartmoor has so much else to offer. For this reason I have selected an itinerary on the eastern moors, between Postbridge and Bovey Tracey, which combines stretches of high and wild moorland with impressive rock features and fascinating historical sites.

The walk is centred on the picturesque old Dartmoor village of Widecombe-in-the-Moor, where a Perpendicular style church with a magnificent hundred-foot high tower presides over a collection of cottages, a fourteenth-century inn and a National Trust information office. Widecombe is popular with visitors to Dartmoor but they don't stray far from the coach park and cafe; nevertheless the village is best avoided on the second Tuesday in September when Old Uncle Tom Cobley and All come to Widecombe Fair.

About one hundred metres past the Old Inn a steep lane runs up to the broad southern extension of Hamel Down. The lane passes under some beech trees before petering out amongst gorse and heather on the edge of the high moor. Rides of springy turf run along the spine of Hamel Down which provides good grazing for Dartmoor ponies, and makes for fast, free walking giving you the opportunity to enjoy the views on either side.

Hameldown Beacon is the first top of the day and it is marked by a low stone inscribed 'Hamilton Beacon'. Various barrows and standing stones are passed on the walk north to Hameldown Tor, 1,732ft/529m, where the grey OS pillar is set beside a huge pile of granite boulders.

A narrow path now runs down through the heather to Grimspound, an exceptional archaeological site and possibly the finest Bronze Age relic on Dartmoor. Here an ancient wall of enormous granite blocks, now tumbled down, encloses four acres of moorland. There is a paved entrance to the enclosure which contains twenty-four hut circles constructed of smaller stones. It is thought that Grimspound was built about three thousand years ago to keep stock in, rather than for defensive purposes. Grimspound has not been developed as a tourist attraction and this makes the site particularly impressive. I found it a moving experience to approach Grimspound through wet, clinging mist and suddenly be confronted by the massive lichen encrusted boulders, left where they had fallen thousands of years ago, emerging from the tangled bracken, brambles and heather.

A spring runs close to the north side of Grimspound and this is followed up the hillside until a line of decayed wooden posts mark the route to King's Barrow on King Tor. These posts were erected in 1940 to deter German gliders from landing on the flattish moor. The barrow is a round earthwork covered with heather and green turf; a deep depression within is lined with quartzite boulders and it makes a useful shelter for lunch on a windy day.

On the east side of King Tor the plantation at Heathercombe is clearly visible and a path leads through a gap in the trees to meet a tarmaced lane, running steeply down to the B3344 Manaton to Moretonhampstead road.

Just beyond the road junction, a track on the right runs past Ford farm, passes through a wood and contours round the northern slopes of Cripdon Down to emerge under Bowerman's Nose on Hayne Down. This extraordinary thirty-foot rock pinnacle looks, in silhouette, just like the head of an old man with a thrusting chin and a very prominent nose. The origin of the name Bowerman is not known. In addition to Bowerman's Nose, Hayne Down sprouts a motley collection of weird granite tors; it is a fine viewpoint for the wooded valleys and knobbly high moors of eastern Dartmoor. South across a shallow valley rises Hound Tor, so named because the long line of rocks on the skyline of the moors is said to resemble a pack of hounds, although I cannot see the likeness.

From the 1,299ft/395m, top of Hayne Down a descent should be made through the thick bracken to the large stone barn in the valley. Easier slopes then lead up to Hound Tor. The principal feature on the tor is a wide chimney, closed at the top by a massive chockstone. On the arête above perch a line of crazy pinnacles.

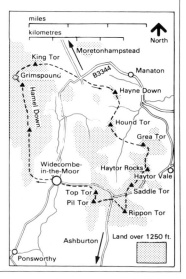

Maps O.S. 1:50,000 Sheet 191; O.S. 1:63,360 Tourist Map 'Dartmoor'; O.S. 1:25,000 Outdoor Leisure Map – 'Dartmoor'.
Grading A varied walk exploring some of Dartmoor's most impressive granite tors. Some tough going over rough heather moorland and boulder fields, but the walk can be cut short at many convenient places.
Start / Finish Widecombe-in-the-Moor (718769).
Distance / Time 14 miles/7 hours.
Escape Routes Numerous. The route crosses several roads and the moors can be descended easily in almost any direction.
Telephones Widecombe-in-the-Moor, Haytor Vale, Manaton and Heatree.
Transport Railway Stations at Exeter and Newton Abbot. Bus service Exeter – Moretonhampstead – Bovey Tracey. Only one bus a week (Wed) connects Widecombe with Bovey Tracey and Newton Abbot.
Accommodation Hotels at Bovey Tracey and Haytor Vale. B & B at Widecombe. Youth Hostels at Steps Bridge (Dunsford) and Bellever.
Guidebooks 'Dartmoor' by K. Lowther and R. Hammond (Ward Lock); 'Dartmoor For Walkers and Riders' by H. D. Westacott (Penguin); 'Crossing's Guide to Dartmoor' by B. Le Messurier (David and Charles); 'The Penguin Guide to Dartmoor' by H. D. Westacott (Penguin); 'The Great Walks of Dartmoor' by T. Bound (Obelisk Publications); 'Exploring Dartmoor' by F. H. Starkey (Penwell Ltd, Callington, Cornwall); 'Worth's Dartmoor' (David and Charles).

Hound Tor with Haytor in the distance.

Away to the east, across a wooded valley, the gigantic twin granite tors of Haytor Rocks stand on the highest point of Haytor Down. The valley should be crossed just south of the woods near the excavated site of a deserted medieval village; then a scramble up exceptionally rough slopes of large boulders, strewn about chaotically and partly

High Man, the smaller of the two outcrops at Haytor Rocks.

overgrown by bracken, leads to Grea Tor.

An ancient tramway crosses the moor south of Grea Tor, this was built in 1820 to carry granite from the quarry below Haytor. The granite was shipped from Teignmouth and was used for the arches of London Bridge and for the columns of the British Museum. The tramway was constructed of long sections of granite which were laid parallel across the moor, with chiselled flanges to take the wheels of horse-drawn wagons. Exposed sections are still clearly visible. Man's uses of natural resources on the moor, whether the huts and enclosure at Grimspound, the numerous standing stones or, far more recently, the granite rails of Haytor Down blend harmoniously with the wild moor and in no way detract from the beauty of the landscape.

Haytor Rocks are the most impressive landmarks on Dartmoor and their ascent is popular. To facilitate the climb, the eastern tor has steps hacked out of the granite, while the steeper western tor has suffered the indignity of drilling and subsequent erection of iron stanchions. The rocks of Haytor provide the best rock climbing on Dartmoor, particularly the western tor which has vertical routes up to one hundred feet in length.

Half-a-mile further south, Saddle Tor towers up from an area of green, cropped

Walkers survey the Dartmoor scene from the Logan Stone. Hound Tor and Grea Tor are the prominent outcrops in the background.

turf; it too offers some hard routes up its splendid overhanging north face.

Continuing the walk the tors come thick and fast. Rippon Tor is a pronounced summit at 1,560ft/475m, and in clear weather gives views across Devon from the Teign estuary in the south to the Bristol Channel in the north. Swinging west towards Widecombe-in-the-Moor, Foal's Arrishes, a group of eight hut circles is passed before the rocks of Pil Tor and Top Tor emerge fifteen feet above the heather. These tors are rarely visited but make a pleasant finale before the descent to Widecombe, clearly seen in the valley below.

Hound Tor – so called because its rocks are said to resemble a pack of hounds.

THE EXMOOR COAST PATH

The Exmoor Coast Path between Minehead and Combe Martin is a mere 35 mile section of Britain's longest footpath, the 520 mile South-West Peninsula Coast Path. I have chosen this particular stretch for the unique combination of seascape with the open moorlands, wooded valleys and rushing streams of Exmoor, which fall steeply into the Bristol Channel.

The hills of Exmoor shelter the coast from the worst of the winter gales, and the Gulf Stream ensures a temperate climate, thus vegetation grows profusely providing an ever changing diversity of environment. At times the path runs through dank, mossy woods of oak, elm and sycamore, at others it winds between extensive banks of brilliant rhododendrons and, when it passes through the pretty villages of Bossington, Porlock Weir and Lynmouth, palm trees can be seen thriving in many gardens.

But for me the walk is memorable for the narrow path, which clings precariously to the steep hillsides, leading you dizzily above the rocky shore many hundreds of feet below. In September the holiday crowds had disappeared and I walked for mile after mile without passing a soul, enjoying the aroma of the luxuriant gorse, heather and bracken, while an abundance of blackberries, bilberries, hips, haws and sloes ripened in the warm sunshine.

The walk should not be rushed; allow two days with an overnight stop at Lynmouth. This way you will have plenty of time to visit the many fascinating places which lie on, or just off, the main path: the old churches, inns, lighthouses, harbours, smugglers' coves, woods, beacons and villages, and to treat yourself to a farmhouse cream tea.

The official Coast Path does not always take the most imaginative or exciting route and by making a few deviations the quality of the walk can be enhanced. I shall recommend some of these deviations, but otherwise the main path is clearly waymarked with wooden pointers and white acorns and no detailed description is necessary.

Minehead has an air of graciousness and elegance; no chippies or amusement arcades sully the sea front and the Butlin's Camp sprawls on the headland well to the east of the bay. As you pass the line of old cottages on the west side of the harbour a flight of steps and a sign to North Hill indicate the start of the walk. The path passes through Culver Cliff wood and then breaks out onto open heathery slopes which culminate in the spectacular viewpoint of Selworthy Beacon 1,010ft/308m. Here you will enjoy your first taste of some of the most entrancing wild country in England, where the sleepiest of villages nestle in deep, wooded combes under the barren moorlands of Dunkery Hill, highest point on Exmoor. Selworthy, lying one mile south of the beacon, with its white-washed church and thatched cottages, is said to be the prettiest village in England.

To the south-east the gently rolling Brendon Hills merge into the broad backbone of the Quantocks, while to the north the faint blue outline of the Welsh coast may be discerned; only the factories at Aberthaw across the Channel, and the nuclear power station at Hinckley Point mar the perfection of the scene.

Bossington Hill overlooks the wide shingle beach of Porlock Bay and, after a descent of Hurlstone combe to the thatched cottages of Bossington, you can walk along the bank of plate-like stones for two miles into Porlock Weir. The inner harbour of Porlock Weir is protected from the elements by a lock gate and this, together with several beautiful old inns, makes the village popular with yachtsmen.

At the toll road a stone archway marks the continuation of the coast path to Lynmouth. The first stage of the walk takes you through the oak woods of Ashley Combe and Yearnor until, quite suddenly, you arrive at a clearing in the trees and a tiny medieval church with a

Maps O.S. 1:50,000 Sheets 180 and 181; O.S. 1:63,360 Tourist Map 'Exmoor'.
Grading A magnificent coastal walk along a switchback, narrow and at times exposed path.
Start / Finish Minehead (971470); Combe Martin (576473).
Distance / Time 35 miles/allow 2 days with an overnight stop at Lynmouth. Minehead to Lynmouth 8-9 hours. Lynmouth to Combe Martin 5-6 hours.
Escape Routes Numerous.
Telephones Minehead, Bossington, Porlock Weir, Lynmouth, Hunter's Inn and Combe Martin.
Transport Railway Stations at Taunton and Barnstaple. Bus services from Taunton and Exeter to Minehead. Daily bus service Combe Martin to Ilfracombe and Barnstaple. Note there is no link between Combe Martin and Minehead.
Accommodation Ample. Hotels/Guest Houses Minehead, Lynmouth and Combe Martin. Youth Hostels at Minehead, Exford, Lynton and Ilfracombe.
Guidebooks 'Somerset and North Devon Coast Path' by Clive Gunnell (H.M.S.O.); 'The South West Way' by Peter Dawson (Macdonald); 'Exmoor' by S. H. Burton (Hale); 'Somerset and North Devon Coast Path' obtainable from Exmoor N.P.A., Exmoor House, Dulverton, Somerset; 'The South West Way' by South West Way Association (E. G. Parrott, Torquay).

Right: The North Devon coastline north-east of Lynmouth showing Sillery Sands and Foreland Point.

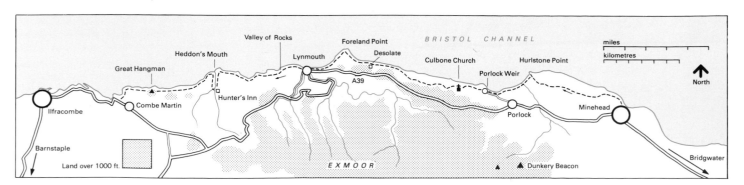

The North Devon Coastal Path near Cow and Calf, west of Woody Bay.

miniature spire. This little gem is Culbone Church, reckoned to be the smallest parish church in England; recently it was used as a set for the film *Lorna Doone*.

Continue walking through Culbone and Embelle woods using the lower, alternative, path and descend to the boulder-strewn beach under Sugarloaf Hill. It is a welcome change to escape from the leafy canopy to the shore and the crump of breaking waves and, unless the tide is high, you can proceed a mile westwards to near Glenthorne House. When you reach a rudimentary breakwater of bleached stakes re-enter the wood and skirt the house and its walled gardens. Now pass under a stone arch, whence a good path zig-zags back up the hillside to rejoin the official route prior to a truly magnificent three mile stretch of open walking above Countisbury Cove to Foreland Point, where 800ft cliffs fall straight into the sea.

A wide grassy path hugs the cliffs above Lynmouth Bay and then descends steeply to the little village which has been almost completely rebuilt since the tragic flood of August 1952. 1952 had been a wet summer

The Valley of Rocks near Lynton where a string of castellated rock towers separate the cliff edge from a small inland hollow

and Exmoor was already saturated when an astonishing ten further inches of rain fell in a ferocious storm. The East and West Lyn rivers meet just above the town and a wall of water, stones and slurry swept through the streets. Gigantic boulders smashed houses like matchwood and even the Rhenish Tower overlooking the harbour was demolished. 35 people drowned in the flood and Lynmouth is still haunted by the memory of the disaster.

A well constructed path, the North Walk, runs round the headland above Lynmouth and leads into the Valley of Rocks, a glaciated valley overhung with rock towers and pinnacles. In order to reach the North Walk from Lynmouth harbour walkers should swallow their pride and take the Cliff Railway, an ingenious Victorian invention which uses water and the force of gravity to hoist you up 500ft.

Leaving the Valley of Rocks the path skirts the top of Woody Bay, rounds Highveer Point, and then descends to the river Heddon at Hunter's Inn. Ignore the official signs and walk along the west bank of the river to the old lime kiln beside the sea at Heddon's Mouth. This is a wild little inlet where the waves boom between towering cliffs, but a way can be found up the steep nose of heather and scree to meet the main path at East Cleave.

Four miles of exhilarating walking above a jagged coastline of rock teeth and skerries leads to the Great Hangman which casts 1,000ft cliffs straight into the sea. As the cliff path approaches Great Hangman it divides; take the path to the right signed Blackstone Viewpoint. This path starts off broad and well beaten, but as it rounds the headland it narrows and becomes increasingly indistinct as walkers, unnerved by the waves crashing hundreds of feet below, have lost courage and turned back. The area has a Slieve League feel about it but, although threadlike, the path is quite safe if you have a head for heights.

By contrast Little Hangman is a sharp, knobbly hill overlooking the windswept Wild Pear Beach of Combe Martin. The path then keeps to the cliff edge all the way into this rather straggly Devon village, a centre for silver mining in the thirteenth century but now best known for its hotel the Pack of Cards, which has 4 floors each with 13 doors and the whole building has 52 windows.

The Exmoor National Park ends at Combe Martin and the village, which has a good bus service to Ilfracombe and Barnstaple, is a convenient place to finish the walk.

Approaching Great Hangman from the east where the cliffs plunge 1000ft to a stony beach.

Heddon's Mouth.

The ruined cottage at Fernacre below Brown Willy.

The view south from Bearah Tor near Henwood towards the TV station on Caradon Hill.

THE GRANITE TORS OF BODMIN MOOR

Cornwall is England's most popular holiday county. Crowds flock to the sandy beaches and coves of the rugged coastline, yet Bodmin Moor is almost entirely deserted. But this was not always the case; in man's progress towards civilisation fundamental changes in his way of life have taken place. Exploration of Bodmin Moor reveals countless relics which show that it was extensively inhabited by Stone Age man, the Beaker people, Bronze and Iron Age man. The high moor was much more hospitable than the dense undergrowth of the lowlands and settlements were easier to defend.

The Romans never succeeded in subduing the Cornish Celts but the moor has many associations with King Arthur, legendary tribal chieftain of the Dark Ages. Some scholars believe that the present town of Camelford was King Arthur's Camelot and it was the waters of Dozmary Pool that closed over the sword Excalibur.

In medieval times small chapels were built on selected sites on the moor, while an expansion of trade stimulated the tinners who were given their own charter by King John in 1201. But it was the discovery of copper in 1837 that significantly changed the character of the moor; railways, chimneys and engine houses were built and shanty towns sprang up. However, well before the end of the century cheap imported copper caused the collapse of the industry and, although an expansion of china clay mining partially filled the vacuum, most developments were further west than Bodmin.

Today we find Bodmin Moor to be a wide tract of high open country, characterised by extensive outcropping of the underlying granite, part of a chain stretching from Dartmoor to the Isles of Scilly. Few fences restrict the grazing of sheep and ponies but remains of the traditional Cornish enclosures, constructed of granite boulders and turf and now covered with a thick tangle of blackberry and honeysuckle, abound on the lower ground. With little or no change in agricultural useage of the moor for thousands of years the results of man's labours remain undisturbed. Thus ancient trackways, tumuli, hut circles, tombs and standing stones are liberally sprinkled throughout the moor and add greatly to its enchantment.

The best way to explore Bodmin Moor in a one day expedition is to tackle a north-south crossing, taking in the highest and most extensive of the granite tors. I found delight in every step of this walk; not only is it packed with interest but, being in the warm southwest of the country, its atmosphere is subtly different from my usual stamping ground in the Northern Pennines.

From Camelford a narrow, tree-lined lane runs straight as an arrow towards Rough Tor, stopping at a small brook under the north facing slopes of the tor. Just off the path, on the right-hand side, a stone monument marks the spot where Charlotte Dymond was murdered by her crippled lover, Mathew Weeks, in 1844. Both are immortalised by Charles Causley's touching ballad on the tragedy. Beyond the monument rise, huge and startlingly white, spoil heaps from the Stannon china clay works.

Rough Tor is a group of three massive granite outcrops, each eroded to give rounded plate-like formations. The crystals of Cornish granite are large and this gives the boulders a wonderfully coarse texture. Harder stones, rolling in hollows in the rock, have produced scoops and pockets which, on my visit, were full of rain water. A plaque on the highest tor records that Rough Tor was given to the nation in commemoration of those men from the 43rd Wessex Division who died in the war. The summit also contains the foundations of a medieval chapel dedicated to St Michael. Rough Tor is now owned by the National Trust.

Brown Willy, 1,377ft/420m, is the highest point on the moor and it rises only a mile away across a shallow valley. It is a long wedge-shaped hill, but its granite tors are less pronounced than those on Rough Tor and it is a less attractive summit. However, the surrounding area of marshes and barren moorland is very wild and has been declared an SSSI.

Descend Brown Willy on the east side and cross the plain which is grazed by semi-wild ponies and Highland cattle, ford the infant river Fowey, beside which there are some old spoil heaps, and ascend Leskernick Hill. This hill is strewn with granite boulders and you pass several distinct stone circles and standing stones.

Maps O.S. 1:50,000 Sheets 200 and 201.
Grading A long walk over high and exposed moorlands. In places the going is very rough and in wet weather it can be boggy. Route finding would be difficult in mist.
Start / Finish Camelford (106837); Minions (261712).
Distance / Time 16 miles/8 hours.
Escape Routes The walk may be terminated at Jamaica Inn on the A30 or at Tressellern Farm.
Telephones Camelford, Five Lanes, Jamaica Inn, Trebartha, Henwood and Minions.
Transport Express bus service Bude to Newquay passes through Camelford. Infrequent bus service from Minions to Liskeard but a regular service from Upton Cross to Liskeard. Train from Liskeard to Bodmin, thence bus back to the start at Camelford.
Accommodation Hotels/Guest Houses at Camelford. Youth Hostel at Tintagel.
Guidebooks 'The Moors of the South West' by Shirley Toulson (Hutchinson); 'Discovering Bodmin Moor' by E. V. Thompson (Bossiney Books); 'Bodmin Moor' by E. C. Axford (David and Charles); 'Cornwall's Structure and Scenery' by R. M. Barton (Tor Mark Press); 'Vanishing Cornwall' by Daphne du Maurier (Gollancz).

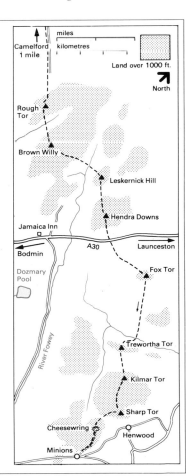

Rough Tor on the north side of Bodmin Moor.

Kilmar Tor.

grounds of the Water Works. Ahead rises the long escarpment of Trewortha Tor and the slopes are extremely rough. You must fight your way through deep bracken, heather, bilberries, brambles, gorse and a chaos of fallen granite blocks. But the effort is worthwhile for the tor is spectacular with many weird and wonderful granite structures including, on the westernmost block, a deep, smooth, cradle-like depression with an additional head-shaped hollow at one end, known as King Arthur's Bed.

The next high-point is Kilmar Tor on Twelve Men's Moor, so named because in the thirteenth century twelve men negotiated grazing rights on the moor. Again, the rocks of the tor are crazily stacked and they are higher and more extensive than any others on the walk.

South of Kilmar Tor a low embankment runs across the moor in an east-west direction. This is an old railway, built in the 1840s for the transport of copper ore, and the granite sleepers can still be seen buried in the heather.

Sharp Tor is a prominent cluster of rocks above the village of Henwood. It is an excellent view-point for eastern Cornwall and, on a clear day, the sea can be seen both to north and south.

Continue over Hendra Downs, where a huge rounded boulder has earned the nickname of the Elephant Rock, and descend to the busy A30 trunk road near Webbs Down. A mile up the road you can see the collection of buildings at Jamaica Inn, made famous by Daphne du Maurier's historical novel of that name.

A good track leads round the north side of Halvana plantation and then an easy ascent lands you amongst the rocks of Fox Tor. The view south from Fox Tor is one of the finest on the whole moor: in the distance the turreted outline of Trewortha Tor and Kilmar Tor emphasises the wild nature of the surroundings, while closer at hand two tumuli and a circle of nine standing stones emerge from the heather.

Cross the road that leads to Tressellern farm and walk through the

Take the path that bypasses Sharptor village and climb steeply to Stowe's Hill. The arrangement of boulders on the summit has been identified as an Iron Age hill fort, but the most spectacular feature is the extraordinary rock on the south side called the Cheesewring. A pile of disc-like boulders are precariously balanced on the edge of a quarry. The name derives from a cider press, the apple pulp being called cheese. The Cheesewring has been a popular curiosity for hundreds of years and the top stone is said to rotate three times when it hears the cock crow.

A broad track now leads to the old mining village of Minions; Bodmin Moor has been crossed and you are left with lasting memories of this romantic, beautiful and long-forgotten corner of England.

Looking north-west from Brown Willy to Rough Tor.

The view east from Nant y Coed, south of Carnedd y Filiast, across Cwm Hesgyn to Graig Ddu.

John Gillham

THE EASTERN MIGNEINT

It had rained ceaselessly for four days, and the last ribbons of snow high up in the Trinity gullies of Yr Wyddfa had melted into the white-capped waters of Glaslyn. The hotel bars were steamy and bright with tinsel and the farmers were undismayed; after all the sheep were down in the valley and the winter was passing nicely. Tomorrow was the shortest day and spring would lie ahead.

But this was little comfort to me, stuck fuming in Helyg, while gales swept down the pass. My dreams of a crisp traverse of the Snowdon horseshoe in bright winter sunshine were in ruins.

Years ago on boisterous club meets the cry would go up on rainy days, 'Soap Gut, it's just the weather for Soap Gut'. Off we'd all go to spend a happy day slithering and thrutching up the slimy runnel that collects much of the water coursing down Tryfan's Milestone Buttress. This reminded me of Harold Drasdo's comment on the Migneint in *Classic Walks*, 'A first crossing ought really to be made by compass in thick mist', he then goes on to describe his feelings of elation when a fence looms up out of the driving rain, breaking the monotony of the featureless, sodden moor.

My mind was made up, come rain or storm it would be the lonely hills of the Eastern Migneint the very next day.

At seven-thirty in the morning only a faint glimmer of light was emerging through the ragged grey clouds, which were racing across the sky, driven by a stiff wind. The inhabitants of Ysbyty Ifan were still asleep, oblivious to the turbulent river Conwy, roaring under the bridge in the centre of the village.

Miraculously the rain was holding off and I made speed up the narrow lane which runs south past a chapel and a row of terraced cottages, before breaking out onto the wind-swept moor. The huge massif of Carnedd y Filiast, 2,194ft/669m, which is the principal summit of the Eastern Migneint, rose dark and brooding to the south, silvery rivulets of water running down its every seam and fold. Clouds were brushing Arenig Fach, six miles to the south-east; the day could go either way, I crossed my fingers and pressed on.

The lane soon gave way to a rough cart-track which leads to Cefn

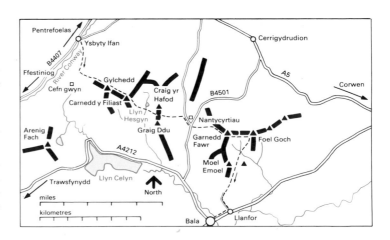

[165]

The north-western slopes of Gylchedd.

gwyn, a deserted cottage surrounded by a cluster of trees. Leaving the track half-a-mile before Cefn gwyn I managed to cross the head waters of the Nant Adwy'r-Llan at a place where it spread out into a broad bed of reeds. Clumps of reeds made inefficient stepping-stones across the oily water but I reached firmer ground at the expense, only, of wet feet.

Saturated hillsides of reeds and peat hags are meat and drink to wild walkers and the Migneint provides the largest area of this type of ground in Wales. Ecologically it is extremely important and it has

Maps O.S. 1:50,000 Sheets 116 and 125; O.S. 1:63,360 Tourist Map 'Snowdonia'; O.S. 1:25,000 Outdoor Leisure Map – 'Snowdonia (Harlech and Bala)'.
Grading A rather boggy walk over rough, featureless and rounded hills.
Start / Finish Ysbyty Ifan (842489); Bala (927361).
Distance / Time 17 miles/8 hours.
Escape Routes Easy slopes descend S from Gylchedd to Llyn Celyn. The route crosses the Bala – Cerrigydrudion road at Nantycyrtiau.
Telephones Ysbyty Ifan, Nantycyrtiau, Llanfor and Bala.
Transport Railway Station at Betws-y-Coed. Express buses Holyhead – London run along the A5 to Pentrefoelas. Weekday bus service Bala – Corwen.
Accommodation Hotels/Guest Houses at Pentrefoelas, Cerrigydrudion and Bala. Youth Hostels at Plas Rhiwaedog (Bala) and Cynwyd (Corwen).
Guidebooks 'The Summits of Snowdonia' by Terry Marsh (Hale); 'On Foot in North Wales and the Peak' by Patrick Monkhouse (Diadem).

been acquired by the National Trust and designated a Grade 1 SSSI by the Nature Conservancy.

Connoisseurs of the Northern Pennines will enjoy themselves hugely on the Migneint because the terrain is very similar. Heavy erosion has produced peat hags and pools of black water, while its acid nature has encouraged mat-grass, moor-grass, cotton-grass and deer's-hair sedge.

The ascent to the plateau of Gylchedd is easy, if wet, and it is not until just below Bryn Cerbyd, 1,895ft/578m, that some outcropping occurs giving better drainage and some shelter. Here the grass is green and cropped and cross-leaved heather gives way to bell-heather.

Rising ground continued to a cairn on Llechwedd-llyfn where the cloak of cloud enveloped me. The gale-force wind was rippling and flattening the coarse grass and hurling drops of sleety-rain against my head. With hood up I proceeded east on a compass bearing towards Carnedd y Filiast while wreaths of mist swirled around giving occasional views south to Llyn Celyn.

I squelched across the moor, a fence leading me in a little over a mile to the considerable summit of Carnedd y Filiast where rocks have again protruded through the peat. Loose stones have been used to construct a wind shelter and a large cairn, bearing a slab of black slate with the letters TI inscribed on one side and CD on the other.

Descending Carnedd y Filiast to the east, down exhausting slopes of knee-deep heather, I passed some old spoil heaps and then emerged beneath the mist into Cwm Hesgyn. Llyn Hesgyn lay below, beautifully situated amongst the hills, three miles up the deserted cwm from the Llyn Celyn dam. A buzzard was perched on a branch of an ancient rowan which overhung the outflowing stream of the lake, and he allowed me to approach within a few yards before soaring lazily away.

Unfortunately the weather had now closed in, and curtains of rain swept me over the pass between Craig yr Hafod and Craig Ddu and down to the road near Ffridd yr Hafod farm. With conditions deteriorating by the minute I turned for home up the lonely road to Tyn-y-rhos, Pentrefoelas and Ysbyty Ifan.

The view across Llyn Celyn to Arenig Fawr from the slopes of Foel-boeth, the southern outlier of Carnedd y Filiast.

Ten wet miles later I was back at the car, changing my clothes in the snug bus-shelter of sleepy Ysbyty Ifan. A palatial establishment seeing that Crosville runs only one bus per week to the village.

Nearly three months passed before I returned to complete the natural extension to the East Migneint traverse. The landscape was still wintry with streaks of snow on the hills and a chill wind blowing; the first lambs were in the fields but a buzzard hovered expectantly overhead.

Fifty metres south of the road junction at Nantycyrtiau, a public footpath sign indicates a farm track which runs through the meadows to the deserted house of Creigwen. Above is open hillside with easy slopes rising to a fence junction and cairn on the summit of Garnedd Fawr.

Garnedd Fawr gives surprisingly good views south to the long line of the Berwyns and Arans, north to Mwdwl-eithin and the Brenig reservoir and west to Carnedd y Filiast and the Arenigs.

Foel Goch, 2,004ft/611m is one mile's easy walk eastwards with stone boundary markers and a fence to follow most of the way. Its lonely summit carries a stone cairn, an OS trig. point and an ancient boundary stone.

The walk could be extended eastwards for another couple of miles but, by now, the tea-rooms of Bala will be beckoning. Descend easy slopes south, ford the Nant Cefn-coch and cross the col between the rounded humps of Moel Emoel and Garw Fynydd. Lanes now lead easily down to the valley of the Dee at Llanfor, half-a-mile east of Bala.

The extensive panorama to the south-west from the summit of Carnedd y Filiast. Arenig Fawr and Arenig Fach are the distant peaks.

MWDWL-EITHIN AND THE DENBIGH MOORS

Map O.S. 1:50,000 Sheet 116.
Grading A surprisingly tough walk through deep heather and across trackless moors.
Start / Finish Cerrigydrudion (953488); Llansannan (933658).
Distance / Time 16 miles/7-8 hours.
Escape Routes The walk may be terminated after crossing Mwdwl-eithin, at the A543, 4 miles north of Pentrefoelas.
Telephones Cerrigydrudion, The Sportsman's Arms and Llansannan.
Transport No local transport to Cerrigydrudion although National Express buses London – Holyhead run along the adjacent A5. Daily bus service (not Sun) Llansannan to Denbigh, Abergele and Rhyl.
Accommodation Hotels/B & B in Cerrigydrudion and Llansannan. Youth Hostels at Cynwyd near Corwen, Oaklands near Betws-y-Coed and Maeshafn.

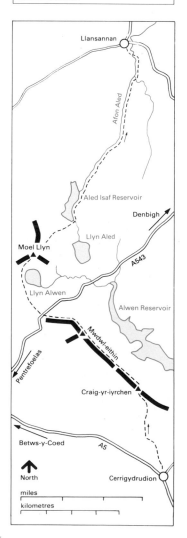

The Clwyd village of Cerrigydrudion stands well back from the A5 and at 8 a.m. nothing stirred. I walked north across fields and along lanes and tracks, passing white-washed farmhouses with slate roofs, where cats lay winking on window sills enjoying the warmth of the sun. It was early October and, in contrast to the persistent rain of previous months, the long awaited Indian summer was breaking records throughout Britain.

Half-a-mile beyond Ty'n-y-gilfach, I left the track and made my way through burnished bracken and then up slopes of cropped grass, where rabbits scurried into their burrows, to reach the rock out-crops and cairns on Craig-yr-iyrchen.

To the east and north the great forests of Clocaenog and Mynydd Hiraethog stretched away monotonously into the distance, although I was relieved to see the familiar bare outline of Moel Fammau and the Clwydian hills rising beyond Ruthin. The eastern part of the Denbigh moors have suffered terribly at the hands of twentieth-century man; the hills have been cloaked in conifers and the valleys dammed and flooded. Thus I turned away west to Mwdwl-eithin and the wild moors beyond the A543 Pentrefoelas-Denbigh road, which are still untouched by the plough.

The ridge leading to the 1,742ft/532m summit of Mwdwl-eithin provides tough walking. In places the heather is nearly waist deep and the rough, bouldery ground discourages even the hardiest sheep, with the result that no meandering trods exist to aid progress. One of the few features above the blanket of heather is a slate boundary stone carrying the inscription Hiraethog Garrec Lwyd. But the open position is invigorating and the views magnificent. As you walk west the wall of the Snowdonia mountains forms an impressive backcloth: Snowdon, Moel Siabod, the Glyders, Tryfan and the Carneddau. South, across the A5, rise Carnedd y Filiast in the Eastern Migneint and the distant Arans. North, beyond the blue water of the Alwen reservoir, the gaunt, derelict shooting lodge of Gwylfa Hiraethog is the only feature on a barren landscape. Perched at the focal point of the walk I found this ghostly ruin unnerving; it always seemed to be watching me, like an evil eye. Even at the end of the day, as I descended the lush valley of the Afon Aled, I glanced back and was shaken to discover I was still in its gaze. The lodge dates from 1908 and at 1,627ft/495m above sea-level it was said to be the highest inhabited house in Wales. Certainly it had the finest view, for on a clear day the occupants could see the Isle of Man, the mountains of Mourne and the Galloway hills. Estate game-keepers lived in the house after it was sold by Lord Devonport in 1925, but since the 1950s it has been derelict.

The exposed summit of Mwdwl-eithin carries a large cairn of rough boulders, a stone shelter and an incongruous OS pillar. Although toy cars and lorries can be seen moving at snail's pace along the A5 away to the south, Mwdwl-eithin is a solitary and proud peak, sufficiently high – thank goodness – to have avoided the ravages of development. No vestige of a path leads to the summit cairn and no boot marks or sweet papers destroy its dignity.

A winter view of the Snowdonia mountains from the

The Denbigh Moors from Mwdwl-eithin with the de

th-eastern end of the Mwdwl-eithin near Cerrigydrudion. The main mountain groups in view are Snowdon (left), Moel Siabod, the Glyders and Tryfan.

hooting lodge, Gwylfa Hiraethog, prominent on the horizon.

On the Denbigh Moors – looking west to a storm-shrouded Snowdonia.

A mile of tussocky grass slopes led me down to the A543 just north of Bwlch Gwyn, but here I made a ghastly error of judgement. In making straight for Llyn Alwen I stumbled into an extensive area of saturated bog. The few clumps of coarse grass provided insufficient support and, having passed the point of no return, I struggled, not only against the elements, but against mounting panic. It was quite the worst stretch of ground that I met, whilst walking many hundreds of tough miles in the preparation of this book. As an added twist of fate, in the middle of the bog, on the largest tussock, lay an adder coiled up and seemingly fast asleep.

By far the best way to reach Llyn Alwen is to keep to the high ground on Pen yr Orsedd and follow the track round to the west side of the lake. Llyn Alwen is beautifully situated in a fold in the hills, and a deserted cottage and boathouse of grey stone on the northern shore add to its charm. As I walked up Moel Llyn, which overlooks the lake, I could see a heron standing motionless in the reeds beside the exit stream.

The peat moors continue over Moel y Gaseg-wen, which is a good viewpoint for the Alwen reservoir, looking like a miniature Kielder in its setting of conifers, and for Llyn Aled where sailing boats were enjoying the freshening wind.

I crossed the bridge at the south end of the Aled Isaf reservoir and followed the access road to the dam at the north end. The reservoir was full to the brim and the waves were spilling over the parapet and cascading down to the gorge below. The main exit stream emerges from a tunnel below the dam and, running through the rocky gorge, becomes the Afon Aled.

The valley of the Afon Aled runs for nearly five miles to the village of Llansannan. It is a deep valley with steep sides which are precipitous in the upper reaches and, throughout its length, it is well

wooded. A plantation of lodge pole pine clothes the central section, but otherwise there is a healthy growth of deciduous trees.

The valley is one of the gems of the Principality, and it is seen to its best advantage when approaching from the bleak moorlands on the south side.

Except in the vicinity of Llansannan there are no paths beside the river and it is necessary to keep to the open, heather slopes above the tree level. Even this route has its problems because, half-a-mile down from the reservoir dam, a tributary stream, coming in from the east, has cut deeply into the hillside forming a ravine, which can only be crossed at the top.

Nevertheless, I found the walk down the valley to be sheer delight. Autumn was early and the leaves were already turning, the bracken was a deep russet and the bilberry leaves brown and curling; yet in sheltered south facing nooks the gorse was still brilliantly yellow.

At the white farmhouse of Bryn a footpath leads down the valley-side to meet a narrow lane. In the afternoon sunshine I dawdled along the muddy track between hedges of hazel and holly, with a profusion of red rose hips and haws, gorging myself with blackberries.

Just before the bridge at Pont y Nant is reached, a gate gives access to a path which passes a ruined cottage, crosses a tributary stream by a foot-bridge and meets the Llansannan path in an oak wood.

The last mile of the walk follows the eastern bank of the Afon Aled under a canopy of oaks, beeches and alders. With the sun streaming through the branches and glancing off the lively water, the scene was perfection. I could only have been in Wales.

Right: The head of the Aled Valley, just below the reservoir.

Inset right: The view north down the Aled Valley.

The view east from Moel Wnion to Aber Falls and the northern spur of Llwytmor.

THE ABER FALLS AND THE NORTHERN CARNEDDAU

Few visitors to Snowdonia make their way into the Carneddau; the easy pickings of Cwm Idwal and Cwm Dyli are preferred to the steep and rough approach to Pen yr Ole-Wen or Pen yr Helgi Du. Yet the spacious plateaus, broad ridges, boulder fields, crags and deep cwms of the Carneddau provide, perhaps, the best walking in Wales.

Five peaks in the central Carneddau are classed as separate three-thousanders and receive some attention from Munro baggers, while discerning rock climbers plod up to Craig yr Ysfa to tackle magnificent routes such as Amphitheatre Buttress, Great Gully, Mur-y-Niwl and Pinnacle Wall. Apart from these intrusions the hills are mostly deserted.

However, the northern Carneddau, overlooking Conwy Bay and the Menai Straights, is an area of wild and desolate hill country which can provide a varied and fascinating expedition. These hills form a perfect horseshoe surrounding the head-waters of the Afon Anafon and Afon Goch which meet at Bont Newydd near Aber; thus they are easily accessible from the A85 coast road.

From the car-park at Bont Newydd a path runs along the east side of the sparkling Afon Rhaeadr-fawr to the Aber Falls. The path passes through woods of oak, hazel, alder, willow, ash and birch; probably remnants of the original native forest which covered much of Wales in ancient times. It is a reflection on the dearth of native deciduous

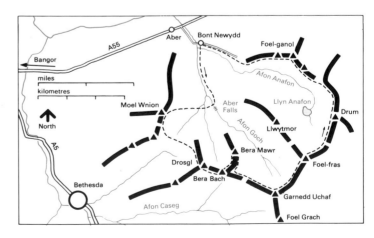

woodlands in Britain that I found it a rare and stimulating experience to walk in summer through these majestic trees, smelling the sap, feeling the texture of the bark and delighting at the shapes and shades of the leaves.

Beyond the woods the river has cut deeply into the Carneddau massif until, on meeting the hard, igneous granophyre of Bera Mawr, it has formed a spectacular waterfall, the Aber Falls (Rhaeadr-fawr). In a series of dramatic leaps, the river plunges 150ft down the rocks in a cascade of white foam. The lower reaches of the Aber valley, up to and including the falls, have been declared a National Nature Reserve and are managed by the Nature Conservancy Council. Above the falls the hills are owned by the National Trust, ensuring this entire area of exceptional scenic quality will be preserved for posterity.

Cross the river at the base of the falls and make for the rounded hump of Moel Wnion, a mile to the west. A path leads as far as the smaller cascade, Rhaeadr-bach, but then you must make your own way up the inexorably steep slopes that lead to the summit plateau of Moel Wnion. The ascent is a big pull from sea-level but it is not without interest. Scabious grows on the valley floor, while higher up the grass is dotted with bedstraw and stonecrop. In late July the heather was in bloom and the bilberries were succulent.

I found that the view from the low stone-built OS pillar on Moel Wnion at 1,902ft/580m extended from the thrusting headland of the Great Orme, across Conwy Bay, Puffin Island and Anglesey to the hills of the Lleyn peninsula. Inland, Y Garn, the Glyders and the distant cone of Yr Wyddfa were outlined against a grey sky. The close proximity of mountains, islands and sea reminded me vividly of the Western Highlands.

Fine open walking leads south to Drosgl, another rounded hill strewn with rough, grey boulders. The pile of stones on the summit is a Bronze Age burial mound, similar to those found on Moel Wnion and Drum. Looking south, beyond Yr Elen, a dramatic view is obtained into Cwm Llafar, ringed by the great circle of cliffs, Ysgolion Duon – the Black Ladders.

Two extraordinary hills lie ahead, Bera Mawr and Bera Bach, turrets of coarse-grained rock splinters piled at crazy angles and reminiscent of Castell y Gwynt on the Glyders. The translation is Great and Little Hayricks, notwithstanding the fact that Bera Bach is the higher of the two.

Marion Teal

Aber Falls.

John Gillham

Steve Ashton

Llyn Anafon and Foel-ganol seen from Foel-fras.

The view from Drum to Foel-fras.

This is wild and rugged country: no paths link the peaks, there is no sign of man, no litter, not even any scuffing of lichen on the boulders, a sure sign of the passage of heavy boots.

Ravens croaked and the wind sighed around Yr Aryg, the rocky outlier of Garnedd Uchaf which lies on the main spine of the Carneddau. But, beyond the summit, a line of cairns and a worn track run down from Carnedd Llewelyn and Foel Grach, leading north to Foel-fras, 3,091ft/942m, the final peak of the Welsh three-thousanders circuit. Foel-fras is the scene of many jubilant reunions with friends and support parties after the gruelling mountain traverse. It is easy to imagine Esme Firbank limping through the white mist to complete the circuit in the astonishing time of 9 hours 29 minutes in the 1930s, evocatively described by Thomas Firbank in *I*

Bought a Mountain.

The cairn on Foel-fras stands beside a magnificently constructed dry-stone wall. In spite of the height and constant buffeting from the elements, this wall is as firm now as the day it was built and I have seen no finer in the hills of Britain.

A gradual descent of easy, grassy slopes round the head of Llyn Anafon leads to Drum where a large stone wind-break has been built. The barren wastes of the high Carneddau plateau have now been left behind and a series of shapely hills with delightful sharp ridges curve north, above the valley of the Afon Anafon, to Foel-ganol. The walking has almost downland quality and the situation is ethereal.

It was mid-afternoon and the tide was out exposing miles of flats

The main Carnedd summits seen from Garnedd Uchaf – (left to right) Carnedds Llewelyn and Daffydd and Yr Elen.

and sandbars in Conwy Bay. From our perch in the hills it looked nearly possible to walk dryshod over the Lavan Sands from Llanfair-fechan to Beaumaris on Anglesey.

We sat on the summit rocks of Foel-ganol, identifying the Iron Age hill fort on Maes-yr-Gaer above Bont Newydd, ancient hut circles and field systems in the Anafon valley and the Roman Road over Bwlch y Ddeufaen. A peregrine glided past the eroded cliffs which fall away on the south side of the ridge, and then made off across the valley towards Llwytmor. We watched it until it became a mere speck in the sky and then we scrambled down the loose west ridge of Foel-ganol. This leads to a narrow lane set between high hedges tangled with brambles, wild raspberries and honeysuckle; one mile's easy stroll to Bont Newydd.

Maps *O.S. 1:50,000 Sheet 115; O.S. 1:63,360 Tourist Map 'Snowdonia'; O.S. 1:25,000 Outdoor Leisure Maps – 'Snowdonia (Snowdon) and Snowdonia (Conwy Valley)'.*
Grading *An easy mountain walk over flattish hills. Route-finding problematical in mist.*
Start / Finish *Bont Newydd (662720).*
Distance / Time *13 miles/6-7 hours.*
Escape Routes *Descend W from Garnedd Uchaf to Bethesda via the Afon Caseg valley. From Drum a descent W leads to Llyn Anafon and a rough road back to Bont Newydd.*
Telephones *Aber and Bethesda.*
Transport *Railway Station at Llanfairfechan on the Bangor to Llandudno Junction line. Regular bus service Conwy to Bangor passes through Aber.*
Accommodation *Hotels/Guest Houses abound in Bangor, Conwy, Llanfairfechan and Penmaenmawr. Youth Hostels at Bangor, Penmaenmawr, Roewen and Idwal Cottage.*
Guidebooks *'Hill Walking in Snowdonia' by E. G. Rowland (Cicerone); 'The Mountains of Snowdonia' by H. R. C. Carr and G. A. Lister (Crosby Lockwood); 'The Summits of Snowdonia' by T. Marsh (Hale); 'Snowdonia National Park Guide' (H.M.S.O.); 'The Welsh Peaks' by W. A. Poucher (Constable); 'The High Mountains of Britain and Ireland' by Irvine Butterfield (Diadem).*

WALKS IN THE LLEYN PENINSULA: THE RIVALS AND MYNEDD MAWR

by ROGER REDFERN

The several lovely hill groups of the Lleyn peninsula are best seen from the golden shores of Cardigan Bay, between Barmouth and Harlech. From those summer beaches I first knew the cones and dips of these lesser uplands, far across the sea to the north and north-west. In certain lighting conditions Bardsey appeared to float above the Irish Sea, a common mirage effect here at the very tip of Lleyn.

Another good viewpoint for these hills is Anglesey's western sea-board. From Llanddwyn Island you look due south for ten miles across Caernarfon Bay to the precipitous, sea-facing profiles of The Rivals, Lleyn's most dramatic heights. To see The Rivals at close quarters Trevor, twelve miles down the Pwllheli road from Caernarfon, makes a good starting point if you have a good head for heights. The great granite quarry that lies high above the sea on this northern flank of the lowest hill, 1,458ft/444m, dominates Trevor and a path leads above the pebble beach below it, towards the point where the great hillsides press out over the waves. To traverse successfully around this bold prow, Trwyn y Gorlech, you must climb to five or six hundred feet above sea-level, making progress across steep turf and short cliffs (easiest in dry weather). There are some fine situations and one gets the feeling of real exploration because there is no continuous path, a pleasant change from the average coastal walk nowadays.

Quite suddenly the angle eases and you come down crumpled, bracken-covered slopes at the mouth of the hidden valley of Nant Gwrtheyrn. Ruined piers and other relics of quarrying litter the quiet shore below the village of Porth y Nant. This place lay empty when

the last family left twenty years ago but now the attractive square of terraced houses are being restored for use by students of the Welsh language. By following the recently realigned track which zig-zags up through conifers, you escape from this narrow defile, and near the top there are superb vistas over the sea to Anglesey. At 900ft a stony track leads northwards towards Bwlch yr Eifl; to the east as you go rise the broad, heather slopes leading to the highest summit at 1,849ft/564m and an easy angled walk takes you to its remarkable viewpoint. It is at a modest altitude but commands most of Lleyn and the seas around it. On a really clear day you will see much of westernmost Snowdonia, the mountains of the Harlech Dome beyond Cardigan Bay, the hills of Anglesey and, maybe, a suggestion of Irish peaks.

Just half-a-mile away to the east of the summit is the top of Tre'r Ceiri, the prize of Yr Eifl and, literally, 'Town of the Giants'. Upon this second hill of the range the hardy Ordovices built their fortification during the centuries of Roman occupation. If you choose to go that way don't miss the small hut circles below the top, and the well built protective rampart in the heather. The Ordovician cattle, sheep and goats grazed the lower slopes and were driven up above the rampart when invasion threatened. It is good to notice the lack of interference by modern man; I hope it will remain so.

From Tre'r Ceiri's cairn, 1,591ft/484m, it is best to traverse towards the north-west, under the highest summit, to Bwlch yr Eifl and go up to the well-chiselled top of the lowest Rival. Here you will see just how close the sea is on the far (western) side, and you will appreciate just how much of this hill was quarried away by the Penmaenmawr and North Wales Granite Company before it ceased operations years ago. There is a way down a steep gully on the northern side which allows you to regain the beach on the return to Trevor; its descent, though, is not easy and a more certain way down is to follow the steep incline of the quarry tramway, which drops to the edge of the village. A third alternative is to take a little path which traverses eastwards below Bwlch yr Eifl to the high-hedged lane connecting Llanaelhaearn and Trevor.

There are other worthy hills on Lleyn, like the square shaped group north-east of Yr Eifl and seen so well from the latter's summits. Their highest top rises craggily to 1,712ft/521m overlooking the main road near Trevor. Then there is Mynydd Rhiw far down the peninsula, a fairly conical hill one foot short of 1,000ft and commanding the broad sweep of beach called Porth Neigwl. At the northern end of this solitary hill are the remains of a stone axe factory.

To get a near view of Bardsey Island you must reach the bare hills of Lleyn's very tip. These last two peninsular hills swing round to the west of Aberdaron.

At a little crossroads half-a-mile west of Aberdaron, walk north-west along a lane to Anelog. At a right bend beyond a cottage go ahead through a gate leading to a farm where varied breeds of poultry range freely. Turn up west towards the sea. At the highest

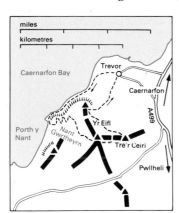

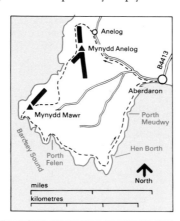

Map O.S. 1:50,000 Sheet 123.
Grading Easy, if steep, walking. A head for heights is an asset for the traverse above the sea between Trevor and Porth y Nant.
Start / Finish The Rivals – Trevor (373468). Mynydd Mawr – Aberdaron (172265).
Distance / Time The Rivals, 6 miles/4 hours; Mynydd Mawr, 8 miles/4 hours.
Telephones Trevor, Llithfaen, Llanaelhaearn and Aberdaron.
Transport Railway Station at Pwllheli. Daily bus services (not Sun) Pwllheli – Trevor – Caernarfon and Pwllheli – Aberdaron.
Accommodation Hotels/Guest Houses at Pwllheli, Aberdaron and Trevor. No Youth Hostels on Lleyn.
Guidebooks 'Exploring Wales' by William Condry (Faber and Faber); 'Walks in Wales' by R. Jones (Hale); 'Rambles in North Wales' by Roger Redfern (Hale).

Looking towards The Rivals from the beach north of Trevor.

Tre'r Ceiri, the eastern Rivals top, provides a splendid vantage point for views across the A499 to Gurn Ddu and Gurn Goch.

The steep slopes of Trywyn y Gorlech provide the most dramatic approach to The Rivals.

Descending Yr Eifl on the return to the granite quarry of the northern top.

The Lleyn coastline at Bardsey Sound seen from the slopes of Mynyedd Mawr.

point turn south up the spine of hill to the summit of Mynydd Anelog, 628ft/191m. There are broad views back to the north-east to the conspicuous Rivals and the open sea.

At the summit of Mynydd Anelog is one of the best low-level views in Wales: to the south-east across pastures to Aberdaron and its bay, and to the south-west into Porth Llanllawen and the cliffs of Mynydd Mawr, with Bardsey beyond. The rolling pastureland of Uwchmynydd is for all the world a piece of western Ireland moved here to western Wales, dotted with white cottages and criss-crossed by rough stone walls.

The route now is to make down towards the sea at Porth Llanllawen, keeping at the edge of the cliffs where the fields end and bracken slopes go down to the shoreline. Where you are forced down to a rocky creek (almost at sea-level), go up the shallow valley with your back to the sea. There is a stile below a tiny, white cottage. Cross a pasture field to another stile, a little left of the overhead electricity line, and turn right onto a farm track. Turn left at the first gate to join a minor road, turning right along this to its official end above the sea.

Follow the concrete track which winds to the top of Mynydd Mawr (National Trust property) where there is a coastguard look-out post.

From here you will enjoy fine views of Bardsey, two miles away to the south-west.

Now follow on round the cliffs, looking for the ancient well and chapel remains not far above the waves. Bardsey is 'the island in the current' where 20,000 saints are said to be buried; three visits to the island equalled one to Rome.

Eventually the inlet of Porth Felen is reached and, at its very head, is a wooden stile giving access to the grassland above the continuing cliff-top. Soon a double fence bars the way ahead, crossing right to the edge of the cliffs. Just before reaching it turn up left and use a galvanised steel gate as a stile into a grassy lane, soon passing two white holiday cottages. These, with the farms under Mynydd Mawr, are the westernmost dwellings of the North Wales mainland. Just after the second cottage turn right at the junction, and this track gives access to the continuing cliff-top path above Hen Borth and Porth y Pistyll. Brambles tend to hinder progress here and there, with a drop into the valley of Porth Meudwy. The path comes to a kissing gate on the lane west of Aberdaron. Turn left for a very short distance to the starting point.

MOEL SIABOD AND MOEL MEIRCH

by SHOWELL STYLES

There are alternative routes up Moel Siabod from Capel Curig but the best and most scenic way is by the East Ridge. For this the best start is from Pont Cyfyng from where there is a rough bridle-path up the lower slopes to below the end of the North East Ridge. A rather easier alternative route of ascent starts here, but the way to the East Ridge bears left and runs almost level above the shore of a small lake, more steeply up on the left of a flooded quarry-hole, and into the marshy cwm that holds Llyn y Foel. Here you see the East Ridge straight ahead, mounting to the summit.

Rounding the lake by a little path above its western shore, you strike up the rough slopes southward to a well-marked notch on the ridge (seen in the photograph opposite) where a bouldery scramble lands you on the rocky crest. Six or seven hundred feet of energetic clambering, nowhere hard, brings you up to the grand crags of the summit after a climb taking between two to three hours from Capel Curig.

This is the highest point of the walk and a good place to examine the topography of the distant Carneddau. The peaks of the Snowdon Horseshoe also look particularly fine from this angle. The view between east and south opens a much wider prospect and in some ways a wilder one, for the infinity of hills and valleys stretching to the horizon holds quieter glens and little peaks which (if one isn't besotted on mere height) have plenty of interest for walker and scrambler. Rolling away to the south-west is a long uplifted wilderness of rock and heather and small lakes rising gradually to Moel Meirch, your next summit.

Descending due west at first and then keeping on down the rounded grassy crest, you are soon looking down on the lonely twin lakes, the Llynau Diwaunedd, hidden away below steep bluffs. The extensive moorlands that fall beyond them into the Lledr valley have been partly tamed by afforestation, but they still give a feeling of space and freedom. From the dip of the Diwaunedd lakes the way climbs over the craggy tops of Y Cribau and – still keeping on the crest with fine views of the Gwynant valley – descends to Bwlch Ehediad. Here you cross one of the oldest trackways in Snowdonia, linking Gwynant to Dolwyddelan, and begin to mount towards Moel Meirch, now some two miles away.

In fine clear weather the crest over Cerrig Cochion gives a long and interesting piece of detailed route-finding, general direction always south, over and round a diversity of rock bluffs and heathery hollows – hard going, and trackless. The summit of Moel Meirch, spiky and scenic, resembles Tryfan in having rock obelisks instead of a cairn, and its surrounding declivities are as wild and lonely as the Rhinogs. It needs just two more feet of height to make it a two-thousander. In mist and rain I would choose the less demanding route up the glen of the Afon Cwm Edno, reached by contouring south-east for half-a-mile from Bwlch Ehediad. Following the course

of the stream and continuing up the trough above, you come upon Llyn Edno cradled on the very crest of the ridge, and have to make almost a U-turn to head north-north-west for Moel Meirch summit, which is reached by a short scramble up heather and rock.

The path for descent starts from a notch in the sharp little ridge between the summit and the lake and at once heads down into the glen of the Afon Llynedno. The scenery here is Wales at its wildest. If you choose to stick close to the stream you will get some mild scrambling and see some fine little gorges and pools, but the higher and plainer path has romantic scenery too. It brings you to walls and stiles and onto the lane at the head of Nantmor.

Now the mountains are behind you but the next section of the route has a wildness and charm of its own. Turn left on the lane for 300 yards and take a waymarked path on the right.

This very small path winds up and down and round, with a stile or two, through hill scenery that has been given a curiously foreign air by the spread of Rhododendron Ponticum. When you have skirted the ancient walls of Hafod Owen, a lonely cottage where Menlove Edwards, most enigmatic of the great rock-climbers, lived for a time, you duck down through a tunnel of rhododendrons and out onto the hillsides above Llyn Dinas. With a final steep descent through a belt of primeval oakwoods the path emerges on the broader track

---

Maps O.S. 1:50,000 Sheet 115; O.S. 1:63,360 Tourist Map 'Snowdonia'; O.S. 1:25,000 Outdoor Leisure Map – 'Snowdonia (Snowdon)'.
Grading An airy and exhilarating walk across rough and rarely visited hills.
Start / Finish Capel Curig (722581); Beddgelert (590481).
Distance / Time 14 miles/7 hours.
Escape Routes Good paths lead down to Nantgwynant from Bwlch Ehediad and Hafodydd Brithion.
Telephones Capel Curig, Dyffryn Mymbyr, Pen-y-Gwryd, Bethania and Beddgelert.
Transport Railway Stations at Bangor and Betws-y-Coed. Bus service Caernarfon – Beddgelert (not Sun). Sherpa bus service (Mon to Sat, May to Sept only) Betws-y-Coed – Capel Curig – Beddgelert. Sunday service stops at Capel Curig.
Accommodation Hotels at Capel Curig, Pen-y-Gwryd and Beddgelert. B & B locally. Youth Hostels at Capel Curig, Llanberis, Snowdon Ranger, Bryn Gwynant and Pen-y-Pass.
Guidebooks 'The Summits of Snowdonia' by Terry Marsh (Hale); 'On Foot in North Wales and the Peak' by Patrick Monkhouse (Diadem); 'The Welsh Peaks' by W. A. Poucher (Constable); 'Hill Walking in Snowdonia' by E. G. Rowland (Cicerone).

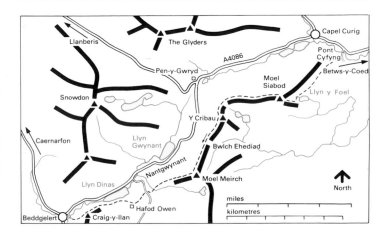

Left: Llyn y Foel and the East Ridge of Moel Siabod.

On the East Ridge of Moel Siabod with Llyn y Foel far below.

that skirts the lake, and turning left on this you come in half-a-mile to the lake's western end where the Glaslyn river issues to flow down to Beddgelert.

Here you have a choice of routes to finish the walk. For those who have had enough up-and-down there is the undemanding path that

follows the left bank of the Glaslyn downstream, with a stretch of lane-walking on the way, and reaches Beddgelert in about two miles. For the walker who wants to prolong his wild walking as far as possible, I commend the ridge-walk over Grib Ddu and Craig-y-llan. This does involve another thousand feet of ascent, but provides a better finish to a grand mountain day. To start it, take the rough path that mounts south-east from the lake's end, up a steep couloir of grass and heather. In the defile above you are again in wildest Wales, and at its upper end you reach a little pass, Bwlch Sygyn. Go right, on a faint but sufficient path, from the top of the pass, threading a way through picturesque rocks and down to the crest of a narrow ridge. Delightful walking along this, with magnificent views, takes you finally up a broader ridge to the top of Craig-y-llan whence you have a bird's eye view of Beddgelert village and the valleys of Glaslyn and Colwyn.

Craig-y-llan has precipitous defences on north and west and a direct descent won't do. A stone wall skirts below the summit on the north, and the key to the way down is a gate in this wall. The path winding down from it brings you right into the village, with no road-walking to spoil the finale.

The view north-east from the summit of Moel Siabod.

Looking north-west to the Glyders, Tryfan and the Carnedds from the summit of Moel Siabod.

ACROSS THE DOVEY FOREST

It is understandable that walkers who do not know the hills of Wales flock to the highest and most spectacular peaks of Snowdonia. But for those who appreciate lonely cwms, broad ridges, freedom from erosion and, above all, peace and solitude, the hills overlooking the Mawddach estuary are without rival. Of these hills I have covered Cader Idris, the Rhinogs, the Arans and Rhobell Fawr in *The Big Walks* and *Classic Walks*, and here I shall turn to the long line of hills marking the northern boundary of the Dovey Forest.

Dolgellau is the county town of Merioneth and was centre of the Gold Rush in 1862, but nowadays it is popular only with farmers, day trippers and charabancs. But the bustle is soon left behind by taking the path which crosses the long north-east ridge of Cader Idris, thence giving easy access to the Dovey Forest hills. At the end of the walk you can find accommodation in Dinas Mawddwy or Mallwyd, or perhaps hitch a lift back to Dolgellau. Sadly the bus service is almost non-existent.

As I walked up the narrow lane towards Tyddyn-Ednyfed at 8 a.m. a bright moon was still hanging over Dolgellau. The trees beside the Afon Aron were heavy with frost and the marshy meadows beside Bwlch-coch farm, where the tarmac ends, were hard as iron.

The path over the ridge to Bwlch Llyn Bach on the Machynlleth road is indistinct and I made my own way up towards the rocks of Gau Graig. Rounding the ridge at about the 1,000ft level I entered the eastern cwm of Gau Graig, which was looking exceptionally fine, with every gully and seam of the crags picked out by the slanting morning sunshine. Below the crags lay jumbled rocks, overgrown with rowan and thorn trees and, extraordinarily, some gorse bushes in flower.

Having crossed the main road at Point 286m I left the cliffs of Craig y Llam on my right and started the long climb up Mynydd Ceiswyn.

Maps O.S. 1:50,000 Sheet 124; O.S. 1:63,360 Tourist Map 'Snowdonia'; O.S. 1:25,000 Outdoor Leisure Map – 'Snowdonia (Cader Idris and Dovey Forest)'.
Grading An easy but exposed walk across mainly grassy and heather-clad hills.
Start / Finish Dolgellau (730178); Minllyn (859140).
Distance / Time 14 miles/7-8 hours.
Escape Routes N from the col W of Maesglasau to the road at Penantigi Uchaf. N from Bwlch Siglen to Tyn-y-braich.
Telephones Dolgellau, bridge near Tyddyn-Ednyfed, Penantigi Uchaf, Aberllefenni and Minllyn.
Transport Railway Station at Barmouth. Daily bus service Barmouth – Dolgellau. Dolgellau – Dinas Mawddwy bus service school days only.
Accommodation Hotels/Guest Houses at Dolgellau, Dinas Mawddwy and Mallwyd. Youth Hostels at Dinas Mawddwy and Dolgellau.
Guidebooks 'The Summits of Snowdonia' by Terry Marsh (Hale); 'On Foot in North Wales and the Peak' by Patrick Monkhouse (Diadem).

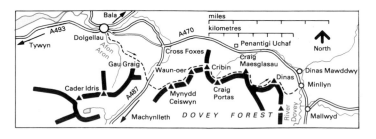

Cader (Cadair) Idris from Waun-oer in the Dovey Forest.

Back now in the chilly shade I looked north to Dduallt and Rhobell Fawr which were bathed in sunshine, and to Aran Fawddwy, capped with snow.

A fence runs along the summit ridge of Mynydd Ceiswyn and I was shocked to see new plantations stretching almost to the ridge. The lesser hills to the south were completely submerged by a green sea of conifers, and I maintained a strict *eyes left* to enjoy the bare rocky slopes and sublime outline of Cader Idris.

Mercifully the remainder of the day's hills, Waun-oer, Cribin, Maesglasau (Maesglase) and Dinas rose well above the forestry and I was able to enjoy easy walking along the high, undulating ridges.

The thin winter sunshine gave no warmth and the sharp air nipped my nose and ears, but the clarity ensured spectacular views ranging from the Brecon Beacons and Plynlimon to Moel Hebog and Snowdon's summits, white with fresh snow. As the sun rose higher, Cardigan Bay shimmered like molten silver away to the west.

Waun-oer, 2,197ft/670m, is a rounded lump when seen from the south side, but it has a perfect east-facing cwm ringed by broken cliffs. Likewise Cribin, Craig Portas and Maesglasau have steep and precipitous faces to the north and east, falling to remote cwms.

On the summit of Waun-oer I found a strange experimental contraption; a collection of solar panels connected to an antenna. The panels were surrounded by a protective wall of turf which had been scavenged from the adjacent hillside. Turf has only a precarious hold on high ridges and, following this act of vandalism, erosion of the undersoil had already started.

A considerable stream has its source on the plateau of Maesglasau and it plunges over the edge of the sheer escarpment into Gulcwm. Recent strong winds had blown the water back up the cliff in a cloud of spray, which had immediately frozen making a fairyland of hanging icicles and a forest of grass stems encased in glass.

From Craig Maesglasau a sheep-path winds down to Bwlch Siglen, the lowest point on the ridge, whence a good track leads to the valley at Tyn-y-braich. But it is worthwhile to complete the whole ridge-walk by climbing the steep, grassy nose of Dinas.

A few more strange aerials sprouted from the flat summit of Dinas, but I preferred to visit the shallow, frozen lake on the north side of the hill before swinging south to the fence junction at Point 423m. It was then an easy descent down slopes of heather and bracken to the valley near Minllyn.

The cliffs of Craig Maesglasau (Maesglase) from near Bwlch Siglen.

The trees were casting long shadows, and the north-facing slopes and the fields shaded by walls and hedges were still white with frost.

It is always comforting to return to the valley after a winter's day on bleak fells, and I was in a relaxed and happy mood as I walked past a row of white-washed cottages with slate roofs, while the homely smell of wood-smoke pervaded the air.

Although it was Saturday I had not seen a soul all day, my feet were dry and I anticipated a large pot of tea at the Red Lion in Dinas Mawddwy. Winter walking has its rewards.

RADNOR FOREST TO LLANDEILO HILL

The Welsh border is crossed at Knighton and at once the lanes become narrower, the hedges higher, the gradients steeper and the villages smaller and further apart. Shropshire's gently rolling uplands give way to a group of hills rising confidently to over 2,000ft. These are the hills of the Radnor Forest (forest in this sense meaning an area set aside for hunting), and from the east they are dominated by the rounded dome of Whimble.

A line of slightly lesser but very wild hills runs south from the Radnor Forest, extending seventeen miles to the valley of the Wye at Erwood Bridge. The combination of these two groups of hills provides one of the longest and loneliest walks in the Welsh Marches.

It was barely 6 a.m. as I walked up the main street of the small Welsh town of New Radnor. A thin white mist hung in the valley, but the few patches of blue sky that appeared were the encouraging precursors to a hot summer's day. A steep lane, Mutton Dingle, leads to a ride through the block of forestry under Whimble and I plodded happily up, swatting flies that were swarming in the still air. By the time I broke out of the trees the mist was rolling away from Great Rhos and exposing the gaunt radio mast on Black Mixen.

Whimble is the most shapely of the Radnor Forest hills but it is seldom ascended; there is no path and no cairn. Glacial action has cut through the Silurian shales leaving a pronounced gap between Whimble and the main massif to the north, the raw shale is exposed in a shattered, layered outcrop called Winyard Rocks. Bache Hill, a mile to the north-east, has its OS pillar built on a high plinth and it is a far better view point. The glorious hill country of the Welsh Borders unfolds to the east with Hengwm, on Offa's Dyke, prominent beyond the Lugg valley.

Walking in the Radnor Hills tends to be rough with deep tussocks, heather and bilberry tugging at your boots at every step. However, there are numerous tracks: some prehistoric, some drovers' roads, some made by sheep and others by heavy tracked vehicles which have crushed the heather. To save energy it is worth following these tracks because there are many miles of rough, tough walking ahead before you reach your destination in the Wye valley.

With boots and trousers soaked by the dew I sat on the OS pillar of

Left: Heading north from Glascwm Hill to Cefn Wylfre.

Maps O.S. 1:50,000 Sheets 148 and 147.
Grading A long walk over rolling hills. Much of the way is trackless and involves ploughing through deep heather and bracken.
Start / Finish New Radnor (212608); Erwood Bridge (090438).
Distance / Time 26 miles/10-12 hours.
Escape Routes Numerous. Tracks lead down to villages on lower ground from many places. Roads cross the line of the walk S of New Radnor and E of Glascwm.
Telephones New Radnor, Forest Inn, Glascwm, Rhulen and Erwood Bridge.
Transport Railway Stations at Knighton and Llandrindod Wells on Swansea – Shrewsbury line, then infrequent bus service to New Radnor. Daily express bus service Cheltenham – New Radnor – Aberystwyth.
Accommodation Hotels/Guest Houses at and around New Radnor. B & B at Erwood. Youth Hostels at Knighton and Glascwm.
Guidebooks 'Walks and More, a Guide to the Central Welsh Marches' by A. Johnson and S. Punter (Logaston Press); 'The Welsh Marches' by R. Millward and A. Robinson (Macmillan); 'Exploring Wales' by William Condry (Faber and Faber).

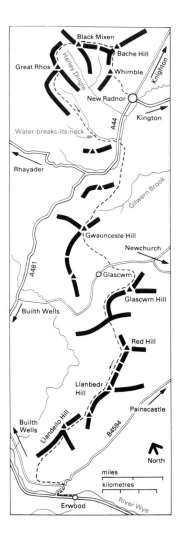

The outcrop and one of several tarns on Llanbedr Hill.

Black Mixen and looked north. Forestry plantations were encroaching ever higher and deeper into the hills; nearby Fron-wen, 1,762ft/537m, was already submerged. Beyond the blanket of firs, Beacon Hill and the Maelienydd were thrown into sharp relief by the early morning sun.

I swung round the head of the deep Harley Dingle valley, which is used for ammunition testing, and ploughed on to Great Rhos, at 2,166ft/600m, the highest hill of the Radnor Forest. The OS pillar stands starkly on the broad summit plateau which is a rather disappointing view point.

On the south side of the Great Rhos plateau there are spoil heaps and some old tracks, one of which leads conveniently down to the col under Fron Hill and then crosses a beck to reach the northern end of the Warren plantation.

A gradual descent through the trees took me to a local beauty spot: a waterfall with the somewhat macabre name of 'Water-breaks-its-neck'. A small stream flows over a fifty foot slab of black, moss-covered rock set in a grotto. Overhanging trees block out the light and the effect is very gloomy.

From the falls an avenue of sweet chestnuts, alder and beech leads, in one mile, to the main road and the completion of the first eight mile loop of the walk.

It was 10 a.m. when I crossed the A44, one mile north of Llanfihangel Nant Melan and started the traverse of the lonely hills south to Erwood Bridge. 'The Day of the Sheep' would be an apt title for this section of the walk, because the entire upland area is extensively

grazed and I saw no human beings on the hills. The small and pretty Welsh sheep lay panting in any shade they could find: under bushes, in deep bracken, behind boulders, walls and tree trunks. My heart went out to these peaceful creatures who were so different from the nervous and scraggy Swaledales and Scottish Blackfaces of the north.

A small plantation on Castle Hill is by-passed on the west side, otherwise the Forestry Commission have not been very active on these hills and walking is unimpeded. From the tarn at Point 415m I made a descending traverse to the Gilwern Brook, a cool, swift flowing stream running between banks of kingcups and overhung in places with giant larches and Scots pines.

Heather slopes now lead to Gwaunceste, 1,778ft/542m, the highest hill in the vicinity and one which commands a delectable view over the green valleys and swelling uplands which roll away twelve miles south to the Black Mountains. Immediately below Gwaunceste lies the exquisite village of Glascwm, with white-washed cottages and a grey stone church standing on a knoll. Its setting, in a deep, wooded valley surrounded by hills, is perfection, and very Welsh.

The walk continues pleasantly over the broad summit ridge of Glascwm Hill passing the reedy Mawn Pools, the nesting place of black headed gulls. At Red Hill the ridge turns to the west, and the final stretch of the walk over Llanbedr Hill and Llandeilo Hill is clearly seen. On the south side of Red Hill stands Manor Stone, a low boundary marker inscribed 'Sir J R B 1882' on one side and 'W de W 1882' on the other.

A green path runs between Rhulen and Llanbedr Hills, a welcome relief from the wiry heather. The path follows a stream which emerges from a spring beside a copse of trees, and then continues through a marshy area of cotton grass and shallow tarns to a picturesque outcrop. Below the rocks lies another tarn, where sheep were lapping the muddy water.

Llandeilo Hill, at the end of the ridge, carries no OS pillar, only another low boundary stone and a cairn with an intriguing notice: 'TWM Tobacco's Grave'.

The hill falls away steeply to the west, the slopes being broken up by a series of rock outcrops, many overgrown with rowan and blackthorn. These cliffs are the first real feature to be met on the day's walk and they make a pleasant contrast to the smooth, green, convex hills further north. From Aberedw the effect is particularly fine.

The view up Harley Dingle to the Great Rhos – Black Mixen ridge.

A wide path leads down through the bracken and scrub to a farm road near another lovely old Welsh church, St Teil's at Llandeilo Graban, one mile from Erwood Bridge.

I swung my legs from the parapet of the bridge; the water gurgled below and I watched a heron fishing up-stream. I finished the last of my sandwiches as the sun dropped behind the ridge above Gwenddwr. A scarlet hot air balloon, released from the Builth Wells Show Ground, drifted silently overhead. Yes, it had been a great day.

The Great Rhos range from the south.

STRATA FLORIDA AND THE TEIFI POOLS

by STEVE ASHTON

This is no ordinary walk. You cannot come once to these hills and make them your own, as you may the rugged peaks further north. Because here the local people have embraced – not denied – their upland heritage. The tides of history have filled the valleys and spilled over onto the seeming wilderness of the high ground. And do so still.

Last stop before the open hillside is Pontrhydfendigaid. To an outsider it consists of little more than two pubs and a tin-roofed garage. But take care not to place its inhabitants too readily. The world of rural Wales is wrapped so tight around its people that they have explored its outer limits. Individualism is alive and well in Pontrhydfendigaid.

The journey on foot begins at the Cistercian Abbey of Strata Florida – the Vale of Flowers – where a single arch rises from the ruins. A vivid imagination will reconstruct the scene of eight hundred years ago.

A slight drizzle filtered through the trees as we began our walk along the lane towards Gareglwyd. Our pace, I recall, was arrogant. Thinking to make a day of it we took a premature rest at the waterfall on the Afon Mwyro. We thought we knew what we were about in these small hills.

From beyond the incline of the fall, when overlooking the farm at Gareglwyd, we broke away from the track and made straight for the first summit of Dibyn Du. The wind thumped a succession of clouds into our shallow ridge as we approached the top. But we held firm and laughed at the rain on our cheeks. Unruly little hills, we thought.

And then all at once we were lost. The summit had been successfully negotiated, and for the continuation of our route to Claerwen we had planned to follow what had promised to be a train of obvious

Map O.S. 1:50,000 Sheet 147.
Grading A rough walk across open moorland which can be rather wet.
Start / Finish The abbey of Strata Florida (746657).
Distance / Time 16 miles/7-8 hours.
Escape Route The track from Claerwen to Strata Florida and Ffair Rhos can be taken as a convenient short cut.
Telephone Strata Florida.
Transport Infrequent daily bus service from both Aberystwyth and Tregaron to Pontrhydfendigaid.
Accommodation Hotels at Tregaron and Pontrydfendigaid. B & B locally. Youth Hostel at Blaencaron near Tregaron.
Guidebook 'Exploring Wales' by William Condry (Faber and Faber).

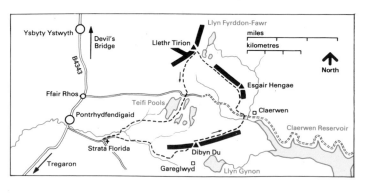

The view east from Dibyn Du across Bryn Trapau to the Claerwen Reservoir.

grass shoulders. But nothing was certain now that the cloud had thickened to a grey, stuck gob. Even the dog was hesitant. An hour later, long after the pretence of being on route had been dropped, the cloud parted for a moment to reveal the distant Teifi Pools. It was all we needed. Within seconds we had stitched ourselves to the hillside with back bearings. Our arrival at Claerwen was assured.

The Afon Claerddu was flooded. At an island, its forces fragmented, we foiled the torrent and gained the Claerwen track with dry boots. As it happened we needn't have bothered. I can't remember who made that fateful decision to strike directly up the slope to Esgair Hengae. One of us must have idly set off that way, the other following blindly. Or it could have been the dog. Anyway, it was a mistake.

It was a marsh, a *flooded* marsh, and inhabited by huge clumps of coarse grass that lay in wait like huddled ostrich. We would clamber onto their backs to keep from sinking, but almost at once they would rise up and shiver their feathers, pitching us back into the swamp. To make matters worse we were mocked throughout by the parallel progress of a dry ridge we might have followed from a short way up the Claerwen track. Our misery was complete, and even the dog – who come to think of it was almost certainly responsible for our predicament – was unusually subdued.

Eventually the great marsh subsided as we began to ascend the Esgair. The clouds lifted, revealing to our backward glance a panorama of impossible wilderness. No road, no house, interrupted the plain weave of the dull green carpet laid over the earth. In one or two places it was buckled and threadbare where it covered some old bones of ancient hills, but otherwise its coverage was complete.

The mood was changing. Squalls now replaced the clinging rain. They came at us in regular sorties, fresh and violent. The few remaining hours of daylight allowed us no more liberties with the route. Our situation had assumed the seriousness of a Scottish winter.

We were on a plateau, between Brynyrhyrddod and the Llyn Du. It could have been the Atlantic Ocean. I can see it now, the greenswell rising and falling around us, the wind thrashing white from the upturned grasses. Ships in a storm, we made the crossing in awe of nature.

It was here we found the mouse. The dog had made the discovery,

Looking west down the Mwryo Valley. The lower slopes of Dibyn Du are on the right.

At the bridge over the Afon Claerwen near Claerwen farm.

unearthing the little animal from its hide-away in a clump of rushes. It emerged wet and bedraggled, a tiny life among an enormous landscape. Pushing the dog to one side, and brushing off my warning, Tony crouched down to pick up the furry thing. 'How cute,' he said, stroking it with his great clumsy fingers. The mouse shivered a moment in his hands and then died of fright. 'You've killed it,' I said, piercing him with the cruel blade of truth. But I could sense his gentle heart break-ing at the very thought. For the sake of morale I retracted the accusation and lay blame instead on the dog. Vicious beast.

The lakes of Fyrddon-Fach marked our passage into a more familiar terrain of ups, downs and arounds. Now we could puff and pant in a convincing manner and measure our progress towards the ridge crest of Llethr Tirion. It was here I thought I saw a figure on a nearby hill

Looking south-east to the Claerwen Reservoir from the slopes of Esgair Hengae.

– the very idea! – but it stayed motionless and proved to be yet another of the ridiculous concrete posts laying claim to Birmingham's water.

Eager now to experience the glowing twilight of our walk, we swept down the graceful ridge curves of Waun Claerddu and hit the tarmac of the Teifi Pools road at a gallop. With that the spell was broken. Had our car been parked here we could have said farewell to all this and roared off into the night. Alas it was not. Instead we trudged east along the road to collect the track that would guide us onto the isthmus between Llyn Teifi and Llyn Hir. There was an eerie silence as we entered into the realm of the Pools.

The mood now took us by the throat. For an instant I fancied we were back in our childhood, exploring again the dismal Lancashire ponds where daring and forbidden deeds were perpetrated.

From the dam at the southern tip of Llyn Teifi we stumbled down through the gloom to gain the stream that would lead us, albeit circuitously, back to the abbey. At the narrows we crossed to follow the pastureland tracks of its right bank, until eventually we came to an ancient track, sunken between hedges and strewn with rubble. It was long disused and we might just as easily have descended a little further to a more comfortable lane. But the dog would have none of it. We were to make hard work of it in the failing light.

At the Teifi Pools.

THE ABERGWESYN COMMON

The announcement in 1984 that the National Trust, with grants from the Countryside Commission and the National Heritage Memorial Fund, had purchased the 16,500 acre Abergwesyn Common meant very little to most people.

But Abergwesyn Common, in Powys, is the wildest area of high heathland in the wildest part of Central Wales. The Common runs for ten miles, in a westerly direction, from a point just south of Rhayader to the Irfon Gorge. On the north side it is bounded by the Welsh Water Authority's Elan Valley holding, thus public access is now assured over an extremely wide area.

Within the Abergwesyn Common lie 2,000ft hills, rivers, ravines, desolate boulder-strewn moorlands, ancient mine workings and natural woodlands of birch, ash and oak. Merlins and the very rare red kite are regular visitors to the Common and the western sector has been designated a Grade 1 SSSI.

Thankfully the Abergwesyn Common will now be saved from moorland reclamation, from overgrazing and from the creeping canopy of conifers which covers much of Powys. Private forestry groups, always eager for land, will have to look elsewhere for their angular plantations of regimented fir trees.

Abergwesyn Common is a lost corner of Britain; tucked away in the no-man's-land between Plynlimon and the Brecon Beacons it is entirely untamed. I found it to be a revelation and a joy and the National Trust could not have spent their money more wisely.

Llanwrtyd Wells is the base for exploring Abergwesyn Common; it is the smallest town in England and Wales and used to be famous for its sulphur springs. Now it is best known as a centre for mountain bicycle tours, walking, pony trekking and an extraordinary marathon race held annually: man versus bicycle versus horse.

A narrow road runs from Llanwrtyd Wells alongside the river Irfon, a tributary of the Wye, through oak woods carpeted with bluebells in spring, and then zig-zags steeply up the Devil's Staircase on its way to Tregaron. This road skirts the southern boundary of the Abergwesyn Common and passes through the village of Abergwesyn, once an important stopping point for cattle drovers, which boasted an inn (The Grouse) and a church. At Abergwesyn the Beulah road branches off right, and in a mile it crosses the Afon Gwesyn at Ty-mawr where there is a post office.

This is a convenient starting point for a circular walk over Abergwesyn Common, which explores some delectable river valleys and includes the ascent of the two highest hills.

It had snowed overnight and two inches of powder snow lay on the road as I drove tentatively along the Irfon valley to Ty-mawr. But

Peat-hagged wilderness in the valley of the Afon Gwesyn on the route to Drygarn Fawr.

patches of blue sky appeared as I walked through Glangwesyn farm, and by the time I emerged from the woods onto the open Common the sun had broken through.

The snow and frost crystals sparkled like gems; it was good to be alive on such a morning and I strode purposefully up the track towards the trig. point on Pen Carreg-dan. Suddenly, with a bang, I found myself flat on my face nursing bruised knees and elbows. In places the snow was lying, as a sugar dusting, over sheets of smooth ice, which had formed during the recent cold-snap. I suffered many more such falls during the day and could easily have broken a limb, the consequences of which would have been serious since I was alone and far from assistance.

Pen Carreg-dan looked over a silent, white world. The rooks were down in the valley trees, the sheep were clustered around the farm gates waiting for hay and only a line of fox tracks indicated any other living creature for miles around. To the north the ground rose gradually to the summit of Drygarn Fawr, nearly three miles away, but the going was tough over the tussocks of coarse grass and I preferred to descend into the valley of the Afon Gwesyn and follow the stream to its source high up on Drygarn.

The stream had cut deeply into the bedrock forming cascades and waterfalls. The rocks were festooned with icicles which flashed with rainbow colours in the sunshine.

Drygarn Fawr, the highest point on Abergwesyn Common, is a whale-backed ridge rising to 2,115ft/641m. It has a line of broken

Map O.S. 1:50,000 Sheet 147.
Grading Rough going over high, trackless moorland. Route finding would be a problem in mist.
Start / Finish Ty-mawr. near Abergwesyn (863534).
Distance / Time 15 miles/7-8 hours.
Escape Route From Bwlch-y-ddau-faen between Drygarn Fawr and Gorllwyn a descent may be made to the Cefngarw Forest.
Telephones Ty-mawr and Llannerch-y-cawr on road to Claerwen reservoir.
Transport Railway Station at Llanwrtyd Wells on the mid-Wales line from Swansea to Shrewsbury (no Sun trains). Postbus from Llanwrtyd Wells to Abergwesyn.
Accommodation Hotels/B & B at Llanwrtyd Wells. Youth Hostels at Blaencaron near Tregaron, Dolgoch and Tyncornel.
Guidebooks 'Exploring Wales' by William Condry (Faber and Faber); Leaflet: 'Walks Around Llanwrtyd Wells' available from the Neuadd Arms Hotel, Llanwrtyd Wells.

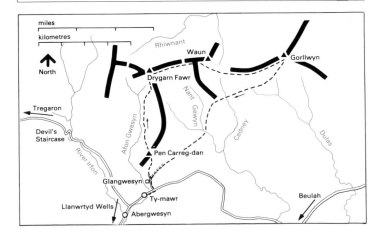

On the Abergwesyn Common.

although a line of concrete posts set deep in the heather acted as a useful guide. Several streams rise on the Common and I blessed the frozen ground as I crossed innumerable areas of marsh and reeds.

Gorllwyn too has a massive stone cairn, built on a knoll five minutes walk from the OS pillar. I sat down briefly by the cairn to wolf some Christmas cake, but the cold was intense and I started to stiffen up. It was only 2 p.m. but the sun was already sinking and I was uneasily conscious of my isolation and vulnerability.

Following even the merest sheep track to ease my way through the energy-sapping tussocks, I headed south-west, crossing the infant Afon Cedney under the hillock of Carnau.

I then climbed the broad shoulder of Esgair-fraith and dropped down to the deep ravine of the Nant Gewyn. The stream was reduced to a trickle and the black walls of the ravine were cased in armour, while pillars of ice as thick as my arm hung down in curtains.

crags on the south side and carries two enormous round cairns, a third cairn lying half-a-mile away to the west. The name Drygarn means Three Cairns. Amongst such illustrious company the concrete OS pillar semed an unnecessary irrelevance.

Four miles to the east my second objective, the rounded hill of Gorllwyn, 2,009ft/613m, looked dauntingly far away across the snow-clad moor. Most of the hills in the middle distance were clothed in forestry but, on the skyline, Cader Idris, the Brecon Beacons and the Black Mountains were clearly visible, the latter emerging above horizontal layers of pink cloud. From the high plateau of the Common, slopes ran down northwards to the ugly concrete dam of the Claerwen reservoir and to the Elan Valley reservoirs.

I could find no vestige of a path across the Common to Gorllwyn,

At Esgair-gul a gate gives access to a path running through the Cefngarw forest and, after crossing a stream, it opens out into a broad ride which eventually emerges from the trees onto open hillside. A good farm track contours round the hill, crossing two streams and passing through oak woods before joining the outgoing route north of Glangwesyn.

The sun had now disappeared and the farmer announced that the temperature had dropped to minus eleven degrees Celsius. My boots, socks, trousers and overtrousers were a block of ice, and I was unable to change them until I had driven fifty miles on the home-ward road, with the car heater at full boost.

The view west from Gorllwyn to Drygarn Fawr.

The Carmarthen Fan escarpment seen from the west.

MYNYDD DU OR CARMARTHEN FAN

You can divide the hills of the Brecon Beacons National Park into four principal masses: the Black Mountains, the Brecon Beacons themselves, Fforest Fawr and the Mynydd Du.

The loneliest mountain is Mynydd Du on the western edge of the Park. Known also as the Black Mountain or Carmarthen Fan, Mynydd Du appears as an enormous lump of high moorland when seen from the valleys running south towards Neath and Swansea, yet it is a fascinating hill and full of surprises. The complex geological structure of the mountain, which is made up of Old Red Sandstone, Millstone Grit, Carboniferous Limestone and coal measures, have produced shake holes, caves, ravines, smooth rocks, boulder fields, outcrops, lakes, marshes, reed beds, coarse moor grass and soft fescues ideal for grazing.

But the outstanding feature of Mynydd Du, which elevates the mountain into the top league in Wales, is a steep escarpment running for over four miles along the north and east sides of the plateau. From the principal summits of Fan Brycheiniog, 2,631ft/802m, and Bannau Sir Gaer, cliffs fall for 600ft into cwms containing small and secret lakes, around which legends and fables have been woven throughout history. The characteristic cut-off silhouette of Mynydd Du when seen from the gently rolling hill country around Llandovery and Trecastle, and from the Usk valley, is one of the best-loved sights in South Wales.

To enjoy the optimum combination of wild moorland, rushing streams, crags and cliff-top exposure, a west–east traverse taking in some of the rarely visited outlying summits is my recommended route.

A convenient starting point is the car-park three miles north of Brynamman at the high point, 1,600ft, on the hill road to Llangadog. George Borrow passed along this road on his way to the inn at Brynamman one exceedingly wet day in 1854. He writes in *Wild Wales*: 'The mist was of the thickest kind, I could just see that there was a frightful precipice on my left, so I kept to the right, hugging the

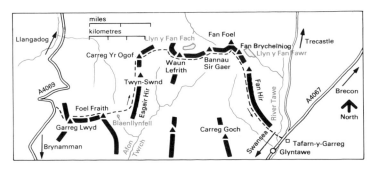

side of the hill. As I descended I heard every now and then loud noises in the vale probably proceeding from stone quarries. I was drenched to the skin, nay, through the skin, by the mist.'

I shared a certain sympathy with George Borrow as I left the warmth of my car and set off through the mist onto the wastes of Mynydd Du, compass in hand. But my familiarity with the high moorland scene, which differs little in the various upland regions of Britain, kept up my spirits. I relished the rough boulders and the substantial cairn on Garreg Lwyd, the squelch of the bogs, the springs and the lively rivulets of melt-water draining the rapidly receding snow patches on Foel Fraith, exposing patches of bright green moss.

Reassured by the appearance in the right place of the marshy pools, Pwll Swnd and Blaenllynfell, from which mallard flew with a tremendous commotion, I scrambled up the rocks to the long ridge of Esgair Hir.

First scoured smooth by glacial action and then fissured and seamed by twelve thousand winters, the grey gritstone rib of Esgair Hir is an extraordinary feature to emerge from the peaty moorland. Broken crags descend to Cwm Sawdde Fechan on the west side, while the northern summit, Twyn-Swnd, is crowned by two huge tumuli marked Carnau'r Gareg-las on the map.

Beyond Twyn-Swnd you pick your way through the rocks to a rough boggy area. The clumps of purple moor grass had died during the winter, for it is one of our few deciduous grasses, and the leaves were a rich apricot colour. But firm, cropped grass soon announced the emerging shelves of limestone on Carreg Yr Ogof, whose high point is incongruously marked by a gleaming white OS pillar.

The limestone beds of Mynydd Du are riddled with underground caves and tunnels. Six miles to the east, in the Tawe valley, the huge cave systems of Dan-yr-Ogof and Ogof Ffynnon Ddu contain over thirty miles of explored passageways, descending in places to a depth of 850ft. Cavers think it possible that connections will be found to Carreg Yr Ogof, or even right through to the west side of the Mynydd Du massif.

Continuing east from Carreg Yr Ogof you arrive at Waun Lefrith, where quite abruptly the great escarpment plunges down to Llyn y Fan Fach. By now the wind had blown gaps in the mist giving me fleeting views over the corniced lip to the lake below. Although it has been dammed to provide water for Llanelli, Llyn y Fan Fach retains an aura of mystery and romance. It inspired a fable of the *Lady of the Lake*. A shepherd boy, passing the lake in the evening, saw a lady emerging from the dark waters. He fell in love with her but she disappeared again and he searched each day for her in vain. But one night he visited the lake by moonlight and she reappeared and fell in love with him.

The view from the eastern end of the Carmarthen Fan escarpment – Bannau Sir Gaer from Fan Foel.

Chris Barber

The edge of the escarpment is followed due east, over the summit of Bannau Sir Gaer, down to a col and then up to the northernmost promontory, Fan Foel. Wind and rain, funnelling up with great force from the cwms below, have eroded the escarpment edge where no turf grows. Fan foel is the best viewpoint for the striated sandstone cliffs, which were carved by the glacier that once filled the Usk valley. A steep path descends the prow of Fan Foel, leading to the Afon Sawddle and Llanddeusant, but you should continue to follow the escarpment edge which now turns south-east.

The day's high point is soon reached on Fan Brycheiniog which carries a cairn and a stone shelter and overlooks Llyn y Fan Fawr.

Two more miles of fine exposed walking along the broad scarp of Fan Hir lie ahead. Due east rises the Fforest Fawr hill of Fan Gyhirych, while to the west a desolate area of streams and hillocks culminates in the wild and deep valley of the Afon Twrch.

I passed close by the farm at Dderi and crossed the bridge over the river Tawe to reach the Tafarn-y-Garreg inn on the A4067. Glancing back I could see the last wisps of cloud rolling off Fan Hir. The bus from Brecon was due in a few minutes time, and I sat on the wall and mused on my eminently satisfying and solitary day on the massif of Mynydd Du.

Left: On Waun Lefrith at the western end of the Carmarthen Fan ridge.

Maps O.S. 1:50,000 Sheet 160; O.S. 1:25,000 Outdoor Leisure Map – 'The Brecon Beacons Western Area'.
Grading A high moorland walk over desolate and sometimes rocky country. The long escarpment of Carmarthen Fan gives superb open walking with expansive views.
Start / Finish Car-park three miles north of Brynamman (732185); Tafarn-y-Garreg (849171).
Distance / Time 13 miles/6-7 hours.
Escape Routes None S of the Carmarthen Fan escarpment. In good conditions the steep path N from Fan Foel could be taken to reach the road at Blaenau.
Telephones Brynamman, Capel Gwynfe and Glyntawe.
Transport Regular bus service Brecon to Swansea passes through Glyntawe. A less frequent service connects this route, at Ystalyfera, to Brynamman.
Accommodation Hotels in Brynamman and Glyntawe. B & B locally. Youth Hostels at Ystradfellte and Llanddeusant.
Guidebooks 'Portrait of the Brecon Beacons' by E. J. Mason (Hale); 'Portrait of South Wales' by M. Senior (Hale); 'The Brecon Beacons National Park' by Margaret Davies (H.M.S.O.); 'The Welsh Peaks' by W. A. Poucher (Constable); 'The Brecon Beacons' by H. D. Westacott (Penguin).

Great Tor at the link between Oxwich Bay and Threecliff Bay.

THE GOWER PENINSULA

As you take the coast-road south out of Swansea towards Mumbles Head you pass through the smart suburb of Oystermouth, with white-painted villas set amongst exotic trees overlooking the bay. Only a hundred years ago Oystermouth was a thriving fishing village with two hundred oyster-ketches working the beds off-shore, but now the oysters have gone and the lovely arc of Swansea Bay is dominated by gigantic industrial complexes at Port Talbot. You may wonder how on earth a coastal walk starting from The Mumbles can possibly qualify for inclusion in *Wild Walks*.

However, as you reach the summit of the hill overlooking the lighthouse on the island of Mumbles Head, it is as if you have passed through a door to a different world. To the west, as far as the eye can see, stretches a wild and rugged coastline of white limestone cliffs, headlands, reefs, coves, inlets, caves, blow-holes and wide sandy bays. The superb Carboniferous limestone was laid down in warm seas over a period of a hundred million years but later, dramatic

Left: Looking east along the Gower coastline from above Mewslade Bay.

movements of the earth's crust, known as the Amorician oregony, buckled and folded the rock, thrusting it up into the ridge of Cefn Bryn which overlooks the coastline of the Gower peninsula.

Springy turf, close cropped by sheep in many places, grows along the top of the cliffs but tangled brambles, gorse and bracken are encroaching. The flora is outstanding with over a hundred flowering species being recorded, including the yellow whitlow-grass which grows in no other place in Britain. Fortunately the Gower coastline is well protected: it has the status of AONB, certain sections are owned by the National Trust, while key areas have been designated National Nature Reserves or SSSIs.

In the height of the summer season the sandy bays are teeming with holiday-makers but, on a Saturday morning in early March, mine was the only car in the vast Mumbles Head car-park and the kiosks and ice-cream parlours were still battened down for the winter.

A stiff breeze from off the Bristol Channel was rapidly dispersing the early mist and, as I followed the narrow path under Rams Tor,

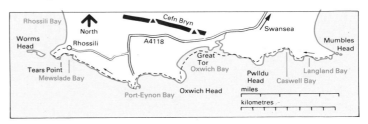

the gorse flowers had opened in the sunshine and the air was heavy with their sweet aroma. Chaffinches and a solitary wren hopped amongst the brambles and I felt spring had arrived in South Wales.

The coast path was deserted save for a lone walker with a dog and a party of student geologists busily examining the rocks of Snaple Point. The tide was out and I could walk right across Brandy Cove, Langland Bay and Caswell Bay where lines of white surf were streaming across the firm sands. This was smugglers' country where casks of brandy from France and chests of tea from Holland were surreptitiously landed and sold for huge profits.

At Pwlldu Bay a shingle bank above the sand was gleaming in the sunshine, and I left the beach to scramble up Pwlldu Head, the highest headland in Gower at just over 300ft. South, across the Bristol Channel, I could just make out the grey outline of the north Devon coast, but my attentions were focussed on the vast sweep of Oxwich Bay two miles away to the west.

I approached Oxwich Bay along the cliff path with a thrill of anticipation. It has the reputation of being one of Britain's finest bays and with the bright sunshine glistening on the wet sand, and prows of white limestone running boldly out towards the breaking waves, I rated it equal to Sutherland's stupendous Sandwood Bay.

The tide was fully out as I jumped down onto the sand at Shire Combe Point and ran with sheer exuberance across Threecliff Bay. Rock climbers provided a splash of colour on the clean, warm limestone buttresses, and I was able to squeeze round the seaward end of the 200ft high Great Tor which divides Threecliff Bay from the main curve of Oxwich Bay.

For an hour I walked along the sand in complete solitude, save for a few oyster-catchers turning over the scallops and razor shells.

At high tide the crossing of Oxwich Bay is an altogether different proposition with headlands, rivers and dunes of marram grass to be negotiated. Behind the dunes lie salt and fresh water marshes managed by the Nature Conservancy Council.

In contrast to the clean sands of the bay, the slopes of Oxwich Point are wooded with oak, ash, elm, hazel and hawthorn. A tiny thirteenth century church, St Illtyd's, is set in a carpet of snowdrops just above high water mark. From behind the church a path winds up

Map O.S. 1:50,000 Sheet 159.
Grading A long and fascinating walk along cliff tops and across bays of firm sand.
Start / Finish Mumbles Head (629874); Rhossili (416881).
Distance / Time 21 miles/8-9 hours.
Escape Routes Numerous.
Telephones The Mumbles, Caswell, Oxwich, Port Eynon and Rhossili.
Transport Railway Station at Swansea. Regular bus services from Swansea to The Mumbles and Rhossili.
Accommodation A wide variety in and around The Mumbles. Hotel/B & B in Rhossili. Youth Hostel at Port Eynon.
Guidebooks 'Portrait of Gower' by Wynford Vaughan Thomas (Hale); 'Portrait of South Wales' by M. Senior (Hale); 'Wales: South and West' by J. B. Hilling (Batsford); 'Exploring Wales' by William Condry (Faber and Faber); 'Walks in Wales' by R. Jones (Hale).

through the trees to Oxwich Point, overlooking wicked reefs on which the ribs of an old wreck lay exposed by the receding tide.

Once round the headland you can descend to sea-level and follow a grassy path above the rocks to Port-Eynon Bay. On the west side of the bay you pass the bramble covered ruins of the Salt House, once a substantial fortified house owned by the Lucas family which became a notorious centre for piracy in the sixteenth and seventeenth centuries.

An exposed traverse leads across the face of Port-Eynon Point; below, the waves were crashing deafeningly on a rock shelf and seals were playing in the surf. Above the roar of the waves I could just hear the clanging of a warning bell on a buoy moored off the point.

Port-Eynon Point provides another of Gower's extravagant views: north-west along five miles of tortured and twisted limestone cliffs, sculptured by the waves and the weather, to the tidal islands of Worms Head, jutting out from the mainland like a hump-backed sea serpent. In a strong breeze, with a wild sea pounding the base of the cliffs sending plumes of spray into a blue sky, there is no finer coastal view in Britain.

This five mile stretch of cliffs contains a host of natural features: pinnacles, arches, caves and blow-holes. Several caves have been found to contain pre-historic remains; the best-known being at Paviland where, in 1823, a human skeleton was discovered which became known as the Red Lady of Paviland. Subsequent tests, including radio-carbon dating, proved the skeleton to be that of a young man who died 18,000 years ago.

A coastal view to the west from near Port-Eynon Point past Overton Cliff to Worms Head.

Richard Gilbert

The path west runs a short way back from the cliffs, but you will not be able to resist walking to the edge of the promontories to watch the surging sea, sucking and pounding at the rocks below.

Notices restricting rock climbing on certain cliffs from March 1st, during the nesting season, were in evidence and climbers were thronging the access-free walls of Thurba Head. It was now late afternoon and the tide had long since turned and was flooding into Mewslade Bay. I climbed to Tears Point and gazed back eastwards towards Port-Eynon Point with the full extent of that amazing coastline bathed in sunshine.

The rising tide had isolated the islands of Worms Head; the channel is called the shipway and the tide allows you a maximum of five hours on the Head. Sadly I had to leave this expedition for another day. Pausing by the coastguard lookout to marvel at Rhossili Bay stretching north for three miles to Burry Holms, I turned inland for a late tea in Rhossili village, my mind reeling at the impressions of such a wild and magnificent walk.

Above and below: Contorted limestone cliff scenery in the vicinity of Horse Cliff at the western end of the walk.

THE SPERRIN SKYWAY

by PATRICK SIMMS

The main Sperrin mountain ridge trends almost east to west forming a subdued range of uplands, partly grassy and partly heathery, straddling the border between Counties Londonderry and Tyrone. Composed for the most part of the Dalradian schists, they possess considerable areas of eroded and ill-drained blanket bog. A general paucity of loughs, corries and rock ridges, combined with the absence of the resistant quartzites, inevitably means that they are overshadowed by the more assertive grandeur of the Donegal Highlands to the west. To sum up, the Sperrins offer a succession of rolling summits with numerous although not heavy dips between.

The walk I describe is essentially all of the singularly unfrequented 'Sperrin Skyway', with the exception of the two eastern tops of Craigagh Hill and Spelhoegh. It is a scenic natural line but in no way a gourmet's route, due to the lack of even modest scrambling. The principal summits, of which five exceed 2,000ft, are difficult to distinguish from afar as numerous supporting flanks running north and south from the main spine belie their true elevation. Their position, however, in the centre of Ulster ensures extensive panoramas ranging from the Mournes and the Antrim Plateau to most of Donegal and the Fermanagh/Cavan uplands. These hills can perhaps be best appreciated more closely from the road on the south side of the Glenelly Valley, where they display their chameleon moods of greens and blues to advantage in the pellucid light of high summer. (Glenelly separates the High Sperrins from a lesser ridge on its south side where a line of summits from Slieveavaddy south of Goles Forest runs westwards to Slievebeg.)

All the 2,000ft summits are included in the walk, starting in the east with Oughtmore and finishing at the head of the Butterlope Glen west of Mullagh-carbatagh, where transport should be left or arranged. The entire traverse is split into three sections by the two

---

Maps O.S. N.I. 1:50,000 Sheet 13; O.S. 1:126,720 Sheet 13.
Grading An easy mountain walk along a series of broad and undulating summits. Straightforward under good conditions. There is much loose fencing wire in places.
Start / Finish Goles Forest (679943); South end of Butterlope Glen (490955).
Distance / Time 18 miles/9 hours.
Escape Routes Southwards to the Glenelly Valley by tarmac roads crossing Sawel and Dart Passes or by any of the valley tracks.
Telephones Plumbridge, McNally's Public House and Mount Hamilton.
Transport No public transport through Glenelly. Bus service from Omagh to Plumbridge (three times daily).
Accommodation Guest Houses at Cranagh. Youth Hostel at Gortin.
Guidebooks 'Irish Peaks' by Joss Lynam (Constable); Irish Walk Guide Vol. 4 'The North East' by Richard Rogers (Gill and Macmillan).

minor road passes of Sawel and Dart, the latter one of the highest in Ireland.

Our walk commences off the B47 which threads the fertile strath of Glenelly east of Plumbridge. Cars can be parked at the riverside picnic site almost opposite the Goles Outdoor Centre, about half-a-mile east of Goles Bridge. On a rare cloudless June day during the atrocious summer of 1985 I ascended for around 500ft, to the musical sounds of the skylarks, alongside the plantation boundary fence over a formerly cultivated field revealing the old 'lazy beds' to the first top of Mullaghsallagh, giving me a close preview of the main ridge as well as a grand view down Glenelly and its riverside moraines far below. I then followed the fence along the broad saddle leading to Oughtmore. Keeping the fence on my left avoided the worst of the energy-sapping peat hags. Below me on the left an oasis of conifers surrounded the isolated Goles farm.

A Londonderry Corporation boundary stone marker indicates the summit. Sawel, 2,240ft/682m, and Dart, 2,040ft/621m, dominated to the west. North-eastwards lay Spelhoegh and Craigagh Hill backed by Mullaghmore with its beacon. South-eastwards the lone outlier of Slieve Gallion was backed by the silvery line of Lough Neagh.

Continuing west the descent led to the col between Oughtmore and Mullaghaneany, where the extensive Altbritain Forest swathes the northern slopes almost attaining the ridge. Passing an over-turned marker stone I gained my first 2,000ft top, where the fence veers north (misleading in mist), and surveyed the long line of the Inishowen Hills topped by Slieve Snaght across Lough Foyle. An easy trot followed to Meenard's peaty summit, 2,061ft/628m, followed by a short level stretch to a second indistinct top, from where a southern spur runs out to Oughtvabeg. A gentle descent from Meenard led over a pair of unnamed tops. I bypassed the first on the left and, on reaching its neighbour, followed the fence down to the cattle grid at the summit of Sawel Pass.

The longest ascent of the walk keeps the fence on the left up the east flank of Sawel. The ground is firmer here, the pale green turf interspersed with bilberries. Nearing the summit the fence veered left but I kept straight ahead to arrive at the trig. point. The spacious summit, which represents about the half-way point of the walk, is a fine belvedere, a place to relax after the last few hours' exertions and the opportunity for a well-earned brew-up. Gazing northwards revealed the conspicuous scarps of Benbradagh, Donald's Hill and Binevinagh forming a kind of geological western extension of the Antrim Plateau, and brooding over the fertile lowland of the Foyle hinterland. Westwards rose the second highest summit, Mullagh-clogha, 2,088ft/626m, beyond Dart Pass. Dart itself appeared satisfyingly close, with a top enlivened by a knuckle of rock – the only substantial outcrop in the Sperrins. The whole western horizon was occupied by the dramatic miscellany of the Donegal Highlands, towards which the eye is constantly drawn on most points along this walk. From Inishowen across the shimmering expanse of Lough Foyle I picked out the Fanad heights and onwards to the Derryveagh range, dominated by Muckish and the pyramid of Errigal. Further to the south-west lay the granite knot of the Bluestacks. Turning due south I could discern the distant Cuilcagh ridge on the Fermanagh/Cavan border beyond the drumlins of south Tyrone.

With the afternoon advancing I left the summit and descended to cross an eroded area of peat. A short uphill stretch took me to the rocky crest of Dart where I disturbed a pair of cronking ravens. The summit crags invite exploration and give a fine retrospective view of Sawel. An easy descent over a nameless top led me to Dart Pass.

Crossing the road I ascended to a nameless outlier where the

Descending Sawel Mountain to the peaty moors leading to Dart Mountain.

accompanying fence joins another at right angles. Now bearing left I continued over haggy ground to Carnakilly – a pair of small knolls en route to Mullaghdoo. Beyond its cairnless top the whaleback of Mullaghclogha loomed ahead, the highest of ten 'Mullaghs' (summits) in the western Sperrins. Here a cross-roads of fences lies beyond a modest pile of stones indicating the summit. I halted for a quick snack at the high noon of the walk.

Three uneventful Mullaghs make up the remaining portion of the walk to the Butterlope Glen. An easy descent and ascent took me to Mullaghasturrakeen, where the summit revealed the notch of the Barnes Gap immediately across Glenelly – a nice example of a glacial meltwater channel. I continued down into an ooze-filled hollow where a gate on the left leads to a track descending the Glenroan valley. Arriving at Mullagh-clogha's summit, the last top of Mullagh-carbatagh is conspicuous less than a mile to the west, capped with a cairn on one of two rocky bluffs. This final summit of the day gave me a fine prospect of the lesser western Sperrins, with the tall TV mast on Koram beyond the concealed glacial spillway of the Butterlope Glen. Moor lough, one of the very few lakes in the Sperrin region, glinted like pewter in the evening sunshine to the right of Balix Hill.

The closing stages of the walk led me to another top a little to the north-west to investigate the site of an ancient chambered cairn. From here I descended over rough but easy graded moorland, keeping a fence and forestry plantation on my left. At the end of a rewarding day I was glad to see my awaiting transport at Butterlope, and lost little time in arriving at Plumbridge for a glass-raising celebration at one of the village's several hostelries.

The southern slopes of Dart and Sawel seen from Cranagh.

SLIEVE LEAGUE AND THE DONEGAL COAST

The Irishman who told me it never snows in April on the west coast must have kissed the Blarney Stone. Martin and I sat in the car at Bunglass while the easterly gale drove snow horizontally against the windscreen and threatened to hurl us into the Atlantic.

A few minutes later Joss arrived hot-foot from Dublin and wound down the window. 'A wild walk you were wanting, was it Richard?' he asked with a wry smile. 'You've certainly chosen your day!'

I tightened my hood and put on a brave smile; two days travelling to Donegal for Slieve League and the finest coastal traverse in Ireland, an expedition delayed until mid-April to ensure a balmy and colourful early spring day. Yet, by a twist of fate, we were back in mid-winter.

From inland Slieve League is an undistinguished hump; rising to nearly 2,000ft it barely warrants a second glance. But, on the west side, the relentless pounding and sucking of the Atlantic rollers have undermined the mountain, causing vast slabs of quartzite to peel away from the cliffs. The entire west coast of Ireland is being slowly eaten away, but nowhere is the effect more dramatic and the scale larger than in south Donegal.

For over two miles Slieve League throws down a line of near precipitous slopes, the maximum height being 1,972ft/601m, from the very top of the mountain. But this is not all; north of Slieve League the rugged, indented coastline continues for a further twenty miles until the broad sands of Maghera are reached in Loughros Beg Bay. This is a coast of islets, jagged rocks, stacks, skerries, bays, cliffs and promontories; the same coast upon which many ships of the Spanish Armada were dashed in 1588.

Although the Bunglass to Maghera walk can be accomplished in a single, long day the village of Glencolumbkille makes a convenient stopping-off point. A variety of accommodation is available in Glencolumbkille, and the extra time afforded by taking two days over the expedition can easily be used for exploring the headlands and coves of this remarkable coast.

The car-park at Bunglass is reached via a narrow, gated road which rises high above the village of Teelin. This is a beautiful and romantic corner of Ireland where many of the white-washed cottages are thatched, hay is stacked in the tiny fields ringed by tumbledown stone walls, piles of peat stand drying under bleached tarpaulins, the aroma of peat fires wafts down the village streets and in summer the hedges are bright with fuchsia, wild roses and honeysuckle.

But our thoughts were far removed from honeysuckle as we staggered under the great buffets of wind and screwed up our eyes against the stinging snow. At times we could steal tantalising glimpses of dripping rock walls and a lumpy, restless green sea far below, but soon we were in cloud and stamping through an inch or two of fresh snow. Joss was wearing training shoes but he had the good sense to carry a ski-stick as a third leg; an enormous help on such a day when balance was at a premium.

Right: The Slieve League cliffs are seen at their finest from the headland at Bunglass.

The Bunglass headland from near the summit of Slieve League.

A short way below the summit of Slieve League the crest of the ridge suddenly steepens and narrows to a rocky arête. This is the famous 'One Man's Pass'. Snow covered and verglased it looked intimidating in the gale, which was now gusting to Storm Force Ten. Exercising discretion we took the easy traverse-line on the east side.

Pushing on past the OS trig. point on the summit of Slieve League the conditions were arctic, with our wet anoraks now frozen stiff as boards. It was frustrating, in our grey world, to be missing the exposure of the Slieve League ridge, but we hurried down on a compass bearing and emerged from the mist on the col under Leahan. In our state of anticipation, even a backward look at the lower half of the Slieve League cliffs was stimulating.

Map O.S. 1:126,720 Sheet 3.
Grading A long walk along a magnificently wild and rugged coastline. Some exposed scrambling is involved on the crest of Slieve League but this can be avoided.
Start / Finish Bunglass car-park (560740); Maghera (660908).
Distance / Time 27 miles/14 hours (6 hours to Glencolumbkille).
Escape Routes Roads down to the coast at Malin Bay, Glen Bay and Port.
Telephones Teelin, Malin Beg, Glencolumbkille and Maghera.
Transport Daily bus service from Donegal to Glencolumbkille via Carrick. No public transport to Maghera but good connections at Ardara (5 miles).
Accommodation Hotels/Guest Houses at Carrick and Glencolumbille. Youth Hostel (An Oige) at Carrick. Private hostel (Dooey) at Glencolumbkille.
Guidebooks 'Irish Peaks' by Joss Lynam (Constable); Irish Walk Guide Vol. 3 'The

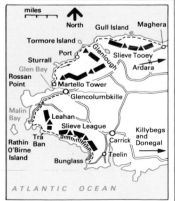

North West, Donegal – Sligo' by Patrick Simms and Gerald Foley (Gill and Macmillan).

Leahan must be traversed at about the 900ft level, but then the cliff top can be regained and followed gently down to Trá Bán (the White Strand), an exquisite horseshoe bay of firm white sand. Ringed by sharp rock teeth and towering buttresses, one containing a natural arch, Trá Bán is a rare jewel on this harsh coast.

A five mile stretch of road now leads round into Glencolumbkille, but this is by no means a tedious grind. The road follows the shore of island-studded Malin Bay before climbing to a superb lookout point for wild Glen Bay and the sheer cliffs of Glen Head.

Dry, warm and in good spirits we peered out of the window of Dooey hostel the following morning to find the clouds had lifted and the first objective of the day, the massive Martello Tower on Glen Head, was clearly visible. The tower was built in the early years of the nineteenth century to provide coastal defence during Napoleon's threatened invasion.

Although the entrance has been sealed and the tower cannot be climbed, the base gives a spectacular view of the numerous reefs and islets, lying in Glen Bay, which were picked out by the boiling surf, and of the Atlantic swell surging against Rossan Point. A fitting backcloth was provided by the snow-capped, whale-backed ridges of Leahan and Slieve League.

From Glen Head the cliffs fall 800ft sheer into the ocean, and obvious cracks in the ground near to the cliff edge emphasise the need for extreme caution.

Again today, the wind was gusting to storm force and endeavouring to blow us off our feet. Ragged grey clouds, driven by a vicious westerly wind were racing in from the Atlantic, and for much of the day we were bent double, fighting to make progress. Maddeningly, without warning, the gusts would cease and we would pitch forward onto our faces in the wet heather. But the day's bonus was the

Atlantic, magnificent in its angry mood, the white horses and thundering waves sending columns of spray high over the wicked black rocks.

Rounding Glen Head the extraordinary headland of Sturrall juts out from the mainland, connected by a razor-sharp and heavily eroded ridge, dropping 600ft on either side. The Sturrall marks the beginning of a stretch of coastline that (barring St Kilda) has rock architecture unequalled anywhere else in these islands. Impossibly steep fangs of rock rear up out of the sea, and even the islets of Toralaydan and Tormore have their green turf guarded by a ring of vertical cliffs. The rock teeth cause the sea to boil and froth, and from a perch high up on the cliffs it is like looking down into a witch's cauldron.

Port harbour and Port Hill on the approach from Sturrall.

Port harbour was empty and devoid of life and activity save for a low cottage, an upturned boat and a tiny concrete jetty. On the north side of the bay, startlingly white cliffs of quartzite rise to Port Hill which overlooks the curved shingle beach at Glenlough. Yet again we drew in our breath at the wild scene of breakers pounding the off-shore stacks and skerries, beneath 800ft cliffs.

Now comes a long descent almost to sea level at Glenlough, followed by a 1,200ft climb over the shoulder of Slieve Tooey to

Tormore Island seen from Port Hill.

The jagged island scenery at Glenlough.

Ascending Port Hill

meet the coast again at Gull Island. In spite of its name, hardly a sea bird was to be seen on or around Gull Island, or indeed anywhere along the Donegal coast. This was in marked contrast to the thousands of nesting fulmars seen on Orkney a week or two earlier.

A wide shelf of heather and dwarf juniper takes you round the north-east shoulder of Slieve Tooey to within striking distance of the sand-dunes at Maghera.

However, the direct route runs above low cliffs containing caves and blow holes, and the narrow, tortuous and exposed sheep track is difficult to locate. The alternative is to climb up yet again to reach easy ground which then descends gently to Maghera. We took the lower route and were delighted to find a colony of purple saxifrage in full bloom, in spite of the desperately unseasonal weather.

If you have not been able to organise transport to meet you at Maghera, you have a further five mile plod along the road to Ardara; a tiresome end to such a magnificent walk. A few pounds for on a taxi would be well spent.

As a postscript to our stormy traverse of the Donegal coast we returned to Bunglass on the evening of the second day to collect the car. The wind had finally torn gaps in the cloud cover and the setting sun was lighting up the stupendous sweep of cliffs falling from Slieve League. With full hearts and satisfied smiles we reluctantly turned our backs on Ireland's finest coastal view and made for Donegal town and supper.

Looking back from Slieve Tooey to Port Hill, Tormore Island and Glenlough.

The descent from Slieve Tooey to Maghera.

THE NEPHIN RIDGE WALK

by TONY WHILDE

Map O.S. 1:126,720 Sheet 6.
Grading A long and arduous day's walk which should only be attempted during the summer months.
Start / Finish The roadside S of Bangor (808203); Mullaranny (802907).
Distance / Time 20 miles/10-12 hours.
Escape Routes At the half-way point a tracks runs from the col between the 1,330ft summit of Nephin Beg and Glennamong, S.E. to the road at Srahmore Lodge.
Telephones Bangor and Mullaranny.
Transport Castlebar is the best centre with buses running north to Belmullet via Bangor and west to Newport and Dooega via Mullaranny.
Accommodation Hotels at Castlebar. B & B at Bangor and Mullaranny. Youth Hostels (An Oige) at Mweewillin, Pollatomish and Lough Feeagh.
Guidebooks Irish Walk Guide Vol. 2 'The West, Clare – Galway – Mayo' by Tony Whilde (Gill and Macmillan); 'Irish Peaks' by Joss Lynam (Constable).

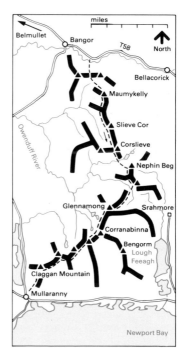

A ninety mile drive in a thick fog was hardly an auspicious start to a day in the hills, but I had little choice with the deadline for copy rapidly approaching. I had been pleased to receive the editor's invitation to write about the Nephins back in May because, though I'd walked the southern part of the range, the northern hills were new ground to me. But on the last Saturday in September, with the wettest summer on record coming to a close and the memories of a previous weekend visit to this Mayo range tent-bound in lashing rain, I felt a twinge of desperation as I approached the still invisible quartzite hills.

I stopped to photograph the mist shrouded Bellacorick power station, an incongruous monolith in a sea of blanket bog, the base screened by mature conifers which looked like toys against the giant cooling tower.

I continued westwards, scanning the expansive bog to the south, contemplating the hours of energy sapping bog trotting ahead of me if I was to approach the hills from this angle. But extensive conifer plantations and the swollen Owenmore River defied access, and it was only at about two miles east of Bangor on the T58 that there was a bridge leading to a small village, and a way onto the boggy approach to Maumykelly.

The days were shortening and, even if the sun drove away the remaining mist, as the weather forecast had promised, my time was limited and splashing through super-wet bogs should be avoided if at all possible. So I continued into the village of Bangor and turned south in the hope of finding a drier route onto the hills. This hope was fulfilled and I discovered a new forestry track just south of Muingnahalloona (850180). A mile or two on the softish track provided the warm up I needed after a couple of hours driving on bumpy west of Ireland roads. The history of the landscape was evident in the cut-away margins of the track. Peat, to a depth of one-and-a-half metres in places, blanketed earlier glacial mineral deposits and at intervals the roots of ancient pines protruded from the peat, just above the mineral soil – testimony to a period, five or six thousand years ago, when much of Ireland was covered with forest. Now man is restoring the sylvan mantle, though with row upon row of alien lodge pole pine, hardly in the manner that nature might have done. Ruined cottages along the way evoked images of harsh times in days gone by.

At the end of the forest track I turned southwards across the wet hillside and, after several hundred metres of uncomfortable drain hopping, I reached the green valley of the Tarsaghaunmore River. Following the north bank I found the going quite easy and relatively dry. The sun was now piercing the haze and the Nephin ridge was, at last, making an appearance. Looking back I noticed a small farm about a kilometre downstream, clearly a more convenient access point than the forest track.

A perky little dipper and then two teal enlivened the walk to the foot of the northern ridge leading to the 2,369ft/722m summit. Bog beans emerged proudly from the shallow pools which graced the

In the Nephin range – approaching Glennamong

The view north from Bengorm to Nephin Beg.

...om the north-east.

bog at the foot of a steep, wet, peaty slope. But this soon gave way to drier ground with short heather. Suddenly, the silence was broken by a cacophony of bleating and barking as a flock of over two hundred sheep was driven down off the hillside into the valley below me. There were sheep, too, when I reached the ridge. This was new to me because in my home territory in Connemara there is little or no vegetation to attract sheep to the bare quartzite ridges of the Bens or Maumturks.

Looking northwards I could now see quite clearly the route I could have taken. Across the bog from the Owenmore River, passing to the west of the small hill (900ft), on to the peat-hagged Maumykelly and thence to the ridge on which I was now standing.

An easy walk in an unseasonably warm south-east breeze (it turned out to be the warmest day of the year in the west of Ireland!) brought me to the 2,369ft/722m, summit (un-named on the half-inch map but called Slieve Cor by some authorities) which must be one of the remotest in the west of Ireland; surrounded as it is by 1,000

[213]

Looking north from Corranabinna past the Glennamong Ridge to Corslieve.

square kilometres of mountains and blanket bog. On top there is a huge cairn (Laghtdamhnbaun) now surmounted by a trig. point, recently constructed as indicated by the fresh remains of cement at the foot of the cairn.

To the north and east the blanket bog stretched into the far distance, punctuated here and there by lakes and new plantations served by intrusive white ribbon-like forestry roads. The lonely cone of Nephin peeped through the haze to the east and the white smoke of the Bellacorick power station wafted gently across the black background of cut-over peat bog – Irish desert. To the west the lowlands of Ballycroy lead the eye to Blacksod Bay and the impressive peaks of Achill Island. The east face of the summit falls away

Bengorm and Corranabinna seen from the eastern shore of Lough Feagh.

steeply to the corrie lake Adanacleveen, one of a series of tarns which enliven the walk across short heather and eroded peat to Corslieve, 1,785ft/544m.

On this occasion, with the short day and more fog forecast for the evening, I descended Corslieve to the old track marked on the map and skirted Nephin Beg, 2,065ft/629m, to the west. But the route to Nephin Beg takes you between the two basins of Scardaun Lough and up onto the north-west spur to a rather uninspiring summit. A straightforward descent, taking in point 1356ft, takes you across the line of the old track and on to the cliff-lined ridge of Glennamong (Gleann an mong, Sedge glen 2,067ft/630m) overlooking, to the west, the attractive loughs Corryloughaphuill and Corranabinna and to the south-east a valley of young conifers leading down to Lough Feeagh.

From the craggy summit 2,343ft/714m (un-named on the half-inch map but called Cushcamcarragh and also Corranabinna) there were fine views of Clew Bay, its profusion of islands set against the sharp cone of Croagh Patrick with its pilgrim path and summit chapel. The western prospect was blanket bog stretching to the sea.

A south-westward descent leads to the final undulating ridge with Lough Anaffrin below to the north. Claggan Mountain, 1,256ft/382m, was the last summit from which I gained just a glimpse of Clare Island guarding the entrance to Clew Bay. To avoid ending up in someone's 'back garden' on the final descent I followed the ridge to Point 675ft and then scrambled down the steep slopes to the road which, in a short distance, took me to the village of Mullaranny.

All in all this is a long and tough day's walk, especially when the bogs are very wet. But the magnificent and ever changing vistas of land, sea, lakes and sky repay the effort. And if it's solitude you want . . .

WEST OF THE REEKS: KNOCKNAGANTEE AND MULLAGHANATTIN

by JOSS LYNAM

To the uninitiated 'Kerry Mountains' mean The Reeks; the more knowledgeable are aware of Mangerton, Brandon, the Caha Mountains; but very few are familiar with the wild, lonely, lake-filled coums west of the Reeks. We walked the eastern, better-known part of this area, Mullaghanattin and Lough Reagh on our honeymoon, in … well, a long time ago. Later (in the sixties) I climbed some of the crags in Coom Reagh, but it was only in the last decade that I explored the series of valleys and ridges echeloned south and west of the Ballaghasheen Pass. It is a wonderful area, and the big problem has been to choose the best route, for it is impossible in one walk to savour everything.

I'll assume you are based in Glencar, and have a car – or preferably two! Drive over the Ballaghasheen Pass (turn your head to look back at the Reeks before the road plunges into the woods on the far side), take the left fork, signposted Waterville, and after a mile turn left again for Lough Derriana. When you come over the shoulder and Derriana comes into view, turn sharp left again, and follow a narrow road (not that the others are exactly broad) along the north shore of the lough, and away up left into Coomavoher. There's plenty of space to park at the end of the road. Fifty yards back, a bog road takes you, almost dry shod, to Tooreenabog Lough, the first of five in the valley, which is as near a paternoster chain as you'll get in nature.

Keep south of the lakes. There's no path, but the occasional sheep track helps you along. As you come over a little rise before the second lake, Lough Adoolig, you begin to appreciate the rocky wildness of this valley. You have had a high ridge to the south of you since you left the car, now the north wall begins to close in. The going gets rougher; you balance precariously on a root just over the water or toil wearily over a spur. Go past the third (very small) lake to the fourth, encircled by crags on three sides. The stream flows down over black, dank, mossy slabs and overhangs. No way there. But you can wind up to the right on steep grass, picking a route between dripping crags until a diagonal rocky rake leads you back to the stream and the fifth lake in a small upper corrie. This is a good place to camp; quite isolated – you can't see the outside world at all, there's dry ground underfoot (nearly level!), and rough dry slabs to scramble on if that is your fancy. The rock (which is Old Red Sandstone), when it isn't damp or mossy is a beautiful pale red-brown, warm and rough, and a delight to climb.

A short ascent takes you over the rim of the corrie onto a boggy plateau, seemingly ringed entirely by summits. This must be one of the loneliest, wildest places in Ireland; two streams drain the plateau, but one (to Lough Reagh) cuts its way through a narrow gorge that is invisible from a hundred yards away, and the other does not advertise its valley either, just gently sinks into Coomeenassig between Knocknagantee and Point 2086. I've been up there at night, and there is not a light to be seen, except when you are exactly in line with the valley to the south, and the lights of Sneem appear, framed between the hills.

Today we turn right, and plug up rocky slopes to Knocknagantee, 2,220ft/676m. From the summit we can gaze down on Eagle's Lough below, and across the foothills to Sneem and the Kenmare River (which is a fjord, not a river at all). Especially if we've camped on the way up, it's a pleasure to see signs of human presence again. We descend a little east of our upward route, contour above Lough Coomeenassig, and climb to Point 2086, sentinel on the east side of the lough. From here a ridge takes us in one-and-a-half miles to the top of Finnararagh (An Fionnbhogach, 'the fair soft one', 2,185ft/665m). A pleasant walk, if it were not for the innumerable rocky barriers across the ridge.

As we walk we can see the plateau on our left break up into a maze of streams, small lakes, rocky knolls, and crags. If you like, you can leave the ridge here and find your way through the maze and down to Lough Reagh. But don't think it is an easy way off; it isn't. There are just two feasible routes down the rock wall supporting the plateau, and they are both hard to find. The best plan is to go round fairly high up onto the slopes of the unnamed 2,100ft/640m, top east of Knockmoyle. Here, some 200ft above Lough Coomalougha, you will find a steep open grassy gully to take you down towards Lough Reagh. Of course if you want excitement, plunge boldly into the maze, and by dint of boulder-hopping, stream-leaping, and some interesting scrambling; you will get to the same place. Having successfully descended, cross the main river above the lough, and pick up a vague path which will take you to a farmyard and the road at the south-east corner of Lough Cloon.

But our route continues from Finnararagh along the narrow ridge between Coomreagh and Coomnacronia over a series of small tops until we climb seriously again to Beoun, 2,468ft/752m. Look back, as

Maps O.S. 1:126,720 Sheet 20; O.S. 1:63,360 'Killarney District'.

Grading A walk with plenty of rough going and route finding problems, especially if the mist is down.

Start / Finish Derriana Lough (629739); Ballaghabeama Pass (752780).

Distance / Time 11 miles/6-7 hours.

Escape Routes From Knocknagantee due W down the ridge to the start. From the col before Beoun (732767) to the Lough Cloon road.

Telephone Glencar.

Transport No public transport nearby. Taxi or car could be hired at Killarney which is well served with rail services to Dublin and bus services to Cork.

Accommodation B & B locally. Hotels in Killorglin and Killarney. Two independent hostels in Glencar. Youth Hostels (An Oige) at Gap of Dunloe and Aghadoe.

Guidebooks 'Irish Peaks' by Joss Lynam (Constable); Irish Walk Guide Vol. 1 'The South West, Kerry – West Cork' by Sean O'Suilleabhain (Gill and Macmillan).

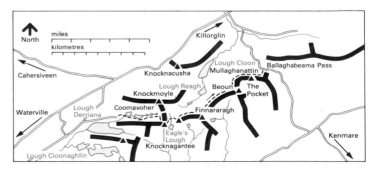

The view north-east from Knocknagantee, across the Knockmoyle plateau, to the distant Macgillycuddy's Reeks.

you walk this section, at the tremendous castellated wall above Lough Reagh. From Beoun the ridge, now pleasantly grassy, undulates along to Mullaghanattin (Mullach an Aitinn, 'summit of the gorse', 2,539ft/773m) highest peak West of the Reeks, and the climax of our walk.

Although our route is mostly hidden, Mullaghanattin is a superb viewpoint. North-east are the Reeks themselves, north is Glencar

and Caragh Lake, north-west is Coomacarrea whose huge northern corries compete for wildness with the route we have followed, while below us to the south is The Pocket, a huge rocky cirque, with the narrowest of exits.

You can choose your descent route. The shortest is to follow the ridge north-east to the road at the Ballaghabeama Pass, where you have, of course, stationed a car. Or you can descend north along the spur east of Lough Eskabehy to pick up the farm track which leads down to the Lough Cloon road one-and-a-half miles below the lake, maybe three miles from Glencar.

If you have to make it a circular walk, park the car below Lough Cloon, reverse the 'escape' route above Lough Reagh, and return over Finnararagh (you can take in Knocknagantee as well if you are really keen) and Mullaghanattin.

The possibilities are endless; all of them are interesting, rough, rocky, and trackless – what more could you want? Well, you could want a good map, and that does not exist; the half-inch is far too small to show enough detail. Many of the names mentioned are to be found only on the old black-and-white one inch maps, but as these are eighty years out of date they are hardly worth buying. The names themselves are suspect; English-speaking surveyors had problems transliterating the Irish names the locals gave them.

Lough Coomeenassig and Knocknagantee.

The stream (and gorgo) above Lough Reagh

The highest of the four lakes of Coomavoher with Knocknagantee beyond.

Approaching Knocknagantee from the west.

Knockmealdown and Knockmoylan from Knocknagnauv.

THE KNOCKMEALDOWN RIDGE WALK

by JEAN BOYDELL

Before I ever set foot on the Knockmealdown Mountains I had been led to believe they were dull, uninteresting and covered in high heather. When I went to see for myself, despite the high heather, I found the ridge an exhilarating walk. A lot of the heather has since been burned to provide grazing for sheep. The ridge straddles the boundary between Counties Tipperary and Waterford. It is flanked on two sides by the Galtee Mountains and the Comeragh Mountains: the patchwork of fields in the lowland between contrasting dramatically. On the third side the River Blackwater flows through Lismore and Cappoquin to the coast.

Finding the eastern half of the Knockmealdown Ridge the more

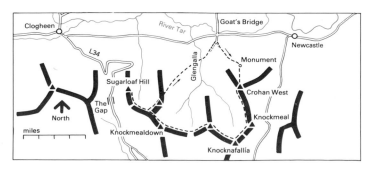

interesting I have chosen a route here from Knockballiniry Forest, just south of Goatenbridge (Goat's Bridge on the maps). In Goatenbridge a road sign-posted for the Liam Lynch Monument eventually reaches a T-junction at the forest where there is space for cars.

Starting off through the forest provides a gentle run-in to the day's walking, even if the road seems to wind eternally upwards, and there are tantalising glimpses between the trees of the plain and distant mountains. Finding the way is no problem – follow the signs for the Monument.

This monument is a small round tower for which the stone was gathered off the surrounding mountainside. Liam Lynch was shot here in 1923 while trying to escape from Irish Free State troops. It is an exposed and lonely spot.

Leaving the monument the climbing starts in earnest. A few metres right of the tower a firebreak heads south-westwards to the fence and more mature trees providing the easiest line, even if rough underfoot, straight to the top of Crohan West. Pause now and again while climbing to look at the plain and the heathery and forested slopes of the low hills stretching towards the Comeraghs.

The ridge and a wall run over a small bump and onto Knockmeal – not to be confused with Knockmealdown Mountain. In the valley on the right forest adds contrast in colour to the grassy green of the rounded end of Knocknagnauv and ravens can be heard croaking as they wheel overhead. Leave the wall for the summit cairn and another view of the plain and eastern end of the range.

The mass of Knocknafallia rises ever more steeply as we descend to the col where a finger of forest claws at the pass. A steep climb it is too, but once on top the ground is carpeted in short springy heather and grass – a delight to walk on. The Cistercian monks built Mount Mellary Monastery on the lower southern slopes of Knocknafallia. It is however a long way down from the ridge and better reserved for a separate visit. Once on this summit attention focuses on the southern side of the ridge for the first time, with the accent changing from mountain to coastal plain.

From Knocknafallia we cross a dip onto the stone-strewn ridge of Knocknagnauv where a wall along the centre provides shelter and is worth bearing in mind as a place to eat. This dip appears to be almost surrounded by mountains with the Crohan West to Knock-meal stretch now parallel.

The line of the wall goes all the way to the Vee Gap and one cannot help wondering why it is there. Was it perhaps a 'folly' of famine times? The steep descent off Knocknagnauv needs concentration with eyes on feet rather than the view. But stop to look across to the corrie nestling under Knockmealdown Mountain with the ridge curving around behind it – a remote and lonely-looking place – and the southern slopes sweeping smoothly to the fields. Once in the col Knockmealdown Mountain rears up ahead with its cliff dropping straight into the corrie from the summit.

(People wishing to escape can take a faint track, right, to the corner of a forestry fence. Across this, stay on a rough forest road for a while, then zig-zag down one of various tracks to a wide forest road which contours around to older forest and winds down the valley to the start.)

Continuing we climb steeply up Knockmealdown Mountain. Lismore and Cappoquin lie at the foot of the ridge, while the coast can be picked out in the distance and from this point the rounded mounds of the western section of the ridge are visible for the first time. A dilapidated hut is a left-over from cable TV although an eyesore and disintegrating it still provides some shelter.

From here the walking over short springy heather is easy. With the narrowness of the ridge and the vistas it is like walking on top of the world. For me this is the most spectacular part of the walk. Because less care is needed for placing feet, attention can wander to take in the tree-edged road to Lismore, winding south from the Vee Gap, and the mountains on either side.

It is worth continuing to Sugarloaf Hill, partly to prolong the pleasant walk along the ridge and partly because it stands aloof. The Galtees are clearly visible as well as the ground already covered, with Knockshanahullion prominent to the west.

(If you have someone waiting in the Vee Gap follow the wall straight and steeply down to the rendezvous. It is a picturesque place with Bay Lough nestling among the rhododendron bushes on the hill-side, with a statue and an old shelter as well as the steep slopes of the mountains which form The Gap.)

Noel Maguire

The southern approach to Sugarloaf.

To return to Knockballiniry Forest you must retrace your steps past the col and the first rise. Where the wall takes a sharp turn right, with a cairn on it, a small path runs almost to the top of Knock Moylan, 2,521ft/768m. From Knock Moylan stay on the ridge for a short while, drop to lower ground towards Roches Hill and then east to the forest edge. The ground is rough and broken making walking tiring, but the scenery is magnificent: The ridge of Knocknagnauv juts into the forested valley of the Glengalla River with Crohan West's stony shoulder behind and the plain spread at their feet.

Turn left along the forest edge to the corner where the fence is easiest to negotiate. Drop alongside it to a break in a wall. Just below the wall cross the fence onto an old track, thence to a clear left turn which winds down through the trees. It is a little overgrown in places but this allows a profusion of wild flowers. Where there is a choice keep left and curve steeply down to a footbridge over the river. The solitude is heightened by the trees and heather-covered slopes rising higher as we descend. A few metres on a second footbridge spans the other branch of the river, leading to the road and down the valley to the start.

Although the Knockmealdown Ridge is not very high – Knockmealdown Mountain being the highest point at 2,609ft/795m – there is a feeling of isolation as the mountains cluster together penetrated by steep-sided valleys. Perhaps the contrast of cultivation around so much of their base accentuates the 'wildness' of the area.

The view north-west from the summit of Knockmealdown, over Sugarloaf to the Galtee range in the distance.

Jean Boydell

Map O.S. 1:126,720 Sheet 22.
Grading A straightforward mountain walk along heather-clad ridges.
Start / Finish Goat's Bridge (008104).
Distance / Time 14 miles/7 hours.
Escape Routes The walk can be conveniently cut short by descending W from Sugarloaf Hill to the L34 road at the Gap.
Telephones Clogheen an Chloichin and Newcastle.
Transport Infrequent local bus service from Clonmel to Clogheen and Newcastle. Daily express bus service Clonmel – Cork (in each direction) passes through Clogheen.
Accommodation Hotels/Guest Houses in Clonmel and Dungarvan. B & B locally. Youth Hostel (An Oige) at Lismore.
Guidebooks Irish Walk Guide Vol. 6 'The South East, Tipperary – Waterford' by Frank Martindale (Gill and Macmillan); 'Irish Peaks' by Joss Lynam (Constable).

THE MANGERTON HORSESHOE

by DERMOT SOMERS

Red splashes on mountain-paths are not all painted by trail-blazers. Those red blotches at the foot of Mangerton are ... blood-stains!

There is a story – but first, a Theme. History has many questions to answer, pools of mystery that lie like corrie-lakes between the ridges of the past ...

> Question: What became of Excalibur?
> Question: What became of Shergar?
> Question: What became of Oisín's
> enchanted horse?
> Question: What's the connection?

The Story So Far: Oisín returned to Ireland on a visit after 30 years in Tír na nÓg – the Land of Youth. He fell off his magic horse in Killarney. The instant he touched the earth he became an ancient man. (Take it or leave it.)

St Patrick (c. 450) baptised him in the nick of time – pagan and christian myths neatly fused as usual.

But what happened to his horse? And where does Mangerton come in?

Now Read On: Some of the local buckos captured the White Stallion for a stud.

But it seems horses from the Land of Youth don't have the normal functions and fluids at all; no need to breed you see. And he had no blood in him either to bind him to the earth for a race-horse. A massive transfusion soon fixed that! They pumped him up with blood from every burnhouse and abattoir in the Kingdom till his body was dark, and tight, and round – flightless as a huge black-pudding.

No bother to them fellows! They were into brain-surgery on greyhounds too before that was fashionable.

But they slipped up this time. It was poisoned blood the poor nag got, full of bile and canker, and not only was all flight grounded but he couldn't run! There was no one to stick for a ransom either.

So the unfortunate creature stumbled down the centuries till at

The view towards Stoompa from Mangerton.

last he ended up, God between us and all harm, with the jarveys.

Now anyone who has been to Killarney knows the jarveys; blood-brothers to all the gondoliers, camel-drivers and ponymen of this world. The most beautiful patch of scenery in the country is entirely controlled by this small group of men, self-appointed to transport American wallets around the lakes in their jaunting-cars. When Neidín (Little Ned) the jarvey got hold of that spavined ould hack he worked him to his knees. He had no expenses – only the odd mug of blood to top the beast up after a nose-bleed, and when the horse-flies were bad.

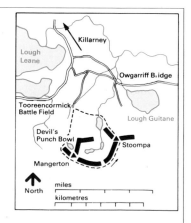

Map O.S. 1:126,720 Sheet 20.
Grading An easy walk over mainly grassy hills.
Start / Finish Road bridge near Tooreencormick Battle Field (984848).
Distance / Time 8 miles/4 hours.
Escape Routes None. The line of the walk is the easiest way on and off the mountain.
Telephone Owgarriff Bridge.
Transport Railway Station at Killarney with a fast link to Dublin. Daily buses from Cork to Killarney.
Accommodation Hotels/Guest Houses at Killarney (4 miles). Youth Hostels (An Oige) at Gap of Dunloe and Aghadoe.
Guidebooks 'Irish Peaks' by Joss Lynam (Constable); Irish Walk Guide Vol. 1 'The South West, Kerry – West Cork' by Sean O'Suilleabhain (Gill and Macmillan).

In his silver-buckled shoes, knee-breeches, and high hat Neidín knew he was sitting on a crock of gold.

One day he was driving round the shore of Lough Leane by the gracious gardens of Muckross on his way to Mangerton Mountain when the horse threw a stumble on the side of the road and spiked his belly on a rhododendron root.

He was bleeding by the bucket, growing paler and paler along the steep road, but the drowsy jarvey saw nothing till he reined in at last, and there between the shafts stood a bright, transparent stallion stamping his silver hooves!

Well the horse threw a buckleap that burst the harness, and away with him up the heathery mountain straight for the Devil's Punch-bowl, and the devil knows where beyond, Neidín after him like the clappers, roaring and shaking his blackthorn stick.

It was a gentle morning on the brown mountain, sunlight and woollen clouds, but Neidín saw none of it, not the golden woods and blue lakes behind, nor the serene grey spire of Killarney Church, nor the tusks and teeth of the mountains west – Torc and the gnashing Reeks, nor the patchworked lowlands stretching north in the morning mist.

[221]

Joe Cronin

Climbing Mangerton from the Devil's Punchbowl.

shortcut up the back of the corrie. The flowing bowl lapped through a channel in the mountainside, and the Lakes of Killarney far below were languidly framed in the deep-cut banks of the stream.

Not for Neidín they weren't! Long before the demented jarvey reached the top he heard the delicate thunder of hooves on the turf above. Out with him below the summit and with every raging hop he saw the Atlantic tearing into the Kerry coast down beyond Kenmare.

The bloodstains were invisible now. They soaked through untrodden turf to the underlying rock. There they await erosion by Wild Walkers.

The enchanted horse was light and easy in himself, hardly touching the ground as he freewheeled by the mighty corries quarried by comets when the planet was bubbling hot – gouged by icebergs when it was frozen cold.

All he saw was his livelihood galloping up the side of Mangerton, sheets of water splashing up from the hooves and arching out like wings beside the shining body. The horse was trying to fly, but he couldn't lift. There was dirty blood in him yet.

Gouts of it splashed on bare rock and stuck – where you see it still today!

When the horse hit the bottomless Punchbowl he veered round the lake and made straight for the summit plateau. Neidín tried a

But the jarvey had his second wind too, and wasn't he drawing up on the magic horse – which only goes to show the speed and the stamina of greed! The cold lakes down in their depths lay glazed with indifference as the chase mounted the ridge towards the bumpy hump of Stoompa.

All of a sudden the sun broke through and turned the black lakes silver. Neidín's blackthorn crashed across the shining rump, the last drop of blood shook free, and the stallion reared away from

Nearing the summit of Mangerton on the westerly approach. The hill in the background is Pt. 2500.

Noel Maguire

On the descent of Pt. 2500 – the Macgillicuddy's Reeks and Knocknagantee groups can be seen in the distance.

Stoompa, soared into the sky, out over Gleann a' Chapaill – the Horse's Glen.

The jarvey was howling rosaries of abuse after the shape in the sky when he heard a wild welcome erupt in the bottomless lake far below. He gaped down and Glory be to God there was his shining steed plunging into the water, down, down through the lake, burning whiter and brighter as it galloped into the heart of light. And when he looked again into the sky there was only a faint reflection

there, a water-dappled decoy dying away.

Illumination struck the jarvey. 'Tír na nÓg' he exulted 'is not up in the heavens at all. It's below in the lake!'

He scrambled and tumbled down, kicked off his buckled shoes, and dived in.

When Neidín was fished out of the Land of Youth they say, 'he was as dead as a shtick!' and there was a hoofprint stamped across his hard, black heart.

Looking north from the col between Mangerton and Stoompa.

INDEX